Galore

...s of Unclerical Life
2021

Gargoyles Galore is not a work of fiction, although some fictional characters are invoked. Rather it is a tapestry of interwoven memories.

Here are some of the more colourful people and events that the author has experienced, reaching back into childhood and covering some fifty years of ordained ministry.

With the aid of anecdotes, historical precedents and cartoons, the aim is to describe life in the church (and a little beyond) as it is, 'warts and all', not as it ideally should be.

In fact, the *Scenes of Unclerical Life* take in much else besides, drawing upon time spent in Africa as well as in grappling with health services and officialdom at home and abroad

---

Rodney Schofield was born at St Albans in 1944. He was initially a mathematics teacher, but in 1971 was ordained for ministry in the Church of England. Apart from serving parishes in Northamptonshire and Somerset, he taught in African seminaries – first in Lesotho, then in Malawi. In 2003 he became a Catholic, subsequently being a parish priest in Dorset, then in semi-retirement continuing to care for St Ambrose' Church in Wye, Kent. He holds a doctorate from the University of Wales Lampeter, and is the author of a number of books, including several published in Malawi for African students. He is married to Sarah, with two children and three grandchildren.

GARGOYLES GALORE

Scenes
of Unclerical Life

Rodney Schofield

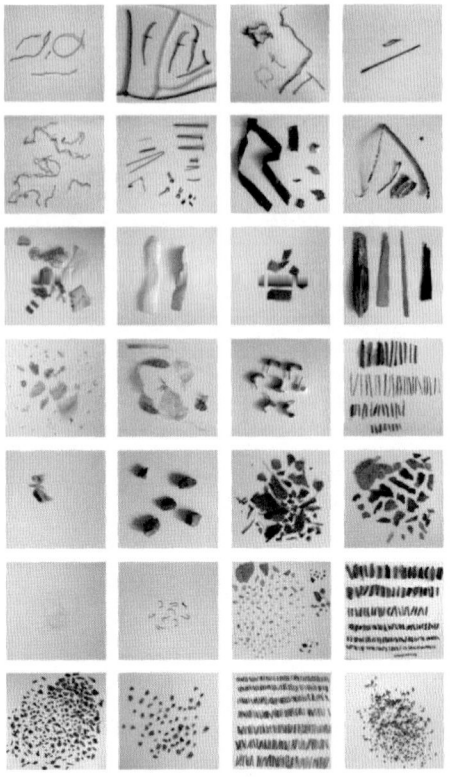

The structuring of this book owes much to our daughter Patricia, whose artwork shown here resulted from sweeping out a derelict hall, and then carefully sifting and sorting the fragments found in the dust.

CONTENTS

Setting the Scene	1
A Cautionary Chronicle	7
Checkpoint Charlies	10
Crazy Convictions	21
Servers and Scones	31
Colourful Clergy	39
Sermon Snippets	50
Commanding Characters	62
Saints and Sinners	76
Sheep Smells	85
Contemporary Crises	96
Quirky Customers	107
Changing Key	120
Scholastic Shocks	131
Christian Coachloads	143
Sink or Swim	151
Quacks and Cures	164
Crucial Challenges	176
Sabbatical Surprises	187
Counting the Cost	197
Catholic Connections	210
Squaring the Circle	224

Dedicated to our grandchildren

Chloe, Cameron and Samuel

who may observe a fine collection of C's and S's

in the chapter headings

SETTING THE SCENE

Mine, I fear, is not a well-regulated mind: it has an occasional tenderness for old abuses.[1]

Anyone first sighting a sighting a Christian church is likely to do so from some distance, when an impressive spire or tower may punctuate the horizon. On closer inspection there may be an imposing structure, and inside sometimes a breathtaking array of arches and pillars surmounted by a lofty vault. It is, however, an atmosphere of serenity that seems to speak most powerfully to the majority of visitors – at least to judge by their comments in the books provided. 'Lovely peaceful atmosphere', they write, or perhaps 'beautiful old church'. Seldom are there comments on the architecture itself, and never (in my experience) upon the details that I find so fascinating, such as the epitaphs of worthy gentlemen of valour who unfortunately met their end while trying to exterminate the natives of some distant land.

Gargoyles are less in evidence than heroic monuments, but just as rich in interest. Unless carved on wooden misericords within an abbey or priory church, they are likely to be far above ground level, embellishing the roof or its supports or its drainage system (these last are properly gargoyles, as others strictly speaking are known as *grotesques*). For the most part they serve an ornamental purpose, but too often go unremarked because of their location; some are even out of human sight in roof spaces, no doubt placed there as a deliberate reminder that nevertheless God's eyes are all-seeing. They depict a wide range of images, from kings and queens, to abbots and less distinguished clerics, to humble workmen; from angelic beings to grotesque animals and demons; from true likenesses to caricatures. By now, so many have weathered that they can scarcely be deciphered. Collectively they symbolise the whole of reality, both good and evil, and remind the observer that the church too is a complex mix of 'wheat and tares'. It is a good church tradition that perfection is God's prerogative; hence Christian art and architecture sometimes incorporate blemished features as a subtle reminder of this truth.

Of course, the presence of the seemingly more malevolent images has met with criticism. In the 12th century St Bernard of Clairvaux, who disliked ornamentation of any kind, objected: 'What are these fantastic monsters doing in the cloisters before the eyes of the brothers as they read? … Surely if we do not blush for such absurdities, we should at least regret what we have spent on them'. Yet they may tell us important truths about ourselves: Thomas Merton, ironically a monk in the Cistercian tradition that St Bernard began, has been described as 'visionary', 'rebel', 'artist', 'a divided

---

[1] George Eliot: *Scenes of Clerical Life* (London, Oxford University Press, 1916) p4

self', 'a troublesome charge', 'guru', 'the nation's conscience' - yet also as 'a dutiful son'. Each one of us is likely to be a similar (although probably scaled down) assemblage of varied personae. Indeed, being prone to mask our failings, any preferred self-image may not always correspond to how others see us and may well be a distortion of the larger actuality – which may be more grotesque than we like to admit. Depicting the elusive multi-faceted character of human nature is a task for artists and sculptors; but even then, as Edgar Degas once observed, 'Il faut laisser un certain mystère autour des oeuvres'.

At one point in the Gospel narrative Jesus quotes verses from a psalm about a stone: 'Have you not read this scripture, "The stone that the builders rejected has become the cornerstone. This is the Lord's doing; it is amazing in our eyes"'. The cornerstone may then have been understood as the central capstone in an arch, or it may have been some different element that held the structure of the building together. The precise interpretation matters less than the fact that it was in some way irregular or misshaped compared with the other carefully cut stones. Even if a gargoyle doesn't contribute to the stability of a structure, it may still have amazing value as a reminder of what the Lord's doings can embrace. A misshapen effigy may remind us of the humble poor or those with disfigured lives for whom he suffered on the cross, as dear to him as the more distinguished line-up of saints whose statues may be prominent elsewhere. What sometimes appears unfamiliar or even unwelcome at first sight may be an angel in disguise; 'Do not neglect to show hospitality to strangers, for thereby some have entertained angels unawares'. Jesus himself reminds us of his reversal of conventional human attitudes: he tells us that 'the first shall be last, and the last first', and that 'whoever wishes to be great among you must be your servant'. So we may recall that mere gargoyles may serve the vital purpose of protecting the rest of the edifice from harm. I was once in Rheims visiting the Gothic cathedral during a heavy downpour of rain: it was a magnificent sight to see the rain flooding off the roof into the lead gutters, thence to be channeled away from the building in cascading waterfalls, each spouting out of a gargoyle's open mouth. The potential damage was deflected, so it struck me, more efficiently than by a downpipe (a legal requirement since the early 18th century) that so easily leaks damp into the adjacent wall. It was an image of the salvific work of the cross - allowing evil and human enmity to do its worst, thereby rendering it harmless.

I recall here a discussion many years ago about the cover design of a forthcoming survey of Christian spirituality. Cheslyn Jones, one of the editors, argued strongly in favour of using Rouault's famous painting of Christ *as a clown*. A clown looks ridiculous, and we laugh when he slips on a banana skin and falls flat on his face. But it's when he's lying contorted in the mud that we recognise him as one of ourselves, and it's knowing that he will climb back on to his feet and carry on performing that gives us the hope of achieving something similar ourselves. The spectacle makes our laughter cathartic. Similarly, in describing the dramatic challenges faced by any theatrical director, Peter Brook commented (in *The Empty Space* p69) that in trying 'to capture the invisible' we must never 'lose touch with common sense'. His model was Shakespeare:

> His aim continually is holy, metaphysical, yet he never makes the mistake of staying too long on the highest plane. He knew how hard it is for us to keep company with the absolute – so he continually bumps us down to earth.

The gargoyles in this book represent a variety of people and circumstances in my life that have come across as a little out of the ordinary, at times engendering some amusement to be shared with others. It is not unkindly meant, even in the pricking of pomposity, which does rather invite a disrespectful response. I hesitate to go to the same extremes as Sydney Smith, when he wrote 'My business is to make the archdeacon as ridiculous as possible'. However, his bark was often worse than his bite: another of his victims admitted it was done with so much drollery that it was impossible for her 'not to laugh and be pleased'. Few of us are actually saints, and it may be healthier to admit our flaws than to deny them.

Indeed, Christian churches have done themselves no good at all in recent times by appearing to suppress both financial corruption and, more seriously, instances of child abuse. It should be remembered that the Bible isn't entirely a manual of respectability: apart from blood-curdling acts of violence, there are intriguing domestic arrangements, including Hosea deliberately setting up house with a shady lady. The gospels too have a remarkable frankness in admitting weaknesses even among the inner circle of twelve disciples: the selfish ambition of James and John, the boasting of Simon Peter, the doubts of Thomas, all spring to mind. There is an apocryphal anecdote that when Jesus ascended into heaven he was greeted by the archangel Gabriel: 'Congratulations, Lord, an excellent task accomplished. May I ask what arrangements you've put in hand to continue the good work?' 'I've appointed a group of apostles to take over'. 'That lot! You're not serious?' 'I have no other plan', was Jesus' firm response. Hence shortcomings and failures were certainly not the end of the story for the chosen Twelve, nor is that the inevitable fate of a latter day church largely made up of sinners.

Alongside the rhetoric of Christian holiness, therefore, these autobiographical sketches (in vaguely chronological sequence) – which began life as talks intended both to entertain and to instruct a group of retired friends – try to tell it as it is, warts and all. I aspire to be worthy of the standard set by the Revd M Conyers Place, who died in 1738: his memorial in St Gregory's Church, Marnhull includes the tribute that he was 'eminently studious, yet remarkably facetious, attached to no party, nor addicted to any cause, but that of truth'. When bishop Blomfield a hundred years later referred derogatively to Sydney Smith as his 'facetious friend' in a speech to the House of Lords, he was subsequently taken to task:

> I hasten with gratitude in this letter to denominate you my solemn friend; but you and I must not run into commonplace errors; you must not think me necessarily foolish because I am facetious, nor will I consider you necessarily wise because you are grave.

Is it a failing to have an irreverent sense of humour? One of St Bernard's pupils was Eugenius III, the pope who preceded Adrian IV, a native of St Albans like myself; he considered frivolity an habitual weakness in the English, whom he otherwise admired greatly. He was certainly right, if the evidence of manuscripts some two hundred years later is allowed: it was in England rather than in continental Europe that their margins came to be embellished with cartoons and such-like drolleries. And it was here too that corrupt clergy were lampooned in the popular carving of Reynard the fox, who after preaching to a flock of geese would make off with one of them slung over his shoulder. Best known of all are Geoffrey Chaucer's *Canterbury Tales*, written in the late 14th century with much humour, including satirical descriptions of priests, friars and other church worthies. A little later St Thomas More is supposed to have prayed for 'a sense of good humour', including 'the grace to be able to take a joke and to discover in life a bit of joy, and to be able to share it with others'.

Yet to illustrate our human follies and failings does not invalidate the grace that restores and renews us. There is great consolation expressed in the Church of England article of religion which reads, 'The unworthiness of the minister hinders not the efficacy of the sacrament'. It's important to add a rider here (not unimportant in a world that idolizes celebrities) viz. 'the popularity of the minister indicates not his true worthiness'. A strange truth I learnt one summer vacation when working at the Royal Observatory in Sussex is that even heavenly bodies are not always perceived correctly. Their light is invariably refracted as it passes through the earth's atmosphere, and at Herstmonceux the detecting equipment itself is subject to the gravitational ebb and flow of the coastal tide. Thus correction tables are necessary to compensate for observational deficiencies: surely a parable of wider application? The Bible itself insists repeatedly that 'My thoughts are not your thoughts, neither are your ways my ways, says the Lord' and warns against judging by human standards.

If some distortion or element of caricature is apparent in any of the gargoyles depicted here, perhaps one should reflect that Christ was misrepresented in the same way himself. He was certainly misunderstood in his own day, even at times by his closest followers. A famous late 2nd century graffiti depicts him as a human-like figure attached to a cross, possessing the head of a donkey. To the left of the image is a young man, apparently a Roman soldier called Alexamenos, shown raising his hand in a gesture of worship. Beneath the cross the caption reads: Αλεξαμενος cεβετε θεον, which is interpreted to mean 'Alexamenos worships [his] God'. This may be considered the earliest and most grotesque 'gargoyle' of them all!

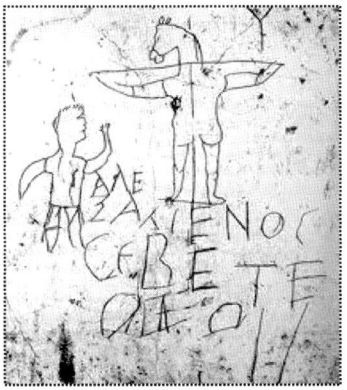

It might also be taken as an archetypal image of each one of Christ's followers (just as in the Roman imperial cult it was often the case that the same statue, apart from the substitution of a different head, sufficed to represent a whole line of emperors).

If any such depiction of the Prophet Mohammed were ever to be drawn, one fears that there'd be protests and rioting across the Muslim world. Yet the folly of the cross goes to the heart of the Christian faith, so maybe Jesus himself would have appreciated the sketch? Indeed, his own sense of humour is occasionally visible in the gospels, with a satirical element present in some of his parables.

> [The kingdom of God] is like a mustard seed, which, when sown upon the ground, is the smallest of all the seeds on earth; yet when it is sown it grows up and becomes the greatest of all shrubs, and puts forth large branches, so that the birds of the air can make nests in its shade.

This is an evident parody on, for example, Nebuchadnezzar's night vision of himself as a mighty tree: no such earthly kingdom in Jesus' understanding can be a match for the invasive, sprawling shrub which God plants himself. Down the centuries those who have given expression to mockery of false ambitions, interrupting our fantasies with a dose of reality, have sometimes been recognised as saints. This is especially true in the Eastern tradition where it is said that holy fools, such as the Russian *yurodivy*, might pelt people with rotten eggs as they emerged from church worship. In England that might overstep the mark, so only one such egg features in what follows.

Does any one of the scenes narrated here matter more than all the others? In Christ's reversal of human values it's not necessarily those endeavours that have occupied a lion's share of time and energy that are ultimately the most significant. Once again this is well understood by artists and writers. Marcel Proust wrote to Pierre Mainguet, the editor of an arts magazine:

> Say to the world, and some of the dissatisfied young men within it, 'Look not just at the Roman campagna, the pageantry of Venice and the proud expression of Charles I astride his horse, but also, have a look at the bowl on the sideboard, the dead fish in your kitchen and the crusty bread loaves in the hall'.

Again, it is intriguing to note that the Portuguese author José Saramango (winner of the Nobel Prize for Literature in 1998) downsized the title of his memoir from *The Book of Temptations* to the humbler *Small Memories* before its publication. Few of the details he records from his childhood days would be likely to command much media attention!

Sometimes a single encounter or an isolated happening can have a disproportionate impact.

**DO NOT FLUSH THE TOILET
DURING EVENSONG
OR THE LIGHTS WILL GO OUT IN CHURCH**

Sanitary arrangements with inbuilt liturgical consequences
as observed in a 1950s Somerset vicarage

Hence trivia from the parish pump are unashamedly included here alongside apparently weighty matters. Small details of personal attitude can mean much more than the expression of lofty ideals; they have the potential to engender fresh hope and perhaps a change of direction, or alternatively to dampen spirits and foster despondency. I believe the great Samuel Johnson would have endorsed this approach:

> There is nothing, Sir, too little for so little a creature as man. It is by studying little things that we attain the great art of having as little misery and as much happiness as possible.

The tomb of St Ignatius puts it even more profoundly in Latin, which translates as

> Not to be confined by the greatest, yet to be contained within the smallest, is truly divine.

A CAUTIONARY CHRONICLE

This feeble imitation of Hilaire Belloc began life as a gruesome entertainment at a parish party, inspired by the Fat Boy in Pickwick Papers who wanted to make his hearers' flesh creep. Whether it's really about irresponsible parenting, obesity, consumerism, capitalism out of control, global warming, the end of the world – or our personal descent into the nether regions – is not for me to say.

Please bear with us while we narrate
The grievous story of the late
Miss Prudence Esmerelda Dickie,
Whose sad demise was somewhat sticky:
For this poor child, if you will heed,
Paid dearly for her shocking greed.
She guzzled slabs of homemade toffee
And washed them down with sweetened coffee.

Her mother must take half the blame,
'Cos ever since her daughter came
Of age to eat she'd fed her Pru
On everything Mums shouldn't do -
Like jam and cream and dairy ices,
Buns and cakes - the hugest slices -
Suet pud and all things stodgy,
A diet best described as dodgy.
Despite becoming spotty-faced,
And rather large around the waist,
She never ate fresh fruit or greens -
And now we join her in her teens.

As we have said, her favourite victual
Was toffee sweetmeats, large or little,
Which mother churned out all day long
With cups of coffee steaming strong.
Each seemed to stimulate the other.
Then came the fatal day when mother
Showed Esmerelda what to do
In making trays of sugary glue.

The time arrived, we need not say,
When Mrs. D was out all day,
And Prudence was not slow to take
Advantage of this lucky break.
Our Esmerelda did not touch
The saucepans, frying-pans and such,
She did not use the casseroles,
Or baking-tins or pyrex bowls.
No, no! with feverish brow and manic zest
'Twas Mum's spin-dryer (acclaimed "the best").

She plugged it in and looked inside -
How vast a volume it could hide!
With glinting eye and toothy grin
She poured twelve bags of sugar in,
Eight pints of milk and eight of cream,
Six pounds of fat - she did not seem
The least bit troubled in her mind
What she eventually might find;
Nine tins of syrup, ten lumps of marge -
'Twere just as well the dryer was large.

So far so good, as yet no hitch.
She closed her eyes and turned the switch.
She held her breath and stared intent
As whirling round the liquid went.
Then with a gurgle of delight
She saw the symptoms now were right -
A frothing sea of sickly brown
Begun to bubble up and down.
It heaved and boiled like something vicious:
The smell however was delicious.

Pru sniffed the air, she sniffed once more.
It never smelt so nice before.
She bent down low and took a lick
At all that toffee sweet and thick.
Just one more taste, then two, then three,
She could not leave the molten sea.

Her lips, her chin, went deeper still,
Down against her weakening will.
'Til suddenly the whirlpool rose
And sealed her eyes and ears and nose.

She tried to leave the oozing muck,
But tighter yet the toffee stuck.
She flayed her arms in struggling grope -
To switch off seemed her only hope.
But when she felt along the dryer
She turned the crucial knob up higher;
The surging wave rotated quicker
And only made the toffee thicker.

Thus Esmerelda breathed her last,
For now the brew was circling fast,
And dashed what thoughts she'd had already
That she'd survive the bog-like eddy.

When Ma returned that night, she found
A topless body on the ground.
It was of course her daughter's torso.
She screamed aloud, but even more so
When in the liquid, brown and red,
She saw a toffee-coated head.

CHECKPOINT CHARLIES

It seems unfair to blame my genes, but I always seem to have had distinct criminal tendencies. The root cause, I suppose, is my impatience when caught up in a queue that edges forward only inch by inch, if at all; and then I start to look for alternative routes, shortcuts, back entrances and any loopholes worth exploiting. You may well question whether it was a wise choice to retire to a village cut off from the outside world by a railway barrier that descends six times in every hour. I do wonder, though, whether my real vocation should have been as a counter-terrorist agent, with a mind naturally evasive of checks and checkpoints.

One of my earliest memories is of visiting my grandmother who lived on the Lancashire coast just north of Blackpool. In the early 50s (and possibly still today) one of the attractions there was riding on the open-topped trams that ran along the seafront. These were designed with a driver's cab at both front and back, and there was a spiral staircase that ran down from the top deck at each end. Getting off the tram from the top you went to the rear stairs, of course; but one day, observing the congestion there, I thought of a much quicker way down – to go via the front staircase, where there was nobody at all. Well, there was nobody actually on the steps, but when I reached the bottom my heart sank because there was the driver of the tram whom I had to pass on the way out. What he said to me, probably aged about 7 years old, is quite unrepeatable; but it taught me two things: (1) never to get off a tram at the wrong end ever again, and (2) next time I wanted to outwit the crowd I really must double-check my plans.

A year or two later began a lifetime's engagement with Britain's stately homes, or shall I say, with their entrances and exits. It all started with a Sunday School outing to Woburn Abbey, home of the Duke of Bedford. As we approached the vast estate down the lanes, I couldn't help noticing a couple of back gates. It dawned on me that of course tractors and the like probably need access apart from the route taken by visitors; and that if a gateway's wide enough for a tractor, it's wide enough for the odd pedestrian or two. Perhaps in theory the driver of the tractor is expected to shut any gates behind him, but my juvenile knowledge of human nature had already come to appreciate that tractor drivers are as fallible as the rest of us and may prefer the easier option of leaving gates open for their return journey. On this particular visit I had no opportunity to test my theory further or to explore the risks entailed; but an encounter in the gift shop did rather prejudice me towards doing this in the future. Having collected all the free leaflets I could find (another long-standing weakness, I regret), I rashly decided to spend pocket-money on an illustrated guide to the Abbey. So I took it to the counter; paid for it; was just receiving it back, when the gaunt, bespectacled assistant popped the surprise question, 'Would you like me to sign it for you?' To which I immediately replied, 'No, thank you'. To no avail! he scribbled in it, and when I got outside I deciphered the scrawl: just one word, *Bedford*. It was a shattering revelation: to think that my seedy-looking sales assistant was actually a peer of the realm. My respect for the landed aristocracy plummeted.

There are certainly some stately homes where rear access is theoretically possible. As this may be legally questionable, I refrain from naming specific establishments. There are others though where ancient rights prevail in the form of public footpaths: a large-scale Ordnance Survey map is always worth scrutinising first. That doesn't, of course, give access to the house itself, but here a different approach might work. It's based on what Bertie Wooster's man Jeeves would have called 'the psychology of the individual'. The psychology of a cash-strapped Duke of Bedford is undoubtedly to make money, and to do so by any possible means (even if African lions have to shiver through our cold, wet summers). We could follow a simple syllogism: (1) Almost all stately homes have *tea rooms*. (2) The visitor's route through the house invariably ends in the *tea room*. (3) But to make even more money, the *tea room* is accessible without buying a ticket for the house itself. Hence, (4) on arrival, go directly to the *tea room*, and from there you may be able to work back through the house against the stream of visitors. However, (5) if an oncoming guide regards you with suspicion, cut your losses and inquire politely where the toilets are to be found; even better, ask directions to the *tea room*.

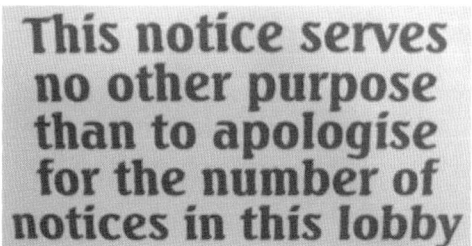

Photographed at Carisbrooke Castle, Isle of Wight
English Heritage[2] thus acknowledges that security notices are a modern aberration.

---

[2] Our true heritage (especially our freedom from the dead hand of regimented procedures) is epitomised in detective fiction, where the police rely upon amateurs like Miss Marple, and *The Mousetrap*'s plot hinges upon a policeman in disguise doing absolutely nothing. Today British bureaucracy (never mind the EU) is ever-increasing — and stifling common sense.

The most uncomfortable encounter I ever had was not in England though, but the States. You will realise that in America today tourists of any description are a huge risk to national security (never mind all the American-owned guns!) and therefore are viewed with great mistrust. A visitor, regardless of his spending capacity, is above all else a potential terrorist threat. So we found when staying in Montana back in 2001. One day, we called first at Little Bighorn where we learnt how battlefield archaeologists have now proved from the pattern of bullets that Colonel George Custer – archetypal American hero – never made a last stand at all, but was killed running away from the Indians. Their version of events was invariably squashed by Custer's widow who long outlived him and created the legend.

We then reckoned there was time to drive on to Bighorn Canyon National Park. As we went up the approach road, a notice barred the way, saying 'National Security Alert – no cars past this point'. It didn't suggest that the visitors centre was closed, but then the authorities probably never envisaged anyone in their right mind walking on from the barrier to reach it (although such was the instruction we'd met the previous day near a renowned Lewis and Clark lookout post on the Yellowstone river). So, after parking in the lot provided, this is what we did, only to have a jeep come in hot pursuit a few minutes later with a frenzied warden pointing his gun at us. He seemed quite unable to grasp that we were pedestrians and therefore, as far as the notice went, perfectly law-abiding. He ordered us to wait while he filed a charge. Ten minutes elapsed, and I thought that maybe he needed help filling in the form; he was plainly not a literary man. But as I approached, paranoia once again gripped his features and he yelled at me, again with a maniacal jerk of his gun, 'Git away from me, you scare me'. Finally his taxing efforts were complete, and we were handed tickets fining us $25 each, but with an appeal procedure listed on their reverse side.

Now the very day after this incident, the American Interior Secretary visited Billings where we were staying, and addressed a public meeting urging Americans not to be intimidated by terrorists, but to get out into their national parks and to use them. The speech was reported in the local paper and gave us a distinct impression that we really ought to be feted as pioneers of the true American spirit, not fined as dangerous foreign intruders. On our return to the UK I sent the cutting to the American Embassy, detailing the off-message behaviour of the warden, which I said rather marred an otherwise enjoyable visit to Montana. There was a charming reply, saying how pleased they were we'd had such a good time – and recommending we paid up. A few weeks later, back in Malawi, I posted off the tickets, opting to stand trial in court. I also pointed out that we couldn't afford the fare back to Montana, so they'd have to fly us over and it might cost them more than $25 each.

To this day on arriving in the States, we're nervous of the immigration authorities in case they've finally caught up with us, which presumably could mean Guantanamo Bay. On the application form for a visa, which you now have to complete in advance, we pay particular attention to the question from the 'intelligence' services which reads something like 'While in the USA do you intend to carry out acts of terrorism – Yes or No', and painstakingly delete the word Yes (as perhaps most others do, apart from strictly truthful members of Al Qaeda). Yet sometimes I ponder whether truthful answers are believed: a school friend just turned 17 applied for a provisional driving licence in the UK. Could he read a car number plate at a distance of 25 yards? No, was his honest admission; but the form was soon returned to him with the unexpected request 'Please alter No to Yes'. He is still contentedly driving around, as blind as a bat. Many years later a parishioner told me a companion tale about his younger daughter, when she was also aged 17. He'd just moved with his family to a diplomatic post in Washington, and in the process of updating the necessary documentation this said daughter had presented her provisional driving licence to an American official in the hope of gaining some kind of driving permit in the States. Not being familiar with the word 'provisional' he had issued her with a full American driving licence – which she proceeded later to exchange in turn for a full British licence. It so happened that she did have a little experience behind a wheel, but theoretically at least could have achieved her final goal without once sallying forth upon the highway!

Although entertaining at times, the inanities of officialdom can have less happy outcomes. Latterly I've realised my own difficulties with American agencies (including dealings with Citibank's call centre, an experience scarcely different from being interrogated under torture by CIA agents) actually pale into insignificance compared with those some of their own citizens endure. A lady named Summer Coish, it is reported, was recruited from the top specifically to engage with local people in Afghanistan, but then:

> She got her first dose of State Department bureaucracy. Although Holbrooke wanted her to get started right away, USAID insisted that she fill out a voluminous stack of security clearance forms that required her to list all of her travel outside the United States and every 'foreign contact' she had had in the previous eight years - no easy feat for someone who had lived overseas much of that time … The forms required so much information that some applicants spent three months completing them… It took four months for Coish to receive her clearance.

Although she was supremely well equipped by previous experience to build local connections and to foster cooperation with as many different parties across the board as possible, she found herself more or less a prisoner in America's diplomatic compound, 'ringed by tall walls topped with razor wire'.

> Embassy rules prevented Americans from leaving the compound unless they had official business... and even then they had to obtain permission from the security office... [Coish] eventually managed to leave nearly every night, but doing so often required creative obfuscation on her security forms to get an exit pass and an embassy vehicle.

So national security concerns effectively thwarted a promising government-sponsored initiative towards reconciliation (and after all, no longstanding conflict has ever been resolved without covert contacts). Are these security fanatics the same ones who, shortly after 9/11, gave a hard time to a 90 year old nun in a wheelchair at an airport checkpoint?

'Creative obfuscation' can on occasion be a very fruitful tactic, as an Anglican colleague in Sherborne discovered (alas, too late to be of advantage to himself) when leading a parish group on a visit to Syria. He himself was more widely travelled than most and had previously visited Israel. Border security agents there had stamped his passport accordingly, which meant that he found himself *persona non grata* when he presented himself to Syrian border control. There appeared to be no alternative other than handing over the entire group into his wife's hands, to embark on the tour without him. Subsequently, however, he discovered that French officials had found a much simpler solution to this 'marked passport' dilemma; they simply pasted a clean sheet over the offending page of the passport, no doubt embossing it with their own rubber stamp. It is not yet clear whether this ingenious idea has been implemented by British officials.

Soon after our own arrival in Malawi, I faced a related problem. A fax came through from customs agents in Lilongwe that our boxes had arrived and could be released as soon as I faxed them a copy of my 'letter of appointment'. Since all arrangements had been made through our missionary society, I had no such letter. It was clear that the Malawian authorities required an official form of some sort from our African bishop. This could potentially have led to a huge delay, and probably more than one visit to diocesan headquarters nearly an hour's journey away. We were, however, staying temporarily with a 'voluntary' priest (Mike, a tobacco and coffee farmer, who in English terms would be described as 'non-stipendiary'). I turned to Mike and said: 'Can you type as I dictate, with the bishop's address to head up the page, then sign it yourself as one of the bishop's officers?' The vital letter was produced in under fifteen minutes, faxed off to Lilongwe, and the very same afternoon permission came through, satisfied that all was now in order. However, any Malawian attempting to visit Britain would not find the experience so easy ...

John Vidal describes rampant discrimination (*The Guardian*, 2018)

The Gumbi Education Fund, a tiny charity set up to help educate children in Malawi, invited Patrick Kamzitu, its administrator and sole employee, to come to Britain this year to give two talks and meet donors. Because he had set up community libraries in villages that had never seen books, he was to speak at the Hay international book festival about how books can change lives.

Getting Patrick a visa from UK Immigration to come for eight days to tell his story was a nightmare of hostility, suspicion, bureaucracy and the exercise of remote power. A long application form had to be filled in online – a costly and hard task in itself for most Malawians who live without computers or electricity and who seldom go to the capital. But Patrick also had to provide his birth certificate, passport, marriage certificate, his children's birth certificates, his employment contracts and several months of bank statements. At the UK end, the Gumbi fund had to issue a letter of invitation, an hour-by-hour itinerary of everywhere he hoped to visit as well as personal and business bank account details. It was not enough. After three weeks and paying £147 online to a company in Johannesburg (which charged £5.48 for each email they sent), his request was refused. The letter stated that his income from administering the fund and working for the Malawi government as a health assistant was not enough to cover his stay in the UK. He was told that because he was a rural health assistant it was unclear why he should have been invited to Hay anyway.

But he was invited to apply again, for another £147. This time, his application was accompanied by a letter of support signed by a member of the House of Lords, the head of a large international charity and an organiser of the Hay festival. Once again he was refused: he had 'insufficient family and financial ties in Malawi' to return there; he appeared to have no savings and could not show that he would not abscond. There was no appeal, nowhere to turn to for official advice, and no chance of any of the £300 being returned. But he could apply again and pay £430 for a quick response.

It means that nearly 97% of Malawians and southern Africans who, like Patrick, earn less than a few thousand pounds a year are not welcome simply because they are not rich. Official figures show that hundreds of people from Malawi are refused visas for similar reasons every year. The Scottish-Malawi partnership, which represents more than 1,000 Scottish NGOs, churches, hospitals, schools and grassroots groups all with links to Malawi, reports that those invited here are being refused entry on offensive grounds every week. And it's not just Malawi. The latest UK figures show one in three Zimbabweans, and one in two Ghanaians are also denied visitors' visas. Yet only 2% of American citizens are denied entry.

There is of course a fundamental rule in all border dealings: never mess with officials, and never gag with them, as their sense of humour is entirely deficient. I learnt the latter truth the hard way, nearly 50 years ago when I went with a university friend on a trip to the Pyrenees. We crossed from Dover to Calais, where immigration wanted to know if we had anything to declare. We exchanged looks before replying that we didn't think so. The French guy then made us take the wheels off the car, poked behind all the seats, looked under the bonnet, had all our gear unpacked. It took another 30 minutes to put it all together again.

And this wasn't the only incident on that trip. My friend's uncle had a small chateau in the foothills south of Pau, within easy reach of the Spanish border. We went across once to visit Jaca, where Spanish brandy was then so cheap that housewives used it as a cleaning fluid. We returned via the mountain border post the following day. It was Sunday lunchtime, so we climbed up steps to the cafe on the French side where we found ourselves the only customers. We ordered a glass of wine each and a paté sandwich. The latter was totally inedible – rock hard stale bread with what careful DNA analysis might or might not have discovered to be paté, spread at most one molecule thick. Despite our best efforts to locate her, the bar-lady had vanished. So we drank up, leaving money on the counter sufficient just to pay for the wine. We returned to the car and were starting to drive off when the gendarme on duty, incited by angry cries from the café's balcony, yelled at us to halt. With his gun pointing in our direction we felt it prudent to do so. There ensued what might have become a major international incident. The bar-lady rejected our aspersions on her cuisine, the gendarme repeated the formula 'to order is to pay', which led us (as true Brits) to ridicule this primaeval way of thinking, and (perhaps tactlessly?) to suggest that the UK was a more advanced civilisation. But mentioning the UK was the magic moment. Suddenly the penny dropped that we were British. Miraculously, despite our overheated defence, all was forgiven and we parted the best of friends. What had happened? The bar-lady had mistaken us for the very lowest form of life, which she hated: the Spanish!

Ironically it was at this very same border post three years later that the tables were turned. With six of us now on board a minibus, we were being checked as we attempted to enter Spain. The official looked menacing as he spoke to us. We produced our passports; he shook his head. We gave him all the vehicle documents; he shook his head. We found our yellow fever immunisation forms; he shook his head. We ransacked our cases for the various insurance policies, medical and otherwise; he shook his head. We were becoming desperate – but finally he smiled, and explained in excellent English, 'All I said to you was "good morning"'.

Nearly 15 years later we found ourselves in Lesotho, where quite often we crossed into South Africa (then at the height of apartheid). The border posts were manned by Afrikaners whose principal object was to detect communist sympathisers. Thus, you were ill-advised to travel with books or videos making any reference to the Marx brothers, as they'd undoubtedly be identified as close relatives of Karl himself. I once foolishly took a book with me entitled *A Christian Critique of Marxism*, and I had a hard time explaining that 'critique' implied disapproval, opposition and censure.

Many of these officials were obviously kin to the archetypal van der Merwe, butt of all South African humour. How do you confuse van der Merwe? Give him two shovels and tell him to take his pick. How else do you confuse van der Merwe? Put him in a rondavel and tell him to stand in the corner. (In case that one's too subtle, it helps to know that a rondavel is the name for a traditional African round hut.) Then again, van der Merwe goes to the railway station, and asks for a return ticket. 'Where to, please?' Van der Merwe replies, 'Back here, of course, man'. And just one more for luck: Van der Merwe goes to the sales and says, 'I'd like to buy this TV set', but the salesman refuses, 'Sorry, we don't sell to Boers'. Van goes home, takes a shower, combs his hair, changes his clothes, goes back and tries again. 'Sorry, we don't sell to Boers'. This time Van goes home, and aims for a complete disguise, dyes his hair, shaves his beard, dons a new suit and tie, puts on fake glasses - then waits for a few days. He goes to the shop, says to the salesman, 'I'd like to buy this TV'. Same reply comes yet again, 'Sorry, we don't sell to Boers'. Van goes nearly crazy with frustration. 'How did you know I'm a Boer?' The salesman says, 'Because that's a microwave'.

A friend of ours, Patrick, a blunt Yorkshireman who ran the campus refectory in Roma, told me of an acrimonious exchange he'd had at the border post. Patrick worked for a South African company and had a border pass to facilitate his regular supply trips. But his wife didn't, and this was a period when the border was barely kept open by the South Africans in response to the Lesotho government's acceptance of aid from (communist) North Korea. Patrick sails through, but then waits an hour while his wife queues. 'This is a b... stupid system', he was heard to mutter. The Afrikaner who heard him hauled him in, and complained, 'This guy called me stupid'. Patrick's irate response: 'I did not call this man stupid. He may well be stupid for all I know, and I'm not saying he's not; but I didn't call him stupid. I said the system was stupid. If I wanted to call this man stupid, I'd say quite plainly, "Man you are stupid". But that's not what I said'. Inevitably they didn't appreciate the subtlety of Patrick's careful verbal distinctions. They removed his border pass and made him queue in future like everyone else.

We did, however, achieve a little triumph of our own around this time, when getting back into Lesotho after a trip into Cape Province. I studied the map carefully and discovered an obscure crossing point way south of the main border post at Caledon Bridge. We zigzagged round the edge of villages and fields to find it, partly via dirt roads and farm tracks. On our arrival at the end of the morning it turned out that we were the first customers of the day. I knew that the blockade was resulting in petrol shortages in Lesotho, so I'd bought two 25 litre cans in Grahamstown and filled them both up to the brim. Obviously we couldn't conceal them, and so were questioned about their capacity. 'Do you realise that you can carry only 20 litres of fuel across the border?' 'Well', I said, 'each of these cans is round about 10 litres, so two of them makes twenty'. 'OK then,' he responded, 'that's fine'. I justified the deception on the grounds that if 'all's fair in love and war' this surely extends to one's dealings with an apartheid regime (especially as 'Boer' rhymes conveniently with 'war'?).

Even though apartheid has ended, I'm not sure that things have changed that much. A few years ago we made a return trip to visit old friends, and had to pass more than once through Johannesburg. Sarah unfortunately had sprained her ankle badly, and we opted for wheelchair assistance at the airport. This meant we were ushered swiftly and painlessly through the first class check point, and that included me as my wife's 'care assistant'. Although I carried hand baggage for us both, never once was it X-rayed or scrutinised. So here's a tip: if you're a suicide bomber in South Africa, wrap a bandage round one of your legs, use a pair of crutches and ask for a wheelchair. It's simplicity itself! Unfortunately the idea has been hijacked elsewhere by the SKI generation (SKI as in 'spending the kids' inheritance'). At a British airport these days it's not uncommon, when the request is made for those with children or with mobility problems to make their way to the departure gate, to see a few of the not-quite-elderly hobble slowly forwards leaning on Leki ski poles, only to collapse the poles once they're presented their boarding passes and then to sprint down to the plane.

My biggest grouse with airports these days though is the restriction on what you can take into the cabin. Most of the time I travel light (not even a ski pole) and have only hand baggage. The problem about this is precisely one item: nail scissors, essential to my very existence. They used to be banned altogether, but at Heathrow they're allowed so long as the blade is less than (I think) 30 millimetres. This is not the case at Bournemouth, whence we sometimes flew with Ryanair. Our MP in Dorset thought like me that the lack of uniformity across the country was nonsensical but found no support in government circles for any change. So one year I took two identical pairs of scissors, taped them together to produce a metallic flower with four petals, fixed it firmly inside my bag adjacent to the metallic handle supports, and prayed that the X-ray machine would be deceived by this slightly unusual ornament. It was! I count that the high point of a life of otherwise largely unsuccessful criminal activity.[3]

Since then I have, however, learnt that security machines have been developed with a superior capacity for suspicion. Returning more recently from Logan airport in Boston, my cabin case was pulled to one side for closer examination: every nook and cranny was searched – but in vain. I inquired of the official what he thought I might be carrying, to which he replied: 'The scan showed a long green line, which tells us you have an explosive device'. 'And what did you actually find?' I asked. 'It was a paperback book', he admitted. In an age when books are becoming a rarity, is their very possession now reckoned to be so dangerously subversive? Curiously, I have had on occasion to dissuade the security staff at Gatwick from calling in a bomb disposal squad to detonate my much-travelled tin of brown shoe polish – while at Heathrow they too now challenge paperbacks, on the grounds that certain fibres found in books can be turned into explosive material: I'd concede that you could start a fire with pages from a book, but wouldn't the smoke alarm go off? And what about the magazines already supplied onboard a plane? I now realise that Evelyn Waugh, whose novel *Vile Bodies* was published in 1930, was a prophet ahead of his time. He describes how his hero Adam lost a whole suitcase worth of books on encountering a British customs officer, who commented:

> Particularly against books the Home Secretary is. If we can't stamp out literature in the country, we can at least stop its bring brought in from outside. That's what he said the other day in Parliament, and I says "Hear, hear".

Today we use sophisticated gadgetry to scan baggage, yet – despite its inevitable limitations – our digital faith increases by leaps and bounds. The lesson of those historic stable doors – i.e. the inescapable *human* factor – has perhaps never been fully learnt? Two years ago I received a fine for speeding on the M20, a motorway on which I had not driven for at least six months. At the time of the alleged incident I had a witness (my wife) that I was in our bathroom at home, the car being firmly locked away in the garage. The accompanying paperwork from the police informed me that the state-of-the-art cameras were checked by 'our highly trained' staff, implying that

---

[3] More modest success was achieved around the same time in Sherborne when I discovered how to gain access to a gated development. Initially when I paid a pastoral visit the gates were opened for me by the parishioner in question, after dialing through to him via the keypad. On leaving, however, I used the large button just inside the gates to effect my own exit. Realising that this was within easy reach of an umbrella extended through the (wrought iron) gates from the outside, you can now guess how I gained entry on future occasions. It saved time (particularly useful in a downpour of rain)!

it would be useless to mount a challenge. I phoned up nonetheless and asked if the photographic evidence could be reviewed. The response was a climb-down: 'they seem to have made a mistake — it wasn't your number plate'. Just to reassure myself I inquired further as to the colour of the car in question?' 'O, you can't make that out at all — the sun was shining'. The obvious way forward, if camera technology has reached its limits, would surely be to ban all driving except on cloudy days?

Yet not long after this episode, by strange coincidence, I discovered from our local community policeman that CCTV recorded footage can also lack precision once darkness has descended. When I heard of night-time thefts in our village, I realized that helpful evidence might be found from the camera positioned at the entrance to our close, given that around 1 am on the night in question a car had been driven noisily past our house but had immediately made its exit in the opposite direction (perhaps because the driver was trying to flee the village and was unfamiliar with the road network?). When I rang to report the incident, imagining that the vehicle's registration number might prove useful in any 'further inquiries', I was at once rebuffed. Such video images would be quite inadequate to provide the required information, so I was informed! (Our neighbours nevertheless persist in thinking that video footage will somehow make them safer, just as they rely on smoke alarms that are frequently being activated by spiders, scent and all things smelly. Yet you can cry 'Wolf!' once too often …)

Is it working?

CRAZY CONVICTIONS
Quand on est jeune, c'est normal de se revolter.
Quand on ne se revolte plus, c'est normal qu'on soit vieux.

Growing up as a Methodist, one was aware of being different: we realised that we stood in a tradition of non-conformity. Whether this was quite what my mother meant on those frequent occasions when she informed me that I wasn't 'normal', I'm not sure. It struck me at times that she might not always be the best judge of normality, given her propensity in later life to dial 999 at three o'clock in the morning in order to summon a policeman to investigate the 'strange noises' she heard in or near her house. This was an often-successful ploy whereby she could invite the constable in and offer him a cup of tea. The ensuing friendly chat would thus help the tedious hours to pass more quickly when she couldn't get to sleep.

I first fulfilled the expectations laid upon me to stand aside from the crowd in a published letter, written when I was about ten years old to *The Methodist Recorder.* My caveat was about a popular children's hymn which began 'There's a friend for little children above the bright blue sky'. It was not the naive assumption that the sky was always blue that concerned me, but the apparent location of heaven in a distant region of the universe. While recognising that symbolic language was being used, nevertheless it seemed to me to present a one-sided view of divine reality. There were repercussions in our local Methodist church, where several elderly subscribers to the newspaper were clearly shocked by this juvenile outspokenness, considering it a manifestation of incipient unbelief. Hymns were after all held by many Methodists to be as sacred as scripture itself.

The next opportunity to flex my muscles came at school, when it was expected that all those in the fourth form and above would spend their Friday afternoons preparing to defend the realm. A small minority of us felt that these schoolboy manoeuvres were misconceived, particularly as rather too much attention seemed to be given to polishing one's kit and then marching up and down the school playground. The object of such activity was presumably to inculcate an ethos of mindless obedience, known in official jargon as *esprit de corps*. Nor was the commanding officer a member of staff who attracted too much respect. He had been our chemistry teacher the previous year, and there was at least one boy in our class who always seem to know far more about the subject than he did. Further, 'Percy' (to give him his nickname) had the curious habit at school lunches of stirring everything on his plate into one unappetising mess. However, despite the fact that his troops never reached active service, army command seemed to appreciate his soldierly abilities. Every few years he gained a higher rank, until at last he became a Lieutenant Colonel. For a Methodist there were yet more profound reasons for not joining in: (1) Percy was known to belong to a pseudo-religion called the Masons, and (2) in any case we were all staunch pacifists. Our punishment was manual labour. We were consigned to shifting barrowloads of soil in the school orchard, supposedly in preparation for an outdoor amphitheatre. After a whole year spent in this Siberian toil, the master in charge (possibly a fan of Sisyphus) discovered that he had misread the plans, so we spent a further year removing earth from our careful mounds to form new dumps elsewhere. I learnt the truth of Bertrand Russell's observation, that there are two forms of work, one being to move inert matter from one place to another oneself, and the second being simply to instruct other people to do this same dirty work! I have a recollection that Stephen Hawking was among those who earned their moral stripes in this weekly activity, although this may be an extrapolation of his sister's presence in my own Sunday School class.

When I subsequently became a teacher at Oundle School for three years, I was obviously useless for CCF duties, so my initial (extra-curricular) responsibility was for the scout troop. Here my ignorance of knots let me down, and at my first camping exercise in the grounds of Chatsworth House I was embarrassed by my inability to handle a primus stove, which I had carefully concealed behind a rocky mound. I think I may have added too much methylated spirit, or so I concluded when flames shot yards into the air, attracting the attention of the troop who sarcastically inquired if I was 'having trouble, sir?' It was a relief to exchange scouting for the Wednesday afternoon social service unit, ever popular with the boys because old ladies whom they visited were often generous with the sherry bottle and cigarettes.

Forty years on, my mis-spent youth also caught up with me as a Catholic priest when I became civilian chaplain at RNAS Yeovilton. I was terrified of mistakenly entering a top secret bunker on site, in case I was shot at dawn shortly afterwards – but my pleas for some induction training were ignored. There were a number of mooted initiatives that might have helped, but it became clear that in the military there is 'many a slip 'twixt cup and lip'. The biggest challenge occurred in a helicopter hangar one Christmas when no one informed me that I'd been allocated the last reading at the annual carol service. The previous carol having ended, my team leader looked across, and said, 'Father Rodney, this is you - you're on now'. The one small snag was that no text was provided and unsurprisingly no Bible was to hand in the hangar. So, in front of the assembled gathering, numbering several hundred personnel, I had to recite from memory the first half of St John's Gospel chapter one. I think I recalled sufficient familiar phrases to bluff my way through, relying on the likelihood of the majority of those present being relatively unfamiliar with the text themselves. When I sat down, the commodore muttered, 'I rather think he owes you a drink or two'.

A particular bane of my military career was the requirement to check email messages on one of the chaplaincy computers. The latter dated back to the Boer War or thereabouts, and took nearly an hour to load up (this is *not* one of my usual exaggerations). There were then discovered at least forty spam messages each day, which the IT department declared impossible to filter out. This raised doubts in my mind about the effectiveness of our defences against inter-continental ballistic missiles, which were surely far harder to cope with? I also received regular official bulletins and other notices, totally riddled with naval acronyms, none of which made any sense to a mere civilian. After a time, I gave up the attempt to keep abreast of strategic plans and allowed the computer to lie fallow. It appears retrospectively that national security was not thereby much endangered.

We were once summoned to a security briefing (supposedly an annual requirement, although it never recurred), and I suggested raising the issue of spam emails. 'Don't even think of it,' said my team leader, 'I should be so embarrassed'. The head of security spent much of the time telling us that the real threat to Britain lay not in Afghanistan but on the internet, where disaffected Muslim youths in Bradford could easily discover how to construct home-made bombs and form a cell group. I nudged the team-leader: 'I was right all along. It is the internet that's the problem' The security chief pointed out that, as a naval officer, if he came across any unattended bags in the camp he would naturally return them to the owner, whereas he regretted that his staff – seconded from the army – would be more inclined to liven up their uneventful lives by initiating a major alert and summoning the bomb disposal unit. 'You think I'm joking?' he asked. 'Only last week,' he said, 'a squadron leader was here for a meeting. He left his briefcase in the office where it was taking place when he went for lunch in the wardroom; when he got back, his case had been blown up, and someone handed him a bill for £100 to redecorate the room'.

At other times, I engaged with officers and other personnel during meals. There were occasionally some who seemed quite to disregard the effect of military operations on civilian populations, and with these I endeavoured (as tactfully as possible) to introduce a more humane perspective. Even so, I recall a highly devout Catholic engineer who took some persuading that killing innocent people was morally unacceptable. There was also a widespread blindness to the effects on other societies of the rampant self indulgence, permissiveness, drink, drugs (and so on) that they too often perceived within the Western world. Is this what we were defending? I asked them. Was it not necessary for self-correction to accompany, if not actually precede, any attempt to impose our so-called 'values' upon others? What was it, in fact, that drove terrorists and extremists in their campaign against the West? Were not some right wing extremists in America – 'Christian' though they claimed to be – just as much a threat to world peace as Muslim fundamentalists?

When I first reached university in much younger days, it was a natural expression of the anti-war mentality fostered in me from an early age (particularly by my father who was a conscientious objector during World War 2) to take part in a CND march in London, as well as to be regular every Friday lunchtime during term to eat War on Want fare consisting of soup, bread and cheese. This again cohered with my childhood upbringing, where reports of missionary work abroad featured regularly at church and indeed in my own growing collection of biographies of outstanding missionaries. The contrast with what I observed in college was sometimes stark. The regular round of meals was adequate to keep students alive, but it seemed to me that there were rather too frequently college feasts when dons and privileged undergraduates (such as myself, on a scholarship) dined extremely sumptuously. In the end, I decided on a dramatic, if entirely futile, protest. I wrote to the Master resigning my scholarship. It didn't change the habits of four hundred and fifty years (which was the age of the college) but was a very tiny witness to the existence of the millions elsewhere who struggled to survive. Yet it may have paid dividends: many years later the college gave a generous grant to our work in Africa.

The next foray had to wait until after I was ordained, when it became possible to test the power of the press. The interest taken in one or two articles written for our parish magazine in Northampton by *The Chronicle and Echo* was actually quite unanticipated. I was fortunate in having possibly the best training incumbent imaginable, who allowed full scope to his curates, including freedom of expression both in the pulpit and in print. I've never (I hope) belonged to the school of vicars who begin their monthly musings with such headline grabbing thoughts as 'Looking out of my study window, I see the daffodils begin to peep through in my garden' (or – far, far worse – 'I can't believe it's nearly Christmas again'), although there's undoubtedly an appreciative market for such soothing sentiments. A more challenging cue comes from Pope Gregory the Great (in his *Pastoral Rule*):

> Negligent religious leaders are often afraid to speak freely and say what needs to be said – for fear of losing favour with people.

What sparked off our local paper were some home truths for our congregation:

In most ways the continuing existence of separate Christian denominations in Far Cotton is unnecessary and unwelcome. It is first and foremost a disgrace that we cannot work and worship together more closely when each church believes most fervently in the unity of Christ and the brotherhood of love. It is a scandal that non-Christians see us so apparently at odds.

Furthermore, it is an expensive schism, entailing the multiplication of costly buildings and equipment. It is wasteful of time and of effort – how many man-hours are spent on church committees in the area each month? Divided among ourselves, we concentrate our strength on keeping up appearances: there seem to be no resources to spare for the conversion of a pagan place.

Yet South Northampton is a pagan place. There are well over 12,000 people within a mile's radius of your door who have little more than the faintest interest in the doings of our different churches. Their knowledge of Christianity is minimal, and what they do know seems irrelevant. Perhaps a good number of the older one would class themselves as Christian, but their days are drawing to a close, and in the younger generation there is great ignorance and apathy.

I hadn't appreciated when typing those thoughts that the phrase 'pagan place' might evoke echoes of the long running soap opera Peyton Place, but it was obviously this resonance that fired up an editorial in the press headed Pagan Northampton: 'South Northampton', it ran, 'may feel it is a little unfair for it to be dubbed Pagan Place – the name given to the area by Far Cotton curate, the Rev Rodney Schofield – for the comments he makes could well apply to almost anywhere in Britain'. A reporter was dispatched to interview local people, and the correspondence columns hummed briefly. No one, however, denied the essential points being made – so perhaps the paper's slightly twisted version of my words was worthwhile.

Indeed, editorial policy seemed remarkably sympathetic to the Christian cause, as a subsequent leading article, responding to further remarks about the quality of religious education in schools, made clear:

PARENTS' DUTY
According to the Rev Rodney Schofield, the curate who caused a bit of a furore recently when he dubbed part of Northampton 'Pagan Place', there are many schools where religious instruction has now virtually ceased.

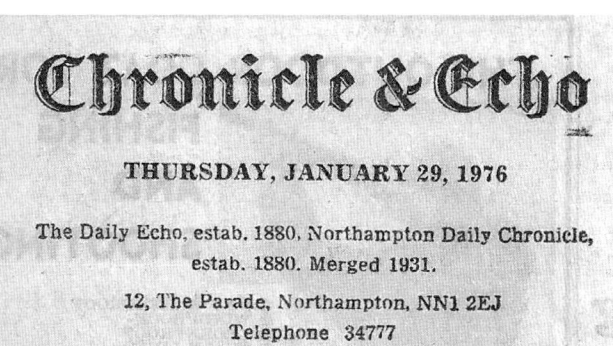

25

[There follows a summary of issues such as bias and indoctrination, the need for children to make their own decisions, the conscience clause that allows teachers to opt out.]

Nevertheless the effect of Christianity on world history is so profound that it can hardly be sidestepped. Even where religious instruction is well presented, however, it must surely be the responsibility of parents to ensure that their children's knowledge is adequate and balanced. As Mr Schofield points out, Christianity cannot expect a privileged position, but equally Christian parents should ensure that the system is not prejudiced against it.

It will be clear from the church magazine extract that Christian unity has long been a priority in my thinking, even though it has sometimes mattered less to others. Indeed, much at the local level depends upon cooperation between the clergy of the various different churches. Some, alas, have no interest in anything not organized by themselves or on their own premises. Or again, there can be excellent relations with a particular priest or minister, but his or her replacement may effectively scupper what has been patiently built up over the years. In some places it is the readiness of lay people to work and pray together that has brought the churches together. However, 'community fellowships' (despite their name) and the more extreme evangelical chapels are usually wary of engaging with others who fail to affirm their supposedly sounder theological principles. In Taunton, where every year Christians combined in a dramatic outdoor procession of the Cross, we tried hard to bring these other churches into the fold, yet they complained that we had no sense of mission to the unchurched. Another project, helping to boost the public libraries of our area with a broader diet of Christian reading to counterbalance the many books in stock about angels, Buddhism, crystals, demonology, earth goddesses (... and so on through the entire alphabet), met with the same objection! My successor as chairman of the council of churches negotiated a deal with these fellowships that our statement of faith, until then a simple reference to the Apostles' Creed, would expand to include clauses such as the inerrancy of scripture. At that point, the Catholic church and several traditional Anglican parishes withdrew their support. (In *Akenfield* – published in 1969 – the Strict Baptist deacon in this Suffolk village remarks that 'The biggest thing which is upsetting us is this Ecumenical Movement. It is getting the Roman Catholics in. If it does this, we must stay at loggerheads because with us the Roman Catholics are completely *out*'.) What may perhaps always be needed is a special envoy from the UN trained in the subtle art of diplomacy!

Garrison Keillor, in reminiscences of his childhood, hardly exaggerates when he describes divisions among the 'exclusive' Brethren in Lake Wobegon:

Once free of the worldly Anglicans, these firebrands were not content to worship in peace but turned their guns on each other. Scholarly to the core and perfect literalists every one, they set to arguing over points that, to any outsider, would have seemed very minor indeed but which to them were crucial to the Faith, including the question: if Believer A is associated with Believer B who has somehow associated himself with C who holds a False Doctrine, must D break off association with A, even though A does not hold the Doctrine, to avoid the taint? [The correct answer is: Yes.]

In less democratic societies a Roman emperor such as Constantine could simply bang Christian heads together.

One of the saddest features of Christian disunity is that it is so easily exported elsewhere. Mission to the Basotho people of Southern Africa was begun in the 1830s by French Protestants. When the British arrived on the scene as a dominant colonial power, it was understandable that Anglican chaplaincies began to appear as well. When, however, the priests who served them began to widen their mission to the native population, the French missionaries pleaded in vain for restraint, on the grounds that converts would then be divided one from another. Catholic centres were soon established as well, so that by the 1980s (during our time in Roma) it seemed that Christian tribalism had taken over: schools and indeed entire villages were branded as 'out of bounds' to other church denominations. I asked our Anglican students if, for example, Roman Catholic children might ever be admitted to an Anglican school: only, they agreed together, if an equal number of Anglican children were allowed to attend some Catholic school.

Other than those churches that exercise local autonomy it is of course necessary for central church authorities to determine the boundaries of acceptable doctrine and practice. The influence of local schemes and the impact of individual voices are then necessarily weaker, but not entirely useless – despite one's suspicion that, while all are equal before God, some are regarded as more important than others in his Church. It was during the rapid transformation of the Church of England in the 1990s from a body in solidarity with Christian tradition to a sect rather more of its own making that I pleaded for some restraint. Clifford Longley expressed the main issue in a nutshell: 'There is a kind of creeping infallibility about the self-regard of an Anglican synod'. By the end of that decade a survey revealed that no more than 25% of liberal Anglicans believed in the virgin birth or the uniqueness of Christ, while scarcely one third gave credence to the story of Jesus' bodily resurrection. Yet this was the very period when such liberals gained ascendancy in our English church affairs – and sadly, during my ten years' service on General Synod, I cannot recall any readiness to pause and hear what Anglicans in the rest of our worldwide communion had to say: hence, the fractured state of that communion today.

Clearly a national newspaper has a wider readership than any local rag, so I penned a number of letters that were published in *The Times*. With 'liberation' theology gaining popularity and sometimes being misused to justify change of any description, I was able to point out on the basis of first-hand acquaintance with archbishop Desmond Tutu (who was being invoked at the time) that he was far less radical than some supposed. I had travelled in the 1980s to Johannesburg, where he was then bishop, for discussions with him prior to admitting several of his Soweto ordinands to Lelapa la Jesu Seminary in Lesotho. His main emphasis, as I clearly recalled, was not on promoting revolutionary ideas nor even liberal practices, but (in his own words) on encouraging 'a sound understanding of the Bible'. This was not particularly apparent in many of the documents which came before General Synod, where the authorities usually cited were synodical reports of slightly earlier date.

In particular, one report, chaired by my own bishop and published as *Something to Celebrate*, offered a new perspective on family life in England. It concluded that all was for the best in this best of all possible worlds; provided, that is, that 'marriage' can be redefined to include cohabitation and 'family' to mean any group of people who happen for the time being to live under the same roof. So I observed (again in a letter published in *The Times*):

> It is a pity that in the more controversial areas [of this report] the Church of England did not apparently take the opportunity to consult with other ecumenical partners. There are statements and conclusions here from which other Christian bodies may wish to distance themselves. And if they do, the credibility of our Christian witness will be impaired.

It was about this time too that strange rites, endorsed again by my own bishop, were emerging. There was 'An Order of Service for Healing the Family Tree', which – no doubt by sheer oversight – had been omitted from the Book of Common Prayer. It was intended for people worried that their ancestors might be exerting a malevolent influence over their lives. In essence this was to be healed by holding consecrated bread and wine over a diagram of the family tree (making the possibly rash assumption that the wicked forebears were listed on it), while reciting a prayer, 'Cleanse our family tree, Father … cleanse us and our generation from any adverse effect of the past'. I impolitely suggested, drawing upon our African travels, that the rite was 'all too redolent of the bones and entrails used in primitive tribal cultures'.

The ecclesiastical ruling classes were not enamoured of such thoughts. Nor did they appreciate an especially blunt communiqué published early in 1996:

> Sir, Anglican bishops may condemn huge lottery wins as 'grotesque' and 'obscene', and bemoan the ill-effects of a scratchcard culture (report, January 1), but I fear their words will

carry little weight until they also renounce taking advantage of the heritage funds that are generated.

This will be a hard and bitter financial pill to swallow, costing the Church millions of pounds. But that, I believe, is the price of moral integrity – or so I was taught in my Methodist upbringing, for which I remain profoundly grateful.

Yours faithfully etc.

Following this, Jim (my bishop at the time) sent a note to the effect that if I wanted to 'get anywhere in the Church of England' I had better stop writing to *The Times*.

Yet an earlier missive printed (on Christmas Eve 1993) under the sub-editor's heading 'Squalls ahead for an ageing Church', which reflected an ongoing concern about vocations to ordained ministry, might have given him a clue about what 'getting somewhere' truly signified. It concluded with these two sentences:

> My own prayer is that young people will not always be wooed by the siren voices of secular opportunity and advancement, but will sometimes respond at an earlier age [countering the trend to older ordinands] to the eternal verities, and discover the rewarding challenge of Christian ministry. It is not a career, and I hope never will be, but an opportunity to live humanly and sometimes to help others a little nearer to their own salvation.

(In fact, before Jim took up his episcopal appointment I had been asked by the then-suffragan bishop to attend a conference at St George's house, Windsor. The day after arriving there I discovered to my dismay that other participants were expecting this course to enhance their rapid 'promotion' within the church – indeed, one man complained that he'd been here previously and had not yet received the archidiaconal status that was plainly his due. I promptly left Windsor and went home!)

The above (1993) letter followed an ill-conceived church report *Order in Diversity*, which had come out earlier that year, claiming that there was a surplus of stipendiary clergy in the Church of England. Not only did I write to *The Times*, but I also lobbied *The Church Times*, which published an article headed 'If they start later they won't last so long', followed by a further article two years later. It was quite obvious that Church House statisticians were useless at doing sums!

> What concerns me is the undue emphasis now being placed upon clergy numbers, whether in service or in training, without regard to clergy ages ... A policy of counting heads without noticing how many hairs remain on those heads will, in the long term, run into trouble ... If ordinands in the 1990s are markedly older than in previous decades we shall reap the consequences the decade after next.

The House of Bishops, however, responded to the report without looking at the longer-term consequences, and introduced restrictions on the sponsoring of ordination candidates, on the grounds that otherwise too many new priests would find themselves unemployed. By early 1996 it was admitted that the apparent surplus was a short-lived phenomenon, arising from some dioceses' financial difficulties. The bishops were then forced into a dramatic U turn.

After the episcopal warning I received in 1996 it was a surprise some two years later to be invited to Blackburn to be interviewed for an archdeacon's post. The question I remember was about the growing Muslim presence in the area: what would I do about it? I recalled my congenial memories of Muslim parishioners in Northampton and described the welcome accorded me in one home that I visited. Despite the fact that I introduced myself as a Christian priest, who came inconveniently interrupting a time of prayer, the family invited me in, turned off their tape recording, provided me with a footstool for my feet and offered me refreshment – 'yet never on any occasion,' I observed to my interlocutors, 'have I found a Christian family at prayer together in their home; nor has any Anglican household provided me with a footstool. So I think our first response to Muslims should be to welcome them as co-religionists, people who believe in God and – at best – attempt to live a devout and moral life. We have more in common with them than with the godless masses, and maybe their practice of prayer even puts us to shame at times'. Needless to say, a different candidate was chosen for the post.

By now, it was becoming clearer that my future calling lay elsewhere. I abandoned the press, and in time took to exploring the dilemmas of the modern age at greater length in books. Africa liberated me to write about third world debt, about superstitious beliefs, about changing pastoral approaches to people looking for some kind of hope and meaning in their lives, and – later on – a re-examination of early church communities (from whom I gained much subversive inspiration). Back in England, I studied the Qur'an in some detail, and offered a series of talks for local laity and clergy alike to attend. It led to an article in *The Pastoral Review*, and eventually to an in-service training course for priests and deacons in the archdiocese of Southwark where I am now based. Much more, however, needs to be done to further Christian-Muslim understanding, and there are encouraging signs that some churches in England are waking up to the challenge. Of course, there are Islamic extremists, just as there are bigots and fanatics in other faiths – and in many walks of life – but learning to appreciate and live alongside those who are different from ourselves is fundamental to the peace and stability both of local communities and of the world at large.

SERVERS and SCONES

Anglicanism has sometimes likened itself to a stool supported on three legs – scripture, tradition and reason. Although bishops and synods may heed contemporary trends rather more readily at times than these customary norms, the same is not necessarily true of local congregations. I recall a priest reporting his early days in a Poole parish: at the Sunday Eucharist he was puzzled to see the servers take a giant footstep (somewhat reminiscent of a Nazi goose step) each time they passed in front of the altar. After a couple of Sundays he ventured to ask a young server what this particular gesture signified, not having encountered it in his previous ministry. The server professed ignorance but said that this was the way he had been instructed when commencing his duties. A teenage server gave much the same reply, as did an older man. So finally he tackled the longest serving of them all, who at last explained the meaning and origin of the rite: 'It goes back,' he said, 'to the early days of this church when a heating pipe ran here, and the altar was in a slightly different position. We always had to step well over the pipe for fear of tripping'. 'Presumably the pipe's been gone for some time now?' was the next question. 'Of course,' came the answer, 'it must be thirty years since it went'. The servers, however, had remained faithful to their liturgical heritage, and made sure each new generation kept it alive.

So too in other ways church life clings to past conventions long past their sell-by date. John Betjeman was perhaps unduly critical when he observed in a letter of March 1950 (commenting on the state of church life he had just encountered in his new village):

> My experience is that there is no Faith in English villages at all, only convention.

Not that he was wholly dismissive, since he opined that 'the convention can be turned into Faith', which is probably true for many of us.

Certainly 'old habits die hard', and one habit particularly hard to change is where people sit in church. It is not an uncommon experience for unsuspecting visitors or newcomers to be asked by the more inflexible regulars to move out of 'their' pew. Even cathedral clergy have been known to cling to their accustomed stalls; I did this myself when, as a prebendary of Wells, I inherited 'Wedmore V' from my deceased father-in-law. Bishops too normally prefer their own thrones; but Pope Francis, renowned for hopping on local buses, may perhaps have related liturgical surprises in store for us (and there is good scriptural warrant for giving children any available seats of honour, which was the preferred practice of Brother Roger in the chapel at Taizé).

At Irchester in the late 1970s there was usually a healthy congregation for our 6.30 pm service of evensong, which numbered a surprising number of retired men. I soon discovered that most of them had once been choirboys – and so were long familiar with the service – and now, having been widowed, had come back to church for the company and for old times' sake. They invariably huddled together in the rear pews, leaving yawning gaps in front of them. So one evening I suggested that they might move forward; to encourage them to do so I turned off the lights at the far end of the nave. That Sunday they reluctantly came nearer, but ever thereafter they sat once again at the back – in the semi-dark!

Front pews of course are seldom filled, and across the Nene at Irthlingborough my friend and neighbour John petitioned for a faculty to remove them, on the grounds that (1) no one ever sat there and (2) weddings and funerals, and sometimes special children's events, were very cramped for space between the nave and the choir stalls. The moment he announced his intention a small conservative group within the congregation moved themselves several pews forward and occupied these front seats week after week, claiming in the end that they had sat there from time immemorial. I believe, however, that his faculty application went through, even if at some personal cost.

Similar intransigence can occur with flower ladies too. The first festival after our arrival in Irchester was for harvest, and in my innocence (but after discovering where flower stands were usually placed) I posted a plan of the church which invited members of the congregation to sign their names in their preferred location. It seemed to me a suitably democratic way of organising the occasion. Names duly appeared on the plan, but then a relatively infrequent church attender arrived on my doorstep furious that someone else had staked a claim on 'her' windowsill. 'Well, there are still vacancies elsewhere in church', I timidly suggested. 'But that's *my* window!' she insisted, 'I've done it for the last ten years'. This, sadly, made a considerable dent in her future church loyalty: I resolved to be much more circumspect thereafter in any such intervention. To this day I wonder about the policy followed in Leeds where my fellow curate in Northampton (now a bishop) had previously served: there, each Saturday evening, the clergy team marched around the church for the vicar to inspect the flowers, and if he was dissatisfied with any display he would order one of his curates to step forward and reposition the blooms under his direction. This courageous policy seems hardly likely to succeed elsewhere?

In my later role with ordinands I spelt out a very simple rule of thumb to allay their fears. 'Surviving as a vicar' I would suggest, 'is not hard *provided* one avoids the three fundamental pitfalls: don't tell primary school children at Christmas that Santa

Claus is a myth; don't preach about pacifism on Remembrance Sunday; and most important (as above) never mess with the flower – or tea – ladies.'

Nevertheless, it is sometimes necessary to act as an umpire when the ladies can't agree among themselves. A year or so after a 'patchwork group' had established itself in our church room at West Monkton an exhibition of their work was staged in the church itself. This brought in many visitors, raised some funds, and facilitated quite a few useful encounters and conversations, even if the interior of the building began to resemble an oriental souk. Teas were also provided in our garden, but here not quite all was sweetness and light: the scones had been baked in several different kitchens, and were of varying sizes, shapes and indeed edibility, meaning that while one person might be served with two large succulent specimens the person following in the queue might be palmed off with a couple of rock-hard miniscule lumps on his or her plate. It rapidly became clear that 'quality control' was needed here, so that all scones would conform to agreed specifications, otherwise (who could tell?) rioting or acts of unseemly violence might ensue. The disappointing fact is that parish teas and the art of baking scones are still not on the curriculum of seminaries and theological colleges, despite the indisputable scriptural instruction of our Lord to St Peter to 'Feed my sheep'. I would not of course deny that this covers more than afternoon teas[4], nevertheless the existence of conflicting views about which recipes should then be used does call for parochial resolution – and who but the parish priest can act impartially in the matter?

Such a role is of course remarkably similar to that exercised by the Holy Father within the Universal Church (this would have been obvious to Miss Marple, who fully understood how her little village of St Mary Mead was the entire world in microcosm). The disputes are different, but the rationale for resolving them as amicably as possible is much the same, viz. to ensure that the outside world's perception of the church is not in conflict with the ethos that she professes; what Christians preach, they should also practise. Very often the rift in church circles is more about doctrines than about scones, but the human factors are very similar. People evolve and then treasure their pet ideas, which they too readily promulgate without regard to what others think. Christianity has been littered with deviant notions

---

[4] Inspiration may yet be drawn from the untainted spirit of the priest celebrated in verse:
    There was a pious young priest
    Who lived almost wholly on yeast,
        For, he said, it is plain
        We must all rise again
    And I want to get started at least.

practically from day 1, and the outcome has generally been further division, to the extent that today there are tens of thousands of different sects across the world, the number of which increases year by year despite valiant efforts to hold churches together or (occasionally) to mend the fences between them.

In reading the Qur'an I was reminded of the particularly contentious times in which the prophet Muhammad lived, and of how in his part of the world there were such acrimonious relationships between the various Christian chefs (I refer here to their clashing Trinitarian or Christological 'recipes'). The Qur'an has repeated references to the 'factions' that proliferated among Christians in the 5th and 6th centuries: for example –

> They have split their community into sects, each rejoicing in their own. [Q 23.53]
> They differed among themselves out of mutual rivalry. [Q 45.17]

The factions were particularly in evidence in Muhammad's part of the world, with the fortunes of different churches very dependent upon the changing political scene. The Byzantines backed *dyophysites* (who held that Christ had two natures, as specified at the Council of Chalcedon in 451), whereas beyond their sphere of influence – as in Egypt and Ethiopia, and among the Syrian Jacobites – the *miaphysites* (who stood by Christ's single nature) more commonly held sway. As if this was not sufficiently mind boggling, a further refinement known as *monothelitism* (which proposed that, even if Christ had two natures, he had but a single will) occupied much debate through much of the 7th century. When Arabs overran Syria and surrounding territories, the blame game then kicked in. Christian writers of all persuasions were agreed that the spread of Islam was a form of divine punishment for the propagation of heresy; but the Chalcedonian author of *The Life of Maximus* thought that *dyothelitism* was the root problem, whereas Anastasios of Sinai conversely considered the fault lay with the Byzantine emperor's stance in favour of *monothelitism*.

Such recondite subtleties can hardly have been helpful in promoting the idea of Jesus as 'the Way, the Truth, and the Life', and are not (as far as I know) keenly debated in any church today. We still adhere to the historic creeds as formulated in the 4th century, but even here the language sometimes reaches beyond our comfort zones. There is a story of a Cambridge philosopher preparing to be confirmed in King's College chapel who asked whether it was legitimate for him to retain certain reservations about phrases within the creeds. 'Yes', came the chaplain's reply, 'all of us are on a learning curve and even bishops can struggle with particular formulations of the faith. It can take time to discover the full wealth of meaning in certain phrases.

What are the clauses that concern you?' 'Well, I can confess without hesitation that Christ "was crucified, dead, and buried". As for the rest, I'm rather less certain'.

Philosophic scruples are not often expressed so honestly, but I fancy may not be particularly uncommon (indeed, I rather imagine the majority of Christians would be stretched to give a coherent explanation of what today is implied by 'the Second Coming', despite its regular affirmation in the main creeds). There are some Christians, both lay and ordained, who would argue as fiercely for their doctrinal views as any 7th century Syrian monk, but they are untypical. In any congregation, for example, there are those who have previously belonged to other denominations, but now attend a different church for various personal reasons (its proximity, the convenience of its service times, its perceived architectural or liturgical merits, the warmth of its welcome or its provision for their children): many of these would probably have little idea as to whether their new church professed significantly different teachings from their previous attachment. I once called on a parishioner who informed me that she gave away her jumble to all and sundry – Anglicans, Baptists, Muslims, Hindus – because 'it's all for the same God really' (which I wasn't willing to query on her doorstep). That is, or used to be, a common point of view; most churchgoers are immune to the niceties of theological debate. Discussions with ordinary parishioners suggest that what draws them into church in the first place can be the desire for 'space' in their lives to be quiet and reflective; what holds them is the friendship that they find and some uplift from the church's worship, but seldom does a creed mean much more than its vital affirmation of God's existence.

Doctrine is of course expressed in the liturgy, and in the hymns (if any) that accompany it. When the Vatican introduced a new English translation of the missal in 2011, there were priestly complaints about the obscurity of its language. Some laity protested too, but they were in a minority since it is the *performance* of the mass that counts for most people. If they like hymns, it may be that the words ring true, but generally it's a familiar – and singable – tune that counts for more. It is worth noting that (alongside purveyors of clerical wear) compilers of hymnbooks are among the most ecumenically-minded Christians today, so that – unbeknownst to themselves – a Catholic congregation may well be singing Methodist words, or vice versa.

There is a limerick which runs as follows:-

> There were three little birds in a wood
> Who always sang hymns when they could;
>   What the words were about
>   They could never make out,
> But they felt it was doing them good.

This is surely the spirit in which hymns were once sung at Gwen Raverat's school. She reports in her classic *Period Piece* (1952):

> The girls' ideas of religion, and even the mistresses' ideas of reverence, were a complete mystery to me. For instance, on the night before a hockey match we always had 'Onward Christian Soldiers' for the hymn at Prayers. It was sung *fortissimo*, and was supposed to ginger us up to martial prowess next day; indeed great importance was attached to the *brio* with which it was sung. This shocked and disgusted me very much indeed; and it made me doubt their sincerity in other ways. I was a very serious person then, and I conceived of religion as a high and spiritual affair, and did not like seeing it made ridiculous, even if I were not a believer myself.

It is unlikely that Gwen's headmistress was deliberately emulating St Ambrose, but he would surely have endorsed the tactics being used. Indeed, in 386 when he faced the prospect of losing one of his churches to an Arian congregation, he staged a sit-in there and kept his flock up to their mettle by composing rousing hymns to be sung (no question for him, though, that the words mattered as much as the music). When the imperial troops backed off, he recorded 'the happiness of all the people present, and their cheers'. Ambrose' contemporaries were equally keen on congregational singing. St Basil considered that 'the grace of music' added to 'the truth of doctrine', and made a comment worthy of any media adviser (read Vance Packard's classic account of advertising techniques in *The Hidden Persuaders*):

> *Charmed* by what we hear, we pluck the fruit of the words *without realising it*.

For his part St Augustine, who had learnt a great deal from his time in Milan with St. Ambrose, reckoned that there was 'nothing better, more useful or more holy' that the laity could do in church than to sing. Hymns in their day were written by men who were highly literate, and the same is true of many of their successors, not least those in the 18th century – for example, Isaac Watts, John and Charles Wesley, Phillip Doddridge and William Cowper. As John Wesley put it:

> When poetry thus keeps its place as the handmaid of piety, it shall attain not a poor perishable wreath, but a crown that fadeth not away.

The following century saw less literary forms emerge, particularly with revivalist songs and negro spirituals from across the Atlantic. Then came Moody and Sankey, who specialised in *clichés* and *mixed metaphors*, just in time for many of their compositions to be included in *Hymns for Malawi*, which was the book still in use at Zomba Theological College nearly 100 years after its first edition ('*Nyimbo za Mulungu*') was published in 1916. So there in Central Africa we were often tossed on *the billowing waves* of a dark and gloomy storm, struggling to find a pilot equipped with a suitable chart and compass: true enough, an early Anglican bishop drowned in Lake Malawi (possibly because he invariably wore a long black cassock), but most Malawians don't live anywhere near it. Alternatively, we might find ourselves wandering across a *desert* – however, the Sahara was a very long way off. Or we'd be struggling up a *barren mountain side* – despite the fact that Mount Mulanje was famous for its cedar trees. Or, if we were lucky enough, we'd be somewhere near a *sheepfold* – yet since sheep are rarely bred in Malawi, a game reserve might have been more appropriate – which had (surely rather extravagant?) *gates of gold*. The real secret though was to be clad in robes washed *white as snow* by the blood of the Lamb – plenty of rain in season, and chilly in the winter, but snow? Hymn-singing – as in 4th century Milan and at Gwen Raverat's school – may often rally people together (and may also distract the congregation from disturbances either within or outside the building), but does it always establish a clear, firmly founded Christian faith? Evidently Dr Mwakanandi, the Presbyterian Principal of ZTC in our time, thought so, because he insisted that students at the college should stick with just ten of the Moody and Sankey variety *and should not allow their future congregations to sing any others.*

Such an attempt to impose a tradition was, however, scarcely enforceable, but the reductionist doctrine that went with it had more enduring popularity. The slogan 'obey God or else' was oft-repeated in the college chapel, and was the Calvinists' rallying cry (sadly, this obsession led eventually to a separate Anglican seminary being formed in Zomba after many years' close collaboration). Was it faith or was it a tribal mantra? And if the latter, was it essentially different from the more complex conventions of Christian churches in other places, or indeed from the catch phrases of other religions?

Who is brave enough to swim against the tide?
asks Michael Sowa

Poetry, or at least an appreciation for the strengths and weaknesses of words, is one of the missing factors in much conventional church life. Mutual misunderstandings and disagreements often arise because the parties concerned are talking at cross purposes, or else fail to recognise the limitations of human language in attempting to express or to probe the divine mysteries. Slogans, mantras and creeds all have their place, but they cease to be helpful when wielded as battle cries. There will be significant subtleties and nuances of thought that also need articulating, which others may have grasped more clearly than ourselves. It may then take 500 years (as with the rift between Luther and the Catholic Church) to reach some kind of mutual agreement.

To achieve reconciliation between the tea ladies of West Monkton in less than 24 hours was thus a remarkable achievement. I am not claiming that the resulting scone recipe was the acme of perfection; worthier of emulation is the process of negotiation through which it evolved. There are matters of weightier import (the ladies themselves would dispute this!) such as Trinitarian doctrine where more extensive dialogue might in time past have resulted in happier outcomes. The impression one sometimes gains is that the proponents of particular theories looked upon God himself as akin to a scone, whose composition could be analysed in similar fashion. Muhammad was quite right to protest about the tri-theism that sometimes took over, and certainly to react against the warring divisions within the church. God's mystery – and that of our Lord – cannot be reduced to any form of words; so if terms such as 'nature', 'person', 'substance', 'begotten', 'proceeds'… are useful in making certain distinctions and clarifications, their meaning inevitably eludes our comprehension. The *apophatic* approach of Greek theologians surely hits the mark.

A Catholic bishop once explained in my hearing that the word 'church' is 'more of a verb than a noun', and he might have said something similar of the word 'God' as well. Our knowledge of God derives from encountering his active presence in our lives, hence how we speak of him needs to reflect this strongly. Thus a mention of the simple word 'love' in the creeds recited so regularly in church might not come amiss. And if we have then to articulate something of Jesus' distinctive being, it is worth recalling a 4th century summary that contradicted the Arians, 'there was not a time when he was not', which has the merit – in English at any rate – of using only simple monosyllabic words.

Could the modern equivalents of the *dyothelites* and the *monothelites* ('Were they dinosaurs?' I hear you asking) ever be brought to shake hands and agree a contemporary statement of our faith? I suspect that in the rabbinical tradition one would have to say first to each of them in turn, 'You are right, and you too are right'. Jesus would then say, 'And your faith comes alive and finds its best expression, not in any form of words, but in works of love and mercy'.

COLOURFUL CLERGY

The village of Wye, where we now live, was once famous for its agricultural college, so that among our friends and neighbours there is a certain familiarity with the concept of a field guide: thus, 'A field guide to edible mushrooms', and perhaps less likely, 'A field guide to rodents and other vermin'. Well, 25 years ago my brother gave me a fascinating book, *A field guide to the English country parson*. It offers potted biographies of some of the more colourful incumbents of recent centuries. The cumulative effect lends considerable credence to the story that when Edward King went to Lincoln as their new bishop he was told: the clergy of this diocese divide into three categories: those who have gone out of their minds; those who are about to go out of their minds; and those who have no minds to go out of.

Bertrand Russell, writing in 1930, considered that 'erratic' behaviour was by then less in evidence within society, having been tolerated more readily in the past particularly from those whose status depended upon birth; hence he urged 'a more deliberate realisation of the dangers of uniformity'. This may have happened in some walks of life, but hardly in the church. The sad thing is, that the eccentric parson is now a threatened species, steadily being eroded from our shores by centralised church officialdom, by health and safety regulations, by a misplaced desire to be up-to-date, in-touch, and generally 'relevant' to modern society. Although the more exotic examples are therefore to be found in the annals, and deserve our homage, here and there even today, as my own experience suggests, some slightly bizarre men of the cloth still exist.

The evolution of the (increasingly rare) clergy species

Undoubtedly the most mocked clergyman of all time is the so-called 'Vicar of Bray'. Starting with the turbulence of the English reformation in the 16th century, some priests lacked any firm conviction other than the desire to stay in post and collaborate with whatever creed was in vogue, be it Anglican, Catholic, Puritan or the prevailing brand of politics. There may have been an actual vicar of Bray (near Maidenhead in Berkshire) whose changing loyalties once made him a figure of fun, but over the years plenty of others were equally free of principles, and merely adapted to the current fashion. The 18th century song named after him runs through the swings and roundabouts of English church life (and contemporary verses ought now to be added – the Vicar of Bray is still alive and crawling in today's church!).

1. In good King Charles' golden time, when loyalty no harm meant,
A zealous high churchman was I, and so I gained preferment.
To teach my flock, I never missed: Kings are by God appointed
And damned are those who dare resist or touch the Lord's anointed.
>   *And this be law, that I'll maintain until my dying day, sir*
>   *That whatsoever king may reign, Still I'll be the Vicar of Bray, sir.*

2. When royal James possessed the crown, and popery came in fashion,
The penal laws I hooted down, and read the Declaration.
The Church of Rome, I found, did fit full well my constitution
And I had been a Jesuit, but for the Revolution.

3. When William was our King declared, to ease the nation's grievance,
With this new wind about I steered, and swore to him allegiance.
Old principles I did revoke; Set conscience at a distance,
Passive obedience was a joke, a jest was non-resistance.

4. When Royal Anne became our queen, the Church of England's glory,
Another face of things was seen, and I became a Tory.
Occasional conformists base; I blamed their moderation;
And thought the Church in danger was from such prevarication.

5. When George in pudding time came o'er, and moderate men looked big, sir
My principles I changed once more, and I became a Whig, sir.
And thus preferment I procured From our new Faith's Defender,
And almost every day abjured the Pope and the Pretender.

6. The illustrious house of Hanover and Protestant succession
To these I do allegiance swear — while they can hold possession.
For in my faith and loyalty I never more will falter,
And George my lawful king shall be — until the times do alter.

In the century after 'George in pudding time' i.e. the 19th century we read of other bizarre goings on. Thus, there was one parson who didn't deign to enter his church for 53 years, meanwhile keeping the local fox-hounds kennelled in his vicarage. Another liked to keep the folk guessing, and so from week to week varied the colour of the communion wine, sometimes red, sometimes white, sometimes pink. One parson disliked church worship altogether and refused to take services, but was fond of people and 'clad in flowered dressing-gown and smoking a hookah' greeted his parishioners in the churchyard. By contrast, another so resented people pestering him that he drove the congregation away and replaced them by cardboard images in the pews; he also surrounded the vicarage with a barbed-wire fence behind which patrolled savage Alsatians. There was an incumbent who equipped his stall in church with its own sanitary arrangements, and one who professed himself a neo-Platonist and sacrificed an ox to Jupiter. The Revd Joshua Brooks, chaplain of the collegiate church of Manchester, who died in 1821, had the habit of breaking off in the middle of the burial service to buy hore-hound drops in a neighbouring confectioner's shop before returning to conclude the service. Easter Monday was a great day for weddings at his church, with large numbers flocking to be married. However, he read but a single service for them all, and with so many couples it was rather difficult to get them lined up in the correct pairs. So his final instruction was 'Now get outside and find your other half'. As for baptisms, Francis Kilvert tells us in an entry of 1874 of an unusual practice earlier in the century about which report had reached him. In the parish of Fordington the font was always bone dry: the incumbent cut out the tedium of fetching water for it by simply spitting into his hand.

Other practices that are probably now discouraged include the quite common custom of boxing the ears of tardy or unruly choirboys, and the poet Robert Herrick's display of temper when he threw his sermon at the congregation for failing to listen. It was this same Herrick who kept a menagerie including a pig that he taught to drink from a pint tankard. Less irascibly, Scott of the Antarctic's brother-in-law Francis Bruce was renowned for carrying live creatures in his pockets, and on occasion would release a dove from underneath his surplice when preaching as a lively illustration of his theme, 'the flight of love'.

Flora Thompson, author of *Lark Rise to Candleford*, describes an aloof 'parson of the old school', plainly based upon a rector (Charles Harrison) under whom she had suffered herself: 'had he not been divinely appointed pastor and master to those little *rustics*'. Since many had ceased attending church, a principal theme of his sermons was the duty of regular churchgoing. 'He would hammer away at that for forty-five minutes, never seeming to realize that he was preaching to the absent.'

The most famous of all Victorian eccentrics was probably Robert Hawker of Morwenstow on the north Cornish coast. In Piers Brendon's biography we read:

> Mr Hawker was rather peculiar in his dress. At first, soon after his induction to Morwenstow, he wore his cassock; but in time abandoned this inconvenient garb, in which he found it impossible to scramble about his cliffs. He then adopted a claret-coloured coat, with long tails. He had the greatest aversion to anything black: the only black things he would wear were his boots. These claret-coloured coats would button over the breast, but were generally worn open, displaying beneath a knitted blue fisherman's jersey. At his side, just where the Lord's side was pierced, a little red cross was woven in the jersey. He wore fishing-boots reaching above his knee ... At first he went about in a college cap; but this speedily made way for a pink or plum-coloured beaver hat without a brim.

For church services, it might be added, he was usually to be found in ornate vestments, sometimes wearing scarlet gloves. As a curate prior to his preferment he kept a tame pig called Gyp which went parish visiting with him. As a vicar he had nine cats which cavorted in the chancel during church services, although one of them incurred excommunication for presuming to catch a mouse on the sabbath day. He also had two pet deer, named Robin Hood and Maid Marion, which is where we can glimpse the inter-necine ploys of church politics. Robin Hood once felled a visiting Low Church clergyman, and pinned him to the ground with his antlers until Hawker came to the rescue. Hawker, as his stylish dress may have suggested, was High Church: he caused the greatest scandal of his life by converting to Catholicism twelve hours before he died.

On the whole, there does seem to be more colour in the lives, as well as in their churches, of clergy in the Catholic tradition. Although I never met him, one 20th century priest exemplifies this to perfection, as described in his obituary:

> Fr Diamond was the sort of parish priest who doesn't exist any more. More catholic than the pope, he gave 23 years to the people of Deptford, living in a condemned slum of a vicarage that was open house to the homeless and the destitute, where many of them also slept. He lived on a bottle of whisky a day and was often found slumped in his chair when he was supposed to be in church conducting a wedding. He was deeply flawed, often exhausted and cranky, but also saintly in a crazily generous sort of way ... He was a great organiser of community events and the Deptford Festival became famous, with its street parties, royal visits, flamboyant firework displays and fun for all on the grandest scale. The pensioners' outing, for example: there had to be a thousand pensioners. A cannon would be fired and twenty coaches would set off, with the narrow high street lined by every infant and primary school, cheering and waving flags, the procession led by a brass band.

Such crankiness is exceptional, but in more muted tones can still be found occasionally. As a boy I remember hearing of the local vicar of St Stephen's who shared his accommodation with teenage desperadoes. Unfortunately for him they stripped the lead off his church roof and then absconded with items from his vicarage. The diocese was not best pleased, nor were the parishioners. Since those days the church has made itself more theft-proof, fire-proof, and (no doubt) people-proof., such are the requirements imposed upon us all by health and safety concerns. We are still not quite animal-proof, although today's clergy usually house fewer of God's furry or feathered friends than did their Victorian forebears (did any of them, however, keep a python as did a Somerset colleague of mine — until one day when it disappeared under the floorboards?). A curious development in recent decades has been the encouragement to bring pets into church. Presumably this derives from an over-zealous commitment to evangelism, although 'pet services' seem to me to rate high on a scale of clerical oddity. I might be persuaded otherwise if I knew more about the sanitary arrangements. But, in any case, what do you say to the poor creatures?

In my early days, in Northamptonshire, I had a neighbouring vicar who kept goats. It was actually something we had in common; but whereas I kept them outside, mainly in the garden, he kept them in the kitchen and allowed them to wander freely through the house. Once we held a deanery chapter meeting there, and we all had to look carefully where we walked or sat. I remember his wife wore gum-boots on an apparently permanent basis (while my own wife still recalls the pungent billy-goat aroma that accompanied her to meetings further afield). Unfortunately this latter day St Francis was not appreciated in his parish; blows were once nearly exchanged at the annual flower festival because the vicar insisted on giving the prize rosettes that his goats had won at agricultural shows elsewhere pride of place on the high altar. Thereafter it was agreed by the parochial church council (1) that the summer fete should no longer be held at the vicarage, but in the churchwarden's garden, and (2) that the vicar should not be permitted to attend. In retaliation, on the day of the fete he manned his own bric-a-brac stall separately in the church porch, but it was apparently not well-supported.

I'm reminded of another clerical colleague who felt obliged to contribute to the success of his annual church fete by making a purchase or two. He invariably bought second-hand crockery, so that by the time he came to retire he had accumulated 128 non-matching dinner plates, 73 side plates, 86 saucers, 62 cups — and, as they say, much much more by way of serving dishes, gravy boats and the like. Grateful parishioners had over the years further enlarged his collection of household goods by passing on to him their redundant appliances, furniture, books and religious artefacts until there was no room to swing a cat. When he retired it took daily trips to the local tip, spread over nearly two months, to empty out his house.

Following one man's obsession with goats, and another's inability to resist what the Romans would have called *impedimenta*, it was refreshing to find the priest of an adjacent parish in Somerset with a more theological fixation. He'd once been at Chichester Theological College, which maintained (until it closed) a fairly High Church tradition. But coming under evangelical influence he'd recently become a born again Christian, which meant that his abiding passion was now to get everyone else born again with him. This had liturgical implications: no longer was he satisfied with an ordinary baptismal font but considered total immersion to be a *sine qua non*. He didn't have a suitable pool in his church (after all, who does?) so he had to improvise. Whenever a baptism was due he'd make elaborate preparations the night before. He'd put out a rectangular array of chairs, sling a plastic sheet over them, and then fill it up with water through a garden hosepipe. Sadly the ensuing bath was never entirely fit for purpose; it leaked, so the church floor invariably became flooded overnight. Those attending one of his services soon got wise to the need for swimsuits, towels and a change of clothes.

Not satisfied with revamping his own parish, he once turned his attention to mine when I was away on holiday. I heard on my return that, with a few like-minded parishioners brought across with him, he'd tested our premises with a divining rod. He had thereby discovered a malevolent *ley line* wreaking spiritual damage and had prayed that we should all be delivered from the bonds of Satan. Naturally, I wrote to him afterwards, thanking him for his kind ministration.

Worthy of mention too are the slightly unusual characters whom I've succeeded in several different places. In my first parish (of 6000 souls) the congregation had been reduced almost to single figures by my predecessor's passion for obscure 18th century hymns ('He ought to have retired years ago', wrote the bishop in his letter of invitation to me). He'd research these in the university library at Cambridge and would then make the congregation sing them — and nothing else. Yes, frequently they would plough through 12 or 15 verses at a time, using authentic, but completely unfamiliar, tunes. All these were supplied on duplicated sheets, since few of the hymns had ever achieved the accolade of being included in a hymnbook. Unsurprisingly church services steadily declined in popularity. But shortly after my arrival in the parish I delighted the local boy scouts with my decision to invest in Hymns Ancient and Modern Revised; the now redundant stacks of paper in the church vestry provided them with their biggest ever recycling opportunity.

In my next parish the congregation was numerically stronger, but it was the finances that had been wrecked. Before accepting the post I'd actually asked Henry (that was his name) if all the bills had been paid. 'O yes,' he'd said. What he didn't tell me was that he'd drained the coffers and borrowed £15000 to pay for extra bells and a new bell-frame. His lifelong ambition had been to have a full peal of eight, regardless of the fact that there were never more than five or six in the belfry to ring them. I think it took some six or seven years to pay off the debts, as well as to reinstate the displaced church clock and to mend the shattered west window (the structural consequence of replacing an 18th century oak bell-frame with a larger rigid metal frame without taking proper advice or indeed obtaining a faculty). Once again, I might add, we inherited a garden that had largely gone to waste, another reminder (if it were needed) that one of the purposes of ordination is to bring order.

There were also stiff challenges to be faced in Lesotho in the 1980s when I was asked to run the seminary there. The warden before me had been given the sack for diverting his energies (and undoubted Christian commitment) from the job in hand. He was a very politically-minded New Zealander who spent most of his time in anti-apartheid activities, including being chaplain to the armed wing of the ANC in exile. Now I'm sure it's just as important for dissidents and terrorists to have spiritual guidance as much as regular soldiers; but when the SADF sent helicopters on a raid across the border to bomb the seminary, both the Lesotho government and the Anglican bishop felt it was time for him to explore new pastures: in the memorable words of a Baptist minister once dismissed from his post by the church meeting, they 'discerned that his ministry had come to an end'.

In the intervening months before my arrival another missionary held the fort, but he had one interest only, which was to master the local language, Sesotho. This limited his ability to attend to the inherited problems of the seminary, and the finances got into an even worse muddle. I had to start account books from scratch, because all that dear Reg had to offer was the odd plastic bag of till slips, augmented on the rare occasions when we met elsewhere (such as at a supermarket in town) with a few scraps of paper from his back trouser pocket. I once lodged overnight with him and discovered that his language learning didn't even cease in the WC. He had a blackboard there with vocabulary to be studied while concurrently being otherwise engaged. When I visited the chamber myself the current topic on the board was the verb *ho rota*, with a note to the effect that – depending on a long or short pronunciation of the vowel – this had two possible meanings. It might mean 'to teach' (thus, I was a *moruti*), but with more of an 'o' sound it signified 'to pass water', which I have usefully remembered to this day.

I must of course confess that Reg's linguistic abilities far surpassed mine, which were limited to a few common greetings and the passable pronunciation of liturgical rites. Nevertheless, I did discover that one can sustain a lengthy conversation in an unfamiliar tongue with the judicious use of occasional guttural noises, such as '*ee*', provided these are accompanied by a smile and a nod of the head. So body language plays a part as well. Yet not even Reg always got it right: I still cherish the recollection of a seminar he once gave in Maseru on *The Sesotho Version of the Eucharistic Prayer*. When he paused for comments from the assembled African clergy, one of them stood up and said, 'You know, it doesn't mean that at all'!

Staying in Lesotho: we had a visiting lecturer at the seminary who may well be considered the most colourful priest I've ever known, far surpassing Ambrose, Henry and Reg, as one or two snapshots of him may reveal. This was Clement, a Kelham Father, who came once a week to Roma to offer New Testament studies. Clement was like Hawker of Morwenstow, eclectic in his choice of clothes — for example, hiking boots, tatty shorts and a red scarf surmounted by a Russian beaver hat. He found ordinary people 'boring', so divided his time between wealthy folk across the border in South Africa where his provincial centre was based and derelict orphan boys in Maseru where a new priory was being established. He had a special devotion to the Blessed Sacrament, and contrary to every ruling of the church always carried on his person a supply of consecrated hosts. This was well known, so that if he called in at a petrol station, after the attendant had filled his tank, he'd say, 'Got any hosts today, father?' and Clement would wind down his window and pop one in the attendant's mouth. Or at a society function in Ladybrand the hostess would announce, 'We're fortunate to have Fr Clement with us again today, so if you'd like to make your communion just go to the other end of the room, but of course — if you prefer — join us for canapes at this end'.

On our first meeting Clement discovered that we'd shipped our Dolmetsch spinet out to Lesotho — which is faintly eccentric behaviour, I grant you, but certainly endeared me to Clement, who declared that he'd bring his flute over some time for us to play together. He did indeed, but it turned out that his flute was just a plain recorder, and that his playing was so *rubato* that I frequently had to omit bars to keep up with him. When his new priory chapel was being dedicated, we attended the service. This featured Clement's very own liturgy improvised on the spot from all the sources he knew — Latin, English, Sesotho, Catholic texts, Anglican texts, old rites, new rites — a gaudy mixture just like his clothes. To his credit the orphan boys were all roped in as servers and choir; but there was a handicapped lad who was a bit slower than the rest, and at the offertory Clement interrupted the hymn to yell across the chapel, 'Hurry up, boy. Don't be so completely spastic!'

You will appreciate by now that there was a theatrical side to his personality, which sometimes took him slightly beyond the bounds of social convention. We once had a sad occasion, the requiem mass of a young priest (I think he was called Fr Paul) who'd been knocked down and killed by a car. Clement was the preacher, and he began his tribute (I don't use the word eulogy here) with dramatic force. 'Fr Paul' he declaimed 'was a stupid man' (pause) 'Fr Paul was an ignorant man' (pause) 'Fr Paul was – wait for it! – an ugly man'. Whatever else he said afterwards, about what a nice man he was, and how people would miss him, and how God loved him, somehow never quite compensated for these initial dramatic assertions. Yet even if Clement could be embarrassingly different, one's eyes always lit up on meeting him: he was never boring.

Although an English bishop was once overheard to say that his most colourful priest, a confirmed alcoholic, was actually a great asset, owing to the fact that his frequent incapacity had induced the laity to be so actively involved as to make his parish the liveliest in the diocese, it's probably true that eccentric clergy these days tend to be shunted overseas, or else gravitate there naturally. No doubt it was my own peculiarities that led me in that direction as well; but I was more than happy to return to Africa as a missionary lecturer in the year 2000. There were hardly any other expatriate Anglican clergy in Malawi, but one American stands out – a widower called Stewart, who'd begun as a secondary school teacher and lay chaplain before being ordained by the local bishop. He was very generous in opening his house in Limbe to our seminarians for the occasional weekend retreat, and it was chiefly there that I got to know him. Stewart was essentially a hangover from the 1960s: he belonged to the hippie generation, characterised by his long pony tail (very grey by now), his addiction to happy clappy songs, and a fierce hatred of all things American. He played the guitar (of course) but was also a painter and the author of a weekly column in one of the national newspapers. The content of his writing didn't vary all that much: in a nutshell, his theme was 'African *good*, anything Western or American *bad*', so you can see why the editor kept him on.

I remember one week how he praised the African community spirit, and their commitment to the family. He noted how the elderly weren't herded out of sight into care homes, but were looked after by their own kith and kin as valued members of the family household. He confessed sadly that he'd fallen short of this ideal himself: after his father had died, he'd invited his mother to come and live with him, but she'd declined and had ended up in an old people's home. The following week's article had a different target, namely, the over-indulgence of Americans who wallowed in bathrooms and spent far too much on soap and shampoo and the like. He proposed his own grandfather as a role model: when the fall came, he'd rub himself all over with animal fat, don his winter woollies, and wouldn't take them off even just once until spring arrived. So he went six months without a wash, a huge saving on soap and water! Putting these successive articles together, I began to suspect why Stewart's mother might have preferred to keep her distance and to live independently of her son.

Yet if his ideas on hygiene were too advanced for many Malawian readers (and I suspect not practised consistently even by himself!), they would undoubtedly have been popular in the ancient Church. The historian Keith Thomas once noted:

> Some early Christians were notoriously dirty on principle. They showed their contempt for the flesh by shunning the luxury of warm baths and allowing their bodies to be tormented with lice … For them, the odour of sanctity was no mere figure of speech.

Indeed, St Jerome famously commented that 'he who has bathed in Christ does not need a second bath'!

Stewart's forceful public distinction between Westernisation and Christianity was nevertheless important in a society unduly influenced by the popularity of the so-called 'prosperity gospel' and prone to interpret spiritual development in terms of growing affluence. The most bizarre example known to me is of the African pastor who argued that, since the soldiers who crucified Jesus cast lots for his seamless robe, it must have been an expensive item — so that here was justification for his own extravagant possessions. More authentic interpretations of gospel teaching continue to have vital importance, as exemplified in another long-standing missionary friend in Malawi. He had no car and few personal chattels, and he invariably negotiated his daily pastoral visits around his far-flung parish on foot. On his own admission he was probably unsuited to other walks of life. A Malawian resident recorded this memory of him:

> One Christmas we had Rodney Hunter, parish priest, to croquet. He wore a straw hat and spoke perhaps the best English I have heard, He had been in the Guards Regiment for his National Service and looked every bit the fine guardsman. He said he was quite hopeless, and was transferred after charging with a bren gun and losing his trousers.

He was a kin spirit to my favourite saint, the 11th century Italian Giovanni Gualberto. Assaulted by robbers who found nothing worth stealing on his person, he suddenly remembered that he had a few gold coins sewn into the hem of his tunic. So he shouted after his assailants as they went on their way, 'Come back, come back, I've something for you after all'. Rodney's only concession to modern styles of living, as I recall, was a CD player that worked off an old car battery.

Shouldn't we expect all clergy (if not the laity too) to exhibit some eccentricities in the topsy-turvy world of faith, where according to St Paul 'God's foolishness is wiser than human wisdom'? A Chewa proverb in Central Africa concurs that apparent human foolishness may be closer to God's wisdom: 'It was the madman who recognised the enemy in disguise'. Or again, as king George II responded on hearing the accusation that James Wolfe was mad: 'Mad, is he? Then I hope he will bite some of my other generals'.

> 'But I don't want to go among mad people,' said Alice. 'Oh, you can't help that,' said the cat. 'We're all mad here'.

Perhaps only a clergyman could have written that.

The Revd John Alington, 1795-1862

> Alington drank strong liquor prior to conducting any worship and often rode a hobby horse up and down the aisles, 'frequently falling off to raucous laughter'. When he started to quote more frequently from love poems than from holy scripture, he was suspended by his bishop.

SERMON SNIPPETS

Samuel Pepys is renowned for his late 17th century diaries. Read them carefully, and he emerges also as a sermon critic of no little distinction. Even though time didn't always permit his attendance at church on a Sunday, he invariably makes a note of the Lord's day; when he does attend, it's clearly the sermon that attracts his attention, unless there are any especially handsome ladies present. Often he's disappointed that the delivery is 'dull', or worse, 'a sorry silly sermon'. He hears 'an unnecessary sermon upon Original Sin' which he declares was understood neither by the preacher nor by the people. He complains another time that the preacher was 'a little overlarge in magnifying the graces of the nobility and prelates'. He finds a stranger in the pulpit, 'a seeming able man', but who offers 'a strange saying' about the resurrection – the idea (emanating from St Augustine) that it's a mightier work to raise an oak-tree from an acorn than to bring a man's dust back to life. He was particularly averse to hearing one Dr Mills, who was usually 'dull' and once made 'a lazy sermon upon Moses' meeknesse'. Bishops are no better and he remarks that there are only two in the whole realm (namely, Hereford and Exeter) 'that the King do say he cannot have bad sermons from'. His vitriol is reserved for the preacher he heard when visiting Bath Abbey: 'a vain, pragmatical fellow' who delivered 'a ridiculous, affected sermon', which made him angry and indeed angered the gentlemen sitting near him.

A vain pragmatical fellow

Yet he can also offer fulsome praise. An 'old dunce' of St Matthew's, Westminster 'did make a very good sermon, beyond my expectation'. He thought highly of a Mr Clifford who gave 'a most excellent good sermon upon the righteousness of scribes and pharisees'. He was impressed in the Queen's chapel when he heard 'a fryer preach with his cord about his middle, in Portuguese, something I could understand, showing that God did respect the meek and humble, as well as the high and rich. He was full of action, but very decent and good'. The best sermon ever came from his favourite, a Mr Frampton:

> The truth is, he preaches the most like an apostle that ever I heard man; and it was much the best time that I ever spent in my life at church. His text, Ecclesiastes xi, verse 8th – But if a man live many years, and rejoice in them all, yet let him remember the days of darkness, for they shall be many. All that cometh is vanity.

For Pepys, this was 'goodness and oratory, without affectation or study'. He has a good opinion too of a Mr Gifford, whose sermon on seeking first God's kingdom he rates 'very excellent and persuasive, good and moral: he showed, like a wise man, that righteousness is a surer moral way of being rich, than sin and villainy'. It might be added that R.L.Stevenson, responding to Pepys' comments, considered this very same sermon far too 'mild'. It emasculated the gospel, making it 'a manual of worldly prudence' by suggesting 'you can make the most of both worlds, and be a moral hero without courage, kindness or troublesome reflection'.

Another Samuel – a Mr Sharp – was visiting Italy a century later, and wrote a series of letters describing the customs and manners of that country, which naturally included descriptions of their religious ceremonies. Writing from Naples in March 1766, he observed:

> Sermons are not the pursuit of the gentry in Catholick countries, and good preachers are therefore uncommon. I had rashly flattered myself I should have gathered much fruit from the pulpit, or at least, that I should have been entertained. At this season of the year [Lent], preachers of the most distinguished parts quit their convents, and spread themselves through the great cities of Italy, to instruct the people, and display their own talents.

Being able to observe these preachers at first hand, he found them much like Pepys' Portuguese friar – men 'full of action'.

> Some of the pulpits here are a kind of gallery, which allows great scope for action: the injudicious preachers do not fail to take the advantage of it; very often in the heat of their discourse running from one end to the other; and it is this excess, this abuse of action, which I object to.

He allows though that it's just a facet of the demonstrative Latin character, somewhat alien to English reserve.

I recall advice received during my own ministerial formation. The lecturer suggested that we should avoid thumping the pulpit. He had done this once when serving in Barbados, causing the pulpit to collapse under him in a cloud of dust and debris. It had been attacked by termites, and until this rude assault it had been held together only through the power of faith, hope and charity. In one of his early livings a scarcely less alarming experience had happened to the great Sydney Smith:

> When I began to thump the cushion of my pulpit on first coming to Foston, as is my wont when I preach, the accumulated dust of a hundred and fifty years made such a cloud of dust that for some minutes I lost sight of my congregation.

On one occasion when I was growing up we too at our Methodist church in St Albans nearly lost sight of the visiting preacher. He gave a vivid, extremely memorable, demonstration of how easy it is to fall from grace and how hard to recover afterwards. He mounted the brass rail that ran alongside the pulpit steps, and slid smoothly down to the bottom, from which scarcely visible abyss he struggled unsuccessfully to pull himself back up. The lesson was not wasted on his audience, at least not on me.

Whereas Pepys knew a good sermon when he heard it, yet a third Samuel – contemporary with Mr Sharp – gave ready advice on putting one together. Samuel Johnson wrote to a young clergyman Charles Lawrence in August 1780: 'The composition of sermons is not very difficult'. So he urged him 'from time to time' to attempt one of his own, instead of adhering to the more common practice of borrowing other people's. 'Few frequent preachers', wrote Johnson, 'can be supposed to have sermons more their own than yours will be'. There follow a few admirable tips:

> In the labour of composition, do not burthen your mind with too much at once; do not exact from yourself at one effort of excogitation, propriety of thought and elegance of expression. Invent first, and then embellish ... Set down diligently your thoughts as they arise, in the first words that occur; and, when you have matter, you will easily give it form: nor, perhaps, will this method be always necessary: for, by habit, your thoughts and diction will flow together.

A contemporary clergyman, Parson Woodforde, had a limited collection of his own sermons which at one time travelled with him. His diary entry for July 20, 1782 records an occasion when he was caught out:

> Yesterday [Mr Thomas] came to ask me to preach for him on Sunday but I could not, as I brought no sermon with me – the last time I was in the country I had some sermons with me and was never asked to preach, therefore I thought it of no use to bring any now.

The novelist George Eliot describes how Mr Gilfil 'had a large heap of short sermons, rather yellow and worn at the edges, from which he took two every Sunday, securing perfect impartiality in the selection by taking them as they came without reference to topics'. His parishioners heard them repeated 'with all the more satisfaction' – since, as Eliot explains, 'phrases, like tunes, are a long time making, themselves at home in the brain'. Whether Dr Chasuble (in *The Importance of Being*

Earnest) had more than one sermon remains uncertain, but Oscar Wilde's portrait of him has an uncomfortably familiar ring:

> My sermon on the meaning of the manna in the Wilderness can be adapted to almost any occasion, joyful, or, as in the present case, distressing. I have preached it at Harvest celebrations, christenings, confirmations, on days of humiliation and festal days.

I'm reminded of my great uncle Edwin, who was organist at the Methodist chapel in Bacup for many years, and who assiduously made notes each week during the Sunday sermon. A visiting preacher returned after fifteen years, and was taken aback when Edwin congratulated him afterwards (with perhaps a touch of insincerity): 'A fine sermon you've given us this morning. I enjoyed it just as much as when I heard it on your last visit'.

As for delivery, Eliot portrayed Mr Gilfil's preaching as having an 'agreeable monotony' which induced pleasant slumber. Although Johnson was usually more concerned with content than with delivery, he was certainly prejudiced against hearing a woman's voice from the pulpit. In his oft-quoted words (on being told of a woman speaking at a Quaker meeting): 'Sir, a woman's preaching is like a dog's walking on his hinder legs. It is not done well; but you are surprized to find it done at all'. Was he querying the intellectual achievement or the temerity of performance?

Pepys clearly appreciated that a sermon isn't a lecture or a spoken screed, nor a theological essay however well composed, but a heart-to-heart apostolic communication – as in Newman's motto that he made his own as a cardinal, *Cor ad cor loquitur*. And it was Newman's mode of speech as much as his mode of thought that within thirty years of Johnson's death uplifted countless hearts as well as minds. Francis Kilvert was encouraged in his own preaching by his father's comment, 'As you were preaching, there came back upon my ear an echo of the tones of the sweetest human voice I ever heard, the voice of John Henry Newman'. Of course, Newman did have something worth saying, and no doubt took trouble to prepare it. Kilvert has a contrasting story of old Mr Thomas the Vicar of Disserth. He would get up in the pulpit without an idea about what he was going to say, and would begin thus:

> Ha, yes, here we are. And it is a fine day. I congratulate you on the fine day, and glad to see so many of you here. Yes, indeed. Ha, yes, very well. Now then I shall take for my text so and so. Yes. Let me see. You are all sinners and so am I. Yes indeed.

Sometimes he would preach about Mr Noe.

> Mr Noe, he did go on with the ark, thump, thump, thump. And the wicked fellows did come and say to him, 'Now Mr Noe don't go on there, thump, thump, thump, come and have a pint of ale at the Red Lion. There is capital ale at the Red Lion, Mr Noe'. For Mr Noe

was situated just as we are here, there was the Red Lion close by the ark, just round the corner. Yes indeed. But Mr Noe he would not hearken to them, and he went on thump, thump, thump. Then another idle fellow would say, 'Come Mr Noe – the hounds are running capital, yes indeed. Don't go on there thump, thump, thump'. But Mr Noe he never did heed them, he just went on with his ark, thump, thump, thump.

With such pulpit orators, who cannot sympathise with Samuel Taylor Coleridge's strictures:

No doubt preaching, in the proper sense of the word, is more effective than reading; and, therefore, I would not prohibit it, but leave a liberty to the clergyman who feels himself able to accomplish it. But, as things now are, I am quite sure I prefer going to church to a pastor who reads his discourse: for I never yet heard more than one preacher without book, who did not forget his argument in three minutes' time; and fall into vague and unprofitable declamation, and generally, very coarse declamation too. These preachers never progress; they eddy round and round. Sterility of mind follows their ministry.

George Eliot had plainly suffered herself from extempore preaching, having one villager remark of Rev Amos Barton:

[Our parson] can preach as good a sermon as need be heard when he writes it down. But when he tries to preach wi'out book, he rambles about, and doesn't stick to's text; and every now and then he flounders about like a sheep as has cast itself, and can't get on'ts legs again.

She contrasts the 'clear ringing tones' of the trumpets that brought down the walls of Jericho with the oratory of the Rev Amos which 'resembled rather a Belgian railway-horn'. One preacher among several who appear in P.G. Wodehouse' novels would – at least in his own opinion – have impressed Eliot: the Rev Sidney Gooch said, 'not once but many times, that he confidently expected, if the fine weather held up, to knock his little flock cock-eyed' Alas, he was thwarted by being knocked about himself during a fight the evening before his sermon was due!

Yet if Coleridge and Eliot were impatient of tedious waffle, Sydney Smith, a noted preacher himself, observed that in the 'crumbling hovels of Methodists' 'the crowd are feasting on ungrammatical fervour and illiterate animation', while the 'stately' churches had 'furlongs of empty pews':

A clergyman clings to his velvet cushion with either hand, keeps his eyes riveted upon his book, speaks of the ecstasies of joy, and fear, with a voice and a face which indicate neither.

One such clergyman was evidently the Reverend Doctor George Tennyson, father of the better-known Alfred. Of his sermons in the early 19th century at Somersby in Lincolnshire, a parishioner is recorded as saying, 'E read 'em from a paaper and I don't know what 'e meant'.

The Reverend William Jones, Rector of Broxbourne, kept a journal that spanned the fifty years 1771 to 1821. He complained in it in 1803 that, from his own experience, the content of contemporary sermons was sadly lacking:

> The name of Christ is scarce ever heard, nor any of the characteristic doctrines of His holy religion. The watchword or catchword (for I hardly know which to call it) is 'Morality'.

(However, in the parish of Brabourne in Kent, it was recorded in a recent volume *Archives and Anecdotes* that the vicar who was heard to mention *Christ* rather often in his sermons alarmed one small boy. The latter had frequently heard his Dad ticking off his Mum when she used the same word at home – no doubt in fits of exasperation! Elsewhere in the same book another preacher is recorded as apparently saying little else but 'Ichabob ... Ichabob ... Ichabob' – even on the most festive of occasions.)

During one academic year in Malawi, I was handed responsibility for the homiletics class. Most students were eager to indulge in public speaking, but were handicapped by a society which judged sermons on their length, rather than on their contents. Having listened to previous student offerings in our college chapel, it had become evident that there was but a single theme to all of them: 'Obey God, or he will punish you'. I was never clear how this constituted 'gospel' i.e. good news, but for them that wasn't the point: what mattered in their view was for how long they could admonish the congregation. It was reminiscent of Mr Pennyfeather's tactics in Evelyn Waugh's *Decline and Fall*, where Mr P offers a prize of half a crown to the boy who writes the longest essay, 'irrespective of any possible merit'. It was difficult to persuade them that there could be any alternative message, and equally difficult to introduce the idea that, more often than not, enough is enough.

A similar culture prevailed in Lesotho, but it was less influenced by Calvinist thinking and the students themselves were more critical of the subject matter. After one Wednesday sermon by a final year Mosotho seminarian, a Xhosa student from the Transkei immediately followed this with a bidding prayer: 'Lord, we pray for people who preach stupid sermons'. While recognising that this might represent serious exegetical appraisal, one could also see that it might equally – and more plausibly – be a reflection of the inter-tribal tensions around at the time. When tackled, the young man in question insisted it was a general petition to the Almighty, with no immediate application in mind. He did perhaps have a point!

I think I prefer the more direct approach I once heard as a student at Cambridge, when well-known public figures gave the Sunday evening sermon at Great St Mary's. It was Ted Heath's turn, and I have no recollection of anything he said. But evidently, Joe Fison the vicar (who later became bishop of Salisbury) had absorbed whatever Ted was trying to say. He stood up in his stall, and shouted across the church,

'Thank you very much, Ted. I think we've all heard enough of that. We'll sing the last hymn now'. And Ted uttered not another word.

Long ago, even the great St Paul, giving possibly his longest sermon ever (lasting till midnight, we're told), had to be halted in full flow. Eutychus was probably the hero of the evening at Troas through his successful if unconscious intervention. He dropped off to sleep and fell out of a third story window to the ground below. Hopefully it taught Paul a salutary lesson, although I wouldn't recommend anyone to imitate his somewhat drastic measure.

Only once have I plotted to bring an end to someone else's sermon. An evening service is always a good time to invite a visiting preacher, and quite regularly neighbouring priests joined us beforehand for tea as well. Alan, who had strange ideas, was somewhat sidelined in our Somerset deanery – and I was warned very firmly that he had (like our students in Malawi) a single theme for all his sermons, which often lasted up to an hour. Forewarned is forearmed, so I enlisted the church choir as angels of mercy. On a signal from me, they were (one by one) to walk slowly out of the church at intervals of five minutes in the hope that Alan would begin to realise that he was losing his congregation. After a quarter of an hour it became evident that he had delivered the core of his message and that nothing fresh was likely to fall from his lips, so the first choir member was detailed to make her exit. To my astonishment the ploy was immediately effective, and Alan's oration came to a rapid conclusion. It was by all accounts the shortest sermon he'd preached for years.

Growing up in the Methodist Church I wasn't however unfamiliar with the sermon sometimes being interrupted by the congregation. A young lady called Gwen, who had some mental disorder, attended in the custody of her brothers. She listened keenly to any words of wisdom offered from the pulpit, and – perhaps as in a Pentecostalist setting – audibly endorsed sentiments of which she approved. The opposite might also happen. I remember the preacher suggesting that we were all miserable sinners, in response to which Gwen leapt to her feet and told him that she wasn't at all miserable: she was a very happy sinner.

Gwen's contributions displayed her attentiveness to the sermon and were motivated by her desire to enhance it further. Only once, in the church of St Ambrose, Wye, have I experienced a similar interruption; a passing reference I made to the topical subject of clerical failures and abuses brought a visitor to her feet. She described in some detail what had once happened to her brother, who had been an altar server. Then she sat down, and I did my best to conclude the homily. She made her communion and left the church immediately afterwards, never to be seen again – no one knew who she was.

Others have told me of more troublesome disturbances, perhaps not unlike the one recounted by Parson Woodforde that took place in Castle Cary in 1770:

> Whilst I was preaching one Thos Speed of Gallhampton came into the Church quite drunk and crazy and made a noise in the Church, called the Singers a Pack of Whoresbirds and gave me a nod or two in the pulpit. The Constable Roger Coles Senr took him into custody after.

There are times, alas, when those listening to a sermon would love to interrupt the preacher, or to contradict him, but are obliged out of courtesy to remain silent. A colleague told me of one Remembrance Service when an army officer had been invited to preach. The gist of his message was that, in his view, society no longer maintained a Christian ethos. In fact, the government had failed to uphold it; schools had failed to teach it; and it was no longer to be found in the Christian churches. Only the army kept Christianity alive.[5] Evidently the vicar of this parish was in complete sympathy with these sentiments, because not only were they published on his website, but not long afterwards a sermon of his own repeated the theme: churchmen, politicians, teachers, lawyers are useless at promoting the kingdom of God, who needs regular soldiers (rather than those of the Salvation Army) to do his work on earth. 'Reminded me of square-bashing', commented my priestly friend, once an army officer himself. Since the clergy are usually spared the painful necessity of listening to other people preach, we agreed that to do so occasionally was a good object lesson, perhaps even a salutary penance.

We are fortunate, however, in generally being spared the marathon orations endured in the Victorian church, as described by Anthony Trollope in *Barchester Towers* (1857):

> There is, perhaps, no greater hardship inflicted on mankind in civilized and free countries than the necessity of listening to sermons. No one but a preaching clergyman has, in these

---

[5] Perhaps he had a point: a pioneering missionary in Malawi (Jack Martin) wrote home in 1928, 'When I was in the army I knew so sure that I didn't bother thinking about it that not one man would let me down, not even drunkards and so-called debauched villains. But here, in a Christian Mission, there is no support and no certainty'. Indeed, Bishop Taylor-Smith had earlier written to the *Daily Telegraph* in 1915 of his 'hope and prayer' that 'the Army might become the greatest missionary society the world has ever known. A nation with such a consecrated body of men ... would prove an irresistible force against all the powers of evil'.

In broad agreement Ronald Blythe recorded a retired brigadier in his *Akenfield* as saying, 'The church is going to pot because of all these young inexperienced parsons. Servicemen make the best parsons. They are men of the world who are used to handling people ... A man shouldn't be a parson until he's in his forties; he can't know about life till then. The best advice I ever had was given me by a padre, you know. Changed my life, you know. "Think of the other fellow", he said – something like that. Made me a different person, you know.'

realms, the power of compelling an audience to sit silent and be tormented. No one but a preaching clergyman can revel in platitudes, truisms, and untruisms, and yet receive, as his undisputed privilege, the sane respectful demeanour as though words of impassioned eloquence, or persuasive logic, fell from his lips. Let a professor of law or physics find his place in a lecture-room, and there pour forth jejune words and useless empty phrases, and he will pour them forth to empty benches. Let a barrister attempt to talk without talking well, and he will talk but seldom. A judge's charge need be listened to perforce by none but the jury, prisoner, and gaoler. A member of Parliament can be coughed down or counted out. Town-councillors can be tabooed. But no one can rid himself of the preaching clergyman. He is the bore of the age, the old man whom we Sindbads cannot shake off, the nightmare that disturbs our Sunday rest, the incubus that overloads our religion and makes God's service distasteful. We are not forced into church! No: but we desire more than that. We desire not to be forced to stay away. We desire, nay, we are resolute, to enjoy the comfort of public worship, but we desire also that we may do so without an amount of tedium which ordinary human nature cannot endure with patience; that we may be able to leave the house of God without that anxious longing for escape which is the common consequence of common sermons.

I was once in my life exceptionally privileged to hear perhaps the shortest sermon ever preached – at least within an English church. It was delivered by Dean Bezzant at a college evensong in the early 1960s, and therefore a century after Trollope's time. We had just sung the Isaac Watts hymn about the saints, who 'wrestled hard, as we do now, with sins and doubts and fears'. We sat down to listen to the Dean, who repeated this line, adding the question 'Well, do we?'. He then sat down as well while we all thought about it for a couple of minutes. Novelties such as this may perhaps be effective if not used too frequently, although the possibility remains that Dean Bezzant had simply forgotten it was his turn to preach. The story is also told of Fr Hope Patten who revived the Anglican shrine at Walsingham, suddenly realising at one Sunday morning mass in July that he had no homily to offer. He stood imposingly before his congregation and announced, 'As is our custom on this the 4th Sunday after Trinity there will be no sermon'.

Once I was present at a confirmation service when it certainly seemed that the officiating bishop's address had been improvised on the spot. He left his episcopal seat, rushed forward towards the candidates with robes flailing behind him, and shouted *'Whoosh!'* It gave every appearance of being a pale imitation of Batman, although it was probably intended to represent the descent of the Holy Spirit at Pentecost – a rather too literal reading of scripture, I felt. Afterwards, however, the children enjoyed rushing up to each other shouting *Whoosh*, so at least something of the bishop's wisdom had registered, and no doubt they'd remain enthusiastic Christians for months and years to come. (Jane Austen noted in her diary that she thought the Vicar of Godmersham was sometimes 'a little too eager' in his delivery, although in his case it was no stunt but heartfelt enthusiasm for the gospel.)

I need to confess here to a Lenten gimmick I once shared with my fellow curate in Northampton. This was much less of a success than we had envisaged, to put it mildly. Each Sunday we delved into a different topic, presenting the pros and cons of relevant Christian teaching. In simple terms, one week I was the goodie and John was the baddie, with our roles reversed the following week. Halfway through the course, a lady stopped at the church door on her way out and congratulated me: 'I did so agree with everything you said this morning'. To which I had to make the embarrassed reply, 'You were really supposed to agree with Fr John today. He said all the right things, whereas I said all the wrong things'.

Needless to say, that wasn't the only occasion when parishioners have misapprehended my meaning, so I obviously still have work to do. On the other hand, it's not uncommon for a throw-away remark to be the one thought that somehow registers with a particular listener, rather than the carefully worked main theme. Such are the mysterious workings of grace, well beyond human devising.

It may be that I was spoilt by hearing some of the great Methodist preachers when I was young. Most memorable of all was the visit of W. E. Sangster. I can't recall the whole of his address, but one vivid illustration remains with me. He spoke of an orchestra in rehearsal, working through a crescendo towards a mighty triple fortissimo climax. Every instrumental section was brought in by the maestro, and everything seemed to be building up as he wanted – until he rapped the rostrum with his baton and stopped the music in full swing. There was a shocked silence: what had gone wrong? The conductor looked across to the woodwinds, to the smallest instrument of all: 'The flageolet is not playing', he said. Further comment or explanation was unnecessary, since everyone listening immediately grasped the preacher's point. Sangster's sermon created just as much an electric atmosphere as the orchestral work in the performance that he was describing. What it demonstrated was the truth that a sermon has the potential to be a divine communication.

This remains true even if more often it is a poorly composed string of pious thoughts, or worse, an unedifying written discourse. (One of God's many wonders can easily be seen by those who devote time to their gardens: one may come across a thin dead-looking strand lying inert, merely straggling across the soil – yet it may still have the capacity to support spring-time growth and amazingly colourful flowers. Such hidden potential can sometimes blossom unexpectedly in those whose words at first seem tediously uninspiring.)

Memorability is a rare quality, which the Congregational divine Philip Doddridge sought to overcome by composing (more than four hundred) hymns mainly intended to summarise the themes of his preached sermons. Structurally they have been compared to Jacob's ladder, which begins on earth and ends in heaven. To imprint his message more firmly upon his hearers' hearts and minds, Doddridge concluded each service with the congregation repeating it in versified song.

I include therefore an attempt I once made to imitate him. The Whitsun hymn that follows aims to reflect Pentecostal teaching, only without the *Whoosh*:

>Lord,
>You were there when worlds began
>and life was thrusting out of naught
>Before the secrets came to man
>You shaped them in your thought.
>>You are Holy,
>>You are Spirit,
>>Creating all untaught.
>
>Lord,
>You were there as man came forth
>and learned to harness nature's wealth;
>Our foolishness will lead to death,
>Your wisdom, life and health.
>>You are Holy,
>>You are Spirit,
>>Enrich us with yourself.
>
>Lord,
>You are here within our life
>Where love and tender feeling flow;
>You guide our hopes, you solve our strife,
>And peace on us bestow.
>>You are Holy,
>>You are Spirit,
>>Let holiness now grow.

I can, however, well imagine such fancy elaborations having a limited appeal. One of E. C. Bentley's *Clerihews* probably sums it up:

>No, Sir', said General Sherman, I did not enjoy the sermon;
>Nor I didn't git any Kick outer the Litany.

To judge by other comments, he was not the only one – as Anne Hughes describes:

We to church this morne, and John did fidget much, he not liking thee passon; which be a new one, who did tell us that hell be nere and we all going there; and that it be wrong to heard monies, for the divell will get it all. Ande he did look so hard at John that I did fear he off from the church wronthefullie. But John did staire back at the man, and fould his armes and look puffed up.

(*The Diary of a Farmer's Wife 1796-1797*)

Or again, Molly Hughes (in *A London Child of the Seventies* — i.e. 1870s) tells the reader of the little that she ever gained from the preachers in St Paul's Cathedral:

> Sermons, of course, were on the endurance side, but had some alleviations. I had a nice long sit down, and as I was seated close to the pulpit I enjoyed the colours of the marble pillars … The sermons were seldom less than three-quarters of an hour. To the preacher it was the chance of a lifetime. He would never again 'address London' … He did not (however) know how his voice would carry under the dome, and we took joy in seeing whether he would bawl, or roar like any sucking dove.

Most note-worthy was her younger brother's comment after yet another sermon 'stiff with learning and far over our heads' — this one on 'Solomon's vision': would he, Molly asked, have chosen wisdom if he had been Solomon. 'Oh, no,' said he, 'I've got enough of that. I should have asked for a new cricket-bat.'

COMMANDING CHARACTERS

Keeping an eye on the Palais des Papes, Avignon

I remember the period [wrote Sydney Smith] when the Bishops never remained unpelted; they were pelted going, coming, riding, walking, consecrating, and carousing.

Every fresh accident on the railroads is an advantage [he also wrote, to a friend in 1842], and leads to an improvement. What we want is, an overturn which would kill a bishop, or, at least, a dean. This mode of conveyance would then become perfect.

In my time (50 years) as a priest, I've known a number of bishops: it might seem impolite to say 'the good, the bad, and the ugly', but you probably know what I mean. My old college dean once put it rather more pungently. Until the Gary Bennett affair in Runcie's day, Crockford's Clerical Directory carried a preface that was theoretically anonymous: Dean Bezzant (mentioned earlier) is reputed to have been the author one year, and to have offered this waspish comment (or something along these lines), 'It has lately become the custom of bishops to preface their signatures with a plus sign; in many cases a minus sign would seem to be more appropriate'. Sydney Smith was more restrained, describing the bishops whom he knew as merely 'feeble'. Those who were flogged by Geoffrey Fisher in his days as Headmaster of Repton, prior to becoming Bishop in turn of Chester and London, then Archbishop of Canterbury, would not however (according to Roald Dahl's memoir *Boy* – if this is credible) have described his floggings and admonitions as anything less than brutal. Today A. N. Wilson's assessment is that bishops are largely 'doleful and illiterate' as John Milton reckoned they always had been. But if that's an exaggeration, we could still agree that there simply aren't as many distinctive characters around as there once were.

There was, for example, Dr Barnes of Birmingham who (in Malcolm Muggeridge's words) 'regarded the Eucharist as a distasteful form of magic'. In Kilvert's day there was the bishop of Hereford who was more high-handed than most, as Mr Pope, the youthful curate of Cusop, found to his cost. Pope arrived late at a confirmation with a single female candidate:

> Pope tried to explain that he was a clergyman and the girl was his candidate, but the Bishop was overbearing and imperious and either did not hear or did not attend, seeming to think he was dealing with a refractory ill-conditioned youth. 'I know, I know,' he said. 'Come at once, kneel down, kneel down'. Poor Pope resisted a long time and had a long battle with the Bishop, but at last unhappily he was overborne in the struggle, lost his head, gave way, knelt down and was confirmed there and then.

A tale is also told about his neighbour the bishop of Gloucester, who by now was both elderly and short-sighted. At confirmations it was his custom to lay hands on two candidates at a time as they knelt before him. On this occasion he'd not realised that there was an odd number of candidates. So, as his left hand touched the last head, his right hand probed a little further to find its anticipated partner. Having found what appeared to be the head in question, he uttered (or muttered) the usual prayer over it. Afterwards, when they told him he'd confirmed the knob at the end of the choir stall, he was so angry he ordered it to be cut off and burnt. But such martyrdom was not to be its fate. They placed it instead in a glass case as the only confirmed wooden protuberance in the Church of England.

An even better anecdote, I think, relates how, twenty years later, Archbishop Frederick Temple was interviewing a young man desirous of being ordained. He decided to give him a pastoral test: 'Let's see how you approach someone on their sick bed. I'm going to be the patient and you can come and visit me'. So the candidate disappears out of the room for a moment, while the archbishop lies down full-length on his sofa. In comes our young man again, who takes one appalled look at Temple, and says, 'Drunk again, Freddie! Get up man and pull yourself together'.

In the modern church the procedures for getting ordained are, as you may imagine, a lot more complicated. You have to get to a selection conference. Mine was a long weekend in Sheffield in about 1967, and when the report came through I discovered it wasn't a straight Yes or No, but a No Decision Made. So I was summoned to the Bishop's Palace in Peterborough to see Cyril. This was my real selection conference which lasted less than 5 minutes. 'Hm,' he said, 'They don't know what to make of you. They don't know why you want to be ordained'. 'Well,' I reflected,

'They all seemed to think that being a Christian teacher was preferable to being a priest, and never asked me what I thought about priesthood. We spent the weekend chairing discussions and giving our views on topical issues'. 'O I see,' said Cyril, 'Do you still want to be ordained or don't you?' 'Certainly I do,' I replied. 'That's all right then', he decided without further inquiry.

Such an interview might well have taken place one hundred and forty years earlier, when Owen Chadwick recalls:

> [The bishop of Norwich] did not ask [William Wayte Andrew] why he sought ordination. That was not a question which any bishop, least of all Dr Bathurst of Norwich, would have asked an ordinand in 1831.

When I encountered Cyril again on my ordination retreat, he took all the candidates for a meal in a local hostelry. As we walked across Peterborough's central market place I can still see the assembled down-and-outs doffing their hats to him as he passed by. Indeed, I retain fond memories of him, because after he retired he kept in touch and wrote to me from time to time. I remember his only regret on leaving office was in having to give up his London club, the House of Lords. At the General Election in the early 70s he instructed his diocesan flock to vote Conservative, on the grounds that Labour wanted to introduce comprehensive schools which, he asserted, were clearly against God's will.

His successor Douglas Feaver was a man of even more pronounced views. He regarded the attempt to abolish capital punishment as a sign of weakening faith in the afterlife; he thought synodical government was a huge mistake by the Church of England, merely encouraging windbags to air their ill-informed opinions. As chairman of our own diocesan synod he would intimidate anyone who rose to their feet, 'Sit down unless you've something to say that hasn't been said already'. One had to be either very brave or very foolish to stay standing. His own views had been formed many years earlier and were not generally susceptible to change – so you knew where you were with him. When Archbishop Coggan launched his Call to the Nation, Douglas sent a message around the diocese, 'You may of course read out the archbishop's appeal in church, but if you take my advice you won't'. He also remained sceptical of the collective wisdom of his fellow bishops. Before the Lambeth Conference met in 1978, he reminded us of the suffering he was about to endure:

> To be incarcerated in Canterbury from 22 July until 13 August, and to catch the echo of every cliché on the nature of episcopacy and on the functions, duties, and, of course, the "role" of bishops, is not a prospect which lightens me with starry eyed bliss.

Douglas was deeply suspicious of committees; for him they were 'more time, money and patience consuming than I have space to describe'. He resisted (for example) any encroachments upon the individual responsibility of a patron for making appointments. One of the 'deadly results' of handing the task to a board might well be a dull uniformity, in which the new incumbent of a parish simply replicated his predecessor:

> Someone who alarmed no-one would be chosen by those who, however well intentioned, have not, nor ever could have, experience in matching a parish's potential with what a particular priest in new circumstances could do. What, too, would happen to those priests who are faithful, hardworking, unknown outside their parishes, and who do not shine at interviews with a committee?
>
> The one who ought to be able to look on the man's heart is his bishop: otherwise David will often be passed over by Eliab and Shammah. The art of finding the right man to do what ought to be done is very different from matching a man with a job: and it is an art, which is given rather than acquired. It is seldom the product of committee compromise.

He certainly allowed, therefore, for the unusual and the unconventional. As he commented on another occasion (in his monthly diocesan letter of September 1979):

> We, Christians, ought not to fit into the ways of the world. We were baptized to be invaders and upsetters of all protective and paralyzing presuppositions. There are dynamic doubts which we can create: and the very sense of helplessness and depressive repetition, which history leaves behind, can bring forth a discontent which is divine; and then there is a door through which the Lord and his Kingdom can come.

Above all else he hated 'schemes', which he hoped had 'had their tedious day'. Slogans, campaigns, any attempt to centralise the Church's business, were anathema to him. Yet all around were those keen to 'blow a whistle', imagining that ordinands would spring out of the ground; or to 'make a statement' as if 'the waiting world will come to attention'; or to 'put up a few signposts' as the principal means of ending moral confusion; or (worst off all!) to 'sound off in the Synod on some social theme' in the expectation that 'all will be put to rights'. It does not work anything, he insisted time and again; it gives the illusion of resolving problems, while in reality merely generating noise and useless activity.

In his personal dealings he was efficiency itself. He was always prompt to answer correspondence and was surprised that other bishops could keep their secretaries occupied past lunchtime. This was really because most of his letters were along the lines of 'Dear Schofield, Yes. Yours sincerely, Douglas Petriburg', or alternatively 'Dear Schofield, No. Yours sincerely, Douglas Petriburg'. He was essentially a Prayer Book man and a fan of the Authorised Version – and woe betide you if you toyed with anything else. He once called on me when I'd been unwell, and asked how things were going in the parish. I remarked that, in conjunction with the Methodists, we'd just completed a door-to-door distribution of St Mark's Gospel (excerpted from the Good News Bible). When he demanded to know what version was being offered, I avoided a direct answer to the question and replied, 'The cheapest', thereby deflecting his wrath.

Only once did I actually clash with him, and this was after completing the annual visitation questionnaire, which was usually issued by the archdeacon but on this occasion was being handled by the bishop himself. As I placed the completed form in its envelope I caught sight of its pompous title page, which read 'Douglas, by divine permission Lord Bishop of Peterborough'. With one stroke of the pen I deleted the word Lord. The next time we met he poked me in the chest and dressed me down: 'I will not have you defacing official documents' – to which I replied, 'Well, in the New Testament bishops are servants, not lords, I believe'. 'The Queen calls me My Lord Bishop so you can as well', he retaliated, shifting the argument rather feebly. 'Ah, but what does the Pope call you?' I rejoined. Answer came there none. Some weeks later a question about ecclesiastical titles was asked in General Synod, and archbishop Runcie's reply was printed in *The Times*, to the effect that he thought in this day and age a restrained simplicity of styling was to be preferred. I clipped this advice out and posted it to Douglas. No acknowledgement was ever received.

It may not surprise you to know that Douglas hadn't been in post for long before a joke started to circulate: What has the diocese of Peterborough got in common with Simon Peter's mother-in-law? (Answer: they're both sick of the fever.) Almost on day one Anglia Television had reached a similar conclusion. They had flown a film crew over in a helicopter from Norwich, intending to get an interview with the newly enthroned bishop broadcast that same evening. The questions were touchy-feely ones about what he liked in his new job, and what he might make of it. Douglas' only responses were extracts which he read out of the Book of Common Prayer from the Ordination of Bishops: not one single personal opinion did he venture to offer. Anglia trashed their recording and vowed never to interview him again. He didn't mind – he thought the press were the personification of evil and warned all of us to steer clear of them.

Early on in his episcopacy he was invited to Northampton Chamber of Commerce, and one of the concluding questions was slightly more focused: 'Now that you're a bishop, what do you notice is really different from being a parish priest?' 'Put it like this,' – and here Douglas was his more candid self – 'I've just taken a morning confirmation in a parish, and had a good lunch (he was ever a hearty eater, usually first at the food), and I'm on my way back to the Palace to put my feet up. I see the lights on in some country church as I pass, and I say to myself, 'There's some poor 'so-and-so' (not the word used, which is unseemly to print!) who's got to turn out again and say evensong'. His audience was nonplussed – shocked by his remark rather than appreciative of the quirky humour. I assume his own family was well used to it: he would regularly refer to his grandchildren as 'the pigs'.

Douglas wasn't much of a touchy-feely person. In church he liked to sit in his chair and then be left alone as far as possible – he hated to have servers hovering around him, and when all was over he made a swift dash for the nearest exit, never mind any procession lining up in more pompous array. I once offered to carry his bag for him after a service, but he declined, saying, 'If I have a free hand, people will want to shake it and I can't stand that'. What he'd have done in an African setting I can't imagine; it was the lovely custom there for clergy on entering any gathering to go round the room shaking hands with absolutely everybody. Nor could Douglas stand smoking: Archie, retired into the diocese after being bishop of Columbo, used to refer to Peterborough as 'the smokeless zone'. Equally he rejected (in fact, *ejected*) dogs, women in trousers, or anyone wearing a colour remotely like his own episcopal purple. I recall one occasion, however, when he met his match. A clergy chapter was being held at Abingdon Vicarage in Northampton; he was met by the vicar's wife whom he greeted thus: 'You can put two things out – that (pointing at the dog) and that (indicating her cigarette)'. She tartly informed his Lordship that out of courtesy to her guests she would keep the dog out of the way, but in her own house she was the one who decided whether she smoked or not. Later that morning, when coffee was due, Pat the vicar called through the door to remind her; reply came there none, as she had stumped out in a rage, leaving the men to make their own drinks!

One had necessarily to train parishioners not to be upset by him. Thus, it was fatal if a helper approached with an offer such as 'Can I get you a cup of tea?' because it would prompt an automatic response, 'You look perfectly capable of it to me'. 'May I get you …' was of course the grammatically correct formula. He had no patience with those who complained of being cold in church: 'In that case wear more clothes', he would say. He expected competence in anyone who had been appointed to hold responsibility, and couldn't comprehend why some bishops might feel the need for the assistance of a full-time suffragan: 'The man's not up to the job', he'd say. He was also dismissive of suggestions that extra diocesan 'specialist' ministries should be created: 'If I acceded to all the requests I get, I'd be sending someone round the vicarages to wipe the babies' bottoms'.

On the whole I think he had a point: some years later down in Somerset, clergy were unsurprisingly bemoaning the shortage of young people in their churches, and when the matter was brought to the attention of the diocesan synod a motion to appoint a youth chaplain was carried overwhelmingly. The financial implications had not been detailed at the synod, and it transpired that the eventual costs were far higher than anticipated; thus, a chaplain would require not only a house, but a separate office in Wells, together with all necessary equipment and indeed his own secretary. Initially, the appointed chaplain ventured forth from Wells to visit parishes and gain first-hand knowledge of the problems being faced. Subsequently, his solution was to stage diocesan events for young people – but as many parishes had few of these, attendance figures were embarrassingly low, leading the diocesan bishop to castigate the clergy for 'not supporting the chaplain'; this seemed a little unfair on those who had not yet managed to rally their youngsters.

Douglas had his own way of engaging with this age group, which perhaps bordered on the unconventional. His jokey quips could leave people quite speechless, as at Overstone Girls School on the occasion of a confirmation, when he remarked, 'It's always difficult to match up mothers and daughters. The trouble is, the pretty girls have ugly mothers and pretty mothers have ugly daughters'. It was his custom on these occasions to interrogate the candidates, first posing a question and then glaring at a particular youngster for his or her response. One soon came to learn that the questions were always the same, and to rehearse Douglas' preferred answer. Thus, he would say, 'Tell me the names of the four gospels', to which most candidates would naturally reply, 'Matthew, Mark, Luke and John'. Their confidence would then be shattered by the bishop's resounding 'No', followed by a pregnant pause, after which he would add, 'We call them SAINT Matthew, SAINT Mark, SAINT Luke and SAINT John'. So, one made a mental note to warn one's future candidates. Next time round, Douglas picked on one of my group with the same question and (I was proud to note) received the 'correct' answer. He was furious: 'Someone told you to say that!' he bellowed.

It's perhaps understandable that when he retired and went to live in Somerset, the bishop of Bath and Wells (Jim, as already mentioned) decided to exclude him from episcopal ministry of any kind. So one summer afternoon a rather forlorn Douglas appeared on our doorstep near Taunton: 'If you need any episcopal services,' he said, 'don't forget to mention to your bishop that I'd be glad to help'. The fact is, that despite the uncompromising exterior there was a gentle soul underneath, who'd once given me the wonderful reassurance, 'What matters in ministry is not any apparent public success, but the particular individuals you manage to help'. It was also encouraging to know that, as he put it, 'the only committed Christians are those in prison'. A clerical friend, Eric Woods, who knew him in these later years, relayed an entirely typical story:

> On one occasion [Douglas] attended the consecration as bishop of a former curate of his at St Mary's, Nottingham. Too old and lane to robe, he sat in the congregation with one of his youngest granddaughters. There came that point when the new bishop disappeared under a sea of hands from other bishops. "Oh granddaddy", cried his granddaughter, "what are they doing to the new bishop?" In a great boom which was heard throughout the cathedral, +Douglas replied, "They are removing his backbone".

I'll come to Jim again in a moment. But first there was the delightful John Bickersteth, who on our return from Lesotho asked but one question, 'Would you like a modern vicarage or an old one?' before appointing me to fill an impending vacancy near the Quantocks. He was the only bishop I've encountered who, having read parish magazines routinely posted to him, then phoned through on the morning of a church event to offer his support. He was soon succeeded by George (as in Carey), who passed like a meteor through the skies of Somerset before gaining the dizzy heights of Canterbury. George always knew he was God's chosen one, to revive Christianity across the land. I was there in the diocesan synod after his appointment to Canterbury had been announced. He told us in these or similar words, 'I knew it was my destiny. I had a dream that God was laying his hand upon me to restore the Church of England'. Luckily for him, God had also informed the Prime Minister about this plan. George had earlier announced himself in Bath and Wells as a bishop-in-mission, making it his aim to get round all the deaneries as fast as possible to give everyone the opportunity of being rejuvenated by his words. First, he visited the clergy, and decided he'd stop at our house for lunch. But there was a significant omen en route: the parish of West Monkton was a mixture of council estates, housing developments, rural hamlets and farms, and as we got nearer the Rectory a flock of sheep blocked the lane and held us up. George unfortunately didn't get the message, but (elsewhere at least) continued at his own breakneck speed. When asked by *Reader's Digest* if it was true that he aimed to run the church 'more as a business', his instant reply was 'Yes, and this is already happening … Jesus was a management expert … He is looking for results'.

SPOT THE ODD ONE OUT
A. Alexamenos' Ass
B. Good Shepherd
C. Lamb of God
D. Management Expert
E. Son of Man
F. Suffering Servant

His (that is, George's) plans included several days in our deanery just a fortnight before Christmas. The clergy told him this wouldn't work, because people were too busy with carols and parties and all the usual Christmas events. He told us it wouldn't suit his programme at any other time, so the mission must go ahead as instructed. Of course, the turn-out was dismal, as we'd predicted – in response to which, we all got a letter dressing us down for not supporting him. When I asked a parishioner who'd actually attended one of his addresses what he made of it, he said, 'Nothing to get excited about: we hear all that from you Sunday by Sunday anyway!'

Having toured the parishes, George then decided to invent a diocesan strategy. It was about all the usual things that vicars are meant to do: a leg-up for young people, something for families, don't forget the elderly, how's your publicity, beef up your services and so on. Then, being democratic, he circulated it for approval to all the churchwardens – but not to the clergy, whom no doubt he'd by now realised might have a few ideas of their own. The churchwardens were naturally anxious to please ('Yes bishop, that's wonderful'), so it all went ahead with a big launch planned at the cathedral. However, before it could take place George's elevation was made public, and so the event was re-jigged to incorporate his farewell. Afterwards the Dean commented, 'We were supposed to be launching the strategy and saying farewell to George: in reality, we launched George and said farewell to his strategy'. Of which, nothing was ever heard again.

To be fair, he was not the only bishop who sought rather too strenuously to exercise leadership. There were plans and schemes elsewhere to whip parishes into line, such as in the neighbouring diocese of Salisbury where the incoming bishop labelled his ideas somewhat alarmingly as a 'vision'. A lesson might have been learnt from nature, in the aftermath of the devastating gales of 1987. Although some authorities drew up master plans for re-forestation, the most successful rejuvenation came from woodland which had been left to fend for itself. Trees and other vegetation started to grow again, and after a few years it was a matter simply to thin out the growth and encourage whichever saplings were destined for long-term maturity. Or to use a different analogy from A.A. Milne: the highly organised Rabbit 'never let things come to him, but always went and fetched them', whereas the more lovable and memorable Pooh Bear waited patiently for inspiration to come from on high. Indeed, Pooh could well claim scriptural warrant:

> The wind blows where it wills, and you hear the sound of it, but you do not know whence it comes or whither it goes; so it is with everyone who is born of the Spirit.

If Jesus can also liken the unpredictable growth of God's kingdom to the spreading of a weed, then episcopal leadership is well summarised by Timothy Radcliffe:

> [It's] about helping the timid to speak up, the minority to have their word, the despised to be heard with respect, and especially those who disagree with you. It's not about control but about the opening the space for God's surprising grace.

As a prebendary of Wells, I had an invitation to George's enthronement in Canterbury, travelling down from Charing Cross on a special train. When we reached the cathedral precincts, there was a police check; those with bags or cases were pulled out of line for closer inspection. As far as I could tell, this meant anyone carrying robes for the procession. Who were they? Certainly not rank and file clergy or laity destined for the side aisles, but the princes of the church heading for the front stalls. In other words, suspicion of murderous intent fell exclusively on the bishops: perhaps George had premonitions of bloody battles in the offing?

One of them, of course, was bound to be over the ordination of women. George favoured women as priests, but not as bishops (although he subsequently changed his mind on the latter issue, as did others). In typically robust fashion he pronounced anyone who disagreed with him to be guilty of 'most serious heresy'. This judgement was directed at opponents within the Church of England, but necessarily it embraced the wider Christian world as well. Thus George became the first modern archbishop of Canterbury to call the Pope a heretic (and subsequently – unless I mistook his meaning – the first retired archbishop to liken the Prime Minister to Adolf Hitler). He modified this a few months afterwards, substituting the milder phrase 'fundamental theological error', which of course made everyone feel so much better. So long as I wasn't a serious heretic, I didn't mind being fundamentally wrong. The unresolved question is whether George's innovative christology (Jesus as 'management expert') is better described as 'most serious truth' or merely as a 'fundamental theological insight'?

Later on, in General Synod, it was interesting to notice his very different approach from that of Robert Runcie his predecessor. Runcie would listen intently throughout a debate and would sometimes rise at the end to give a magisterial appraisal of the various points made. By contrast, George would intervene at an early stage, as if to make any further discussion unnecessary; this was usually counter-productive, since his arguments were then open to critical comment or even plain disagreement.

Down in Kent, the evidence points to his having at some stage issued mounted, signed photographs of himself in full regalia to all the parish churches in his archdiocese for public display. Even now, a decade and two archbishops later, they remain in many places for the faithful to be reminded of their once Great Leader, just as in China there are those who still recall the glory days of Chairman Mao.

His primacy, of course, coincided with the so-called Decade of Evangelism, intended to swell congregations up and down the land. It echoed George's own messianic vision, and throughout the 1990s he wanted everyone to know it was working. It wasn't by any means, but the way round that was to publicise (lies, damned lies and) statistics. He seems to have encouraged (or at the very least, not to have discouraged) his spin doctors in Church House, Westminster to seize upon every tiny green shoot and to blazon them abroad. So although the annual returns of baptisms, confirmations, marriages, and church attendance continued the gentle decline begun in the 1960s, inevitably one or two dioceses would show a temporary year-on-year improvement. It might be that there were (say) 30 confirmations reported for Sodor and Man where the previous year there had been only 24; in which case the headlines would typically ring out, 'Confirmations up by 25%: strong revival of Christian faith now under way'.

I once submitted a paper which pointed out that church attendance figures, although on a downward slope, could be misleading in so far as they failed to take account of the decline in frequency of attendance, and also omitted weekday services. These observations, intended to qualify matters more carefully, resulted in a different method of head-counting but unfortunately allowed the spin doctors to paint an even rosier picture. But not everybody was fooled: it was reported that the PM's Appointment Adviser, after reading the paper, remarked, 'Thank goodness there's at least one person who seems to understand what's happening to the Church of England'.

When George retired he at last admitted himself that things weren't quite so buoyant and explained the reason. He had the vision, he had the plans, but the clergy of the Church of England had let him down. One wonders whether he was ever reminded, as was once explained to an over-zealous monastic community, that 'there's only one Saviour of mankind – and it's not you'. Maybe he didn't properly appreciate the strengths of his potential collaborators? We glimpsed in the diocese how things might have been when he led a pilgrimage to (what for him was) the unfamiliar territory of Walsingham. It was a gesture that was deeply appreciated, because for once he was encouraging others and not imposing upon them. It was an affirmation of spirituality, not always evident in his top-down management style.

I can't claim much familiarity with his successor at Canterbury, beyond a far-off overnight stay with us in Lesotho, when he was newly married and had black hair. He had come with Jane his wife on a South African lecture tour. I was impressed: I can still remember, nearly 30 years later, what he said. The seminarians were even more impressed by Jane, being the first time ever to haved heard a woman give (a) a public talk (b) an erudite talk (c) a talk in a Catholic seminary. Rowan continues to inspire many with his thoughtful books and poems, and his readiness to engage in important public debates – a kindly Christian through and through

George's successor in Somerset was the generally genial Jim, who was neither erudite nor an intellectual, which meant that he couldn't always keep up in a theological discussion and when out of his depth was inclined to get emotional. One of the archdeacons, who'd also served under his immediate predecessors, told me that, whereas there'd always been a robust exchange of ideas in staff meetings, with Jim it was expedient to keep quiet. As occasionally I begged to differ from him, I had no expectation of being one of his protégés. Any references he wrote on my behalf invariably had a sting in the tail, although he did once admit to the same PM's Adviser that he'd been a little 'unfair' once or twice. He much preferred compliant liberals with advanced views like his own. Yet if he was sometimes petulant towards those of us who held more traditional beliefs he usually made up for it afterwards. When, for example, we'd taken ourselves off to Malawi he sent a generous donation towards the roofing of a new church we were helping to build there.

So we were sad that he died of a sudden heart attack in early retirement. After all, life under Jim, if not exactly orthodox, could be entertaining. I think of the time he brought the clergy together for a conference at Swanwick. The opening worship focused on a maypole bedecked with ribbons. First of all we were issued with pencil and paper and instructed to write down our worries and anxieties. They were collected up, and burnt in a metal can near the maypole (if only life itself were so simple!). Then the Yeo Valley Dancers took over. These were middle-aged ladies dressed in black leotards who'd been bussed in from a hundred miles away; why economise on 'wine, women and song' to entertain the troops? They came forward to the maypole; they each grasped one of the coloured ribbons; their dance radiated outwards until all those assembled were within reach of a ribbon. We stretched out our hands, as instructed, each of us holding a ribbon, ecstatically united by the maypole. Unfortunately the cluttered furniture of the chapel allowed only limited manoeuvrability, or we would have danced all night, no doubt in circles.

For churches of Jim's advanced thinking, circle dancing was the coming thing in the 1990s, possibly to emphasise solidarity with Wicca. On another episcopal occasion I really did dance in his company. We were together at a retreat house immediately before the ordination of a number of priests and deacons. The usual worship on these occasions was the sharing of the divine office according to the authorised liturgies of the Church of England, which meant a choice between the old

Prayer Book or the updated modern version. Here we were just a little bit different. First, the chairs were cleared from the chapel, and then we made a large ring, joining hands. A tape recorder played Indian music, which for all I knew was expressing fervent devotion to Krishna or some Hindu goddess. We took one step forward, then one step back, one to the left and two to the right – by means of which (if you're following this carefully) the ring of dancers rotated very slightly anticlockwise. We repeated this again, and again, and again… until at last we were all back in our original places. We then sang a Graham Kendrick song and went for supper. Thus, on the eve of their ordination into sacred ministry, the candidates crossed the threshold into a new multi-faith, indeed cosmic, world – yes, Jim's world.

It was a cutting-edge world too, well spotted by *The Daily Telegraph*:

Bishop Jim drops his shield for an egg

Image consultants have struck in the Church of England. The Bishop of Bath and Wells, the forthright Rt Rev Jim Thompson, has deemed the traditional diocesan logo a touch old fashioned. The St Andrew's cross, emblazoned on a shield, has a long history at Wells. A statue of the apostle holding the instrument of his martyrdom has peered down from the building's great West facade since the 13th century. The new, egg-shaped logo appears on all letter heads from the Bishop's Palace and diocesan communications.

[NB not mine – I used my supply of headed notepaper for shopping lists and other vital purposes; the editor of the diocesan newspaper, known as *The Grapevine*, had a more plausible excuse, pointing out that he couldn't very well change his logo from a bunch of grapes to 'an egg']

'It is designed to reflect a modern, relevant, mission-focused diocese,' says Thompson. 'I hope that all will feel our new face not only projects a new corporate identity but helps in the parish and in personal ministry'.

An unidentified spokeman from Wells Cathedral asked, 'Is it supposed to be an American football?' Less polite suggestions were also rumoured to be in circulation. I was not particularly aware of any ensuing uplift that surged through the diocese, but colleagues may have been reticent in admitting how spiritually helpful they found it.

It seems too that Jim's successor did away with his logo – because, of course, today's world keeps moving on still further. An Anglican magazine reported in 2012 that a priest conducting a wedding rehearsal was told by the bride how the previous week she'd been the crucifer at a confirmation service, where she had an excellent view of the bishop tweeting on his iPad during the liturgy. We hail the dawning of a new *aggiornamento*! And to be fair, he may necessarily have been multi-tasking and catching up on his endless correspondence. (I've known some bishops who, unlike St

Paul – surely the patron saint of letter writers – never reply at all. Congratulations, however, to those who do, or did: Archbishop Rowan Williams and Cardinal Basil Hume come particularly high in the ratings.) Or was he simply testing a pilot version of *Alexa*, as described by Andrew Brown in *The Guardian* (2018) … ?

Amazon assistant *Alexa* is launched

Religion exists to supply the needs that couldn't possibly be bought with money. But *Alexa* is a piece of consumer technology. It exists to make it easy to buy things, listening patiently for you to express a certain kind of wish. What Amazon gets out of this deal is obvious: reliable information about which of its customers are seriously interested in the Church of England; information which can be used to sell them other things.

What's in it for the Church, though? Obviously there is some favourable publicity to be had … There is also the hope that it will reach half-believers, or cultural Christians, who can quickly find their nearest church, or hear a prayer for the day (read by a human being and not a robot). The machine will even say grace before a meal it you ask it to. Why you should want to do so is something Alexa can't explain. I asked it the great question which opens the Westminster Catechism, one of the foundational documents of puritanism: "Alexa, what is the chief end of man?". The answer should be: "To glorify God and enjoy him forever." Alexa was silent!

That isn't surprising. There are all sorts of questions that can [result in a] silence of polished evasiveness. When I asked "does God exist?", Alexa didn't give me an answer. Instead, it talked about what it feels like to believe in God, a surreal experience when I recalled that I was talking to a robot. "It's been well briefed!" said the Church's communications officer. Actually, it's even simpler. The program can only react to words or phrases which it recognises, and then only with formulaic responses.

But this shouldn't be blamed on the Church of England. No large and respectable organisation wants to get into a theological controversy. For a second opinion I asked Google if God exists and the robot voice answered solemnly "everyone has their own opinion about religion". Religions have always taken advantage of technology: the most obvious example is the spread of printed Bibles when printing was young; but throughout the 19th and 20th centuries Christians, and especially missionaries, made use of innovative techniques to get the message out. The word "propaganda" itself originates from the Vatican, while evangelical Christians worked on hymns that would embed their message in unforgettable tunes. In the 20th century it was the American religious right that invented database marketing, while the merchandising skills of charismatic megachurches are almost up there with Disney's.

Even so, the emergence of Alexa is a surprise. Others will have to catch up – Humanists, Muslims, Catholics, evangelicals … It's all invaluable marketing information. The resulting cacophony of canned replies will be indistinguishable from what passes for religious debate online today, but no one will have to type to participate; they can simply speak into the empty air.

SAINTS and SINNERS

A perpetual danger for religious institutions, as for secular society in general, is to divide the world into 'Us' and 'Them', and to categorize issues in black and white terms. The Bible, however, tells us that when God restored a broken world in Noah's day the sign of peace and harmony was a *multi-coloured rainbow*. One of the arias in J.S.Bach's *St John Passion* movingly describes the striped wounds on Christ's back using this very imagery. And again it is highly significant that the Christian Church reveres not one single Gospel writing, but four: while Matthew, Mark, Luke and John hold much in common, we are enriched by the different perspectives that each of them provides. God's revelation can never be reduced to one formulation alone, just as the mystery of his own Being can now only be glimpsed as "in a mirror dimly" – so St Paul explained to the Corinthians – and our glimpses are not necessarily identical.

What is true of God holds also for our perspective on human beings, made 'in his image'. One of the strengths of the Bible is that it doesn't necessarily reduce its more prominent characters to stereotypes, seeing them each as either wholly good or wholly bad. It's worth repeating that the New Testament (to its credit) admits the failings of those who became leading apostles, including of course 'Saint' Paul who initially features as a prime opponent of the early Christian Church. There is likewise an honest admission in the Hebrew Bible that not all the patriarchs conducted themselves admirably at all times. In particular, Abraham and Jacob, along with Moses and Aaron, and later even king David, displayed significant weaknesses such as deceitfulness or tinkering with idolatry. What is of perhaps of greater concern is that subsequent commentators and biblical interpreters were so shocked to learn of these failings that they either explained them away or, in some instances, rewrote the text. The following examples are taken from the books of Genesis and Exodus.

Abraham is first mentioned in the genealogy of Genesis 11, and then in chapter 12 he dutifully travelled from his homeland to live in Canaan. But when famine struck he moved further south for a time:

> Now there was a famine in the land. So Abram went down to Egypt to sojourn there, for the famine was severe in the land. When he was about to enter Egypt, he said to Sarai his wife, "I know that you are a woman beautiful to behold; and when the Egyptians see you, they will say, 'This is his wife'; then they will kill me, but they will let you live. Say you are my sister, that it may go well with me because of you, and that my life may be spared on your account." When Abram entered Egypt the Egyptians saw that the woman was very beautiful. And when the princes of Pharaoh saw her, they praised her to Pharaoh. And the

> woman was taken into Pharaoh's house. And for her sake he dealt well with Abram; and he had sheep, oxen, he-asses, menservants, maidservants, she-asses, and camels.

Evidently Sarah colluded with this deception, which worked very well indeed for her husband, who displays no concern for her at all. In some later versions of the story extra verses were inserted that describe the distress he suffered. But other writers went further by omitting the perpetrated falsehood, and ascribed the separation of husband and wife to Pharaoh's ruthless lust. In the *Book of Jubilees* (2nd century BC) we read that Sarah was taken by force – *five years* after they had arrived in Egypt. In the following century Philo of Alexandria says that Pharaoh "sent for the woman and, seeing her extraordinary beauty, paid little regard to decency or the laws enacted to show respect to strangers". The 1st century BC *Genesis Apocryphon*, found at Qumran, reiterates this theme, and describes Abraham "weeping greatly" on the night that Sarah was taken away by force. Nevertheless, he probably cheered up when he saw the flood of sheep, oxen, asses and servants heading in his direction – although a much later midrash *Lekh Lekha* takes a different view and describes Abraham complaining to "the Master of the universe" for inflicting disaster upon him without prior notice.

Lying seems to have become embedded in the family genes, or so we may speculate on account of the way **Jacob** subsequently tricked his father Isaac into giving him his blessing and hence the greater part of his inheritance. In this he was aided and abetted by his mother Rebekah:

> Jacob said to Rebekah his mother, "Behold, my brother Esau is a hairy man, and I am a smooth man. Perhaps my father will feel me, and I shall seem to be mocking him, and bring a curse upon myself and not a blessing". His mother said to him, "Upon me be your curse, my son; only obey my word, and go, fetch [two good kids] to me". So he went and took them and brought them to his mother; and his mother prepared savoury food, such as his father loved. Then Rebekah took the best garments of Esau her older son, which were with her in the house, and put them on Jacob her younger son; and the skins of the kids she put upon his hands and upon the smooth part of his neck; and she gave the savoury food and the bread, which she had prepared, into the hand of her son Jacob. So he went in to his father, and said, "My father"; and he said, "Here I am; **who are you, my son?**" Jacob said to his father, "**I am Esau your first-born**. I have done as you told me; now sit up and eat of my game, that you may bless me". But Isaac said to his son, "How is it that you have found it so quickly, my son?" He answered, "Because the Lord your God granted me success". Then Isaac said to Jacob, "Come near, that I may feel you, my son, to know whether you are really my son Esau or not". So Jacob went near to Isaac his father, who felt him and said, "The voice is Jacob's voice, but the hands are the hands of Esau". And he did not recognize him, because his hands were hairy like his brother Esau's hands; so he blessed him. He said, "Are you really my son Esau?" He answered, "I am". Then he said, "Bring it to me, that I may eat of my son's game and bless you". So he brought it to him, and he ate; and he brought him wine, and he drank. Then his father Isaac said to him, "Come near and kiss me, my son". So he came near and kissed him; and he smelled the smell of his garments, and blessed him.

This biblical story hardly provided its hearers with a worthy example to be followed. Scribes and rabbis felt this was warrant enough for modifying the text, or at least for revisiting its punctuation, not featured at all in ancient Hebrew writing. The sentences in bold type offered a way out. The dialogue between Jacob and his father became "Who are you? my son?" with the reply, "I am. Esau is your first-born." This version, or one very like it, was preferred in the *Book of Jubilees*, as in several midrashim, which thus presented Jacob as perfectly truthful. It left Isaac as seemingly somewhat naïve or dim-witted, but this was explained away by the argument that God intended Jacob to succeed his father and so temporarily weakened Isaac's powers of perception. *Jubilees* reads, "there was an ordering from heaven to turn his mind astray". This dispensation was "a blessing", suggests Philo, "that not a wicked man but one deserving of blessings might obtain it." Other writers concurred with this judgement, claiming that Esau as a "skilful hunter" (Genesis 25.27) was obviously a wicked killer in contrast to Jacob who was "a quiet man, dwelling in tents": this is not quite the way Genesis portrayed them, particularly when we read that Jacob refused to feed his starving brother unless he first sold him his birthright, and in their final encounter is generously forgiven by Esau.

Rebekah hardly stands out here as an impartial and honest mother, and not long afterwards we encounter another woman whose morality is also questionable. After Jacob found himself deceived into taking Leah as his wife, he struck a bargain with his father-in-law Laban to marry **Rachel** as well. When he had prospered sufficiently, he left Laban – without notification – and headed back south for Canaan.

> Laban had gone to shear his sheep, and Rachel stole her father's household gods. And Jacob outwitted Laban the Aramaean, in that he did not tell him that he intended to flee.

On discovering this – and the loss of his household gods – Laban pursued him and eventually caught up with him. Jacob as it happened knew nothing of the theft, but allowed Laban to search his tents. Rachel quickly hid them in her camel's saddle, and sat herself on it, pleading "Let not my lord be angry that I cannot rise before you, for the way of women is upon me". Defeated in his search, Laban struck a deal with Jacob, and they parted, if not quite amicably, at least peaceably. By now, we are not surprised that later commentators tweaked the story so as to exonerate Rachel. Their common explanation was that in *taking* (but not *stealing*) the idols she was saving her father from idolatry: this was St Ambrose's version in the late 4th century, as also that of the slightly later Syrian bishop Theodoret. The 1st century Jewish historian Josephus, however, acknowledged the theft (in his *Jewish Antiquities*) but explained it as an attempt by Rachel to have divine help in the event of Laban catching up with them – thus, "they might have recourse to [the idols] in order to obtain a pardon". This would seemingly make Rachel not only a thief but an idolater as well!

Idolatry surfaces again in the Book of Exodus with **Aaron**, the brother of Moses. When the Israelites were in the Sinai wilderness he somehow colluded with them in creating the Golden Calf while Moses was otherwise engaged:

> And he received the gold at their hand, and fashioned it with a graving tool, and made a molten calf; and they said, "These are your gods, O Israel, who brought you up out of the land of Egypt!" When Aaron **saw** this, he built an altar before it; and Aaron made proclamation and said, "Tomorrow shall be a feast to the Lord".

Not an easy text to manipulate, interpreters noted that the Hebrew letters in the word for 'saw' could alternatively be read as 'was afraid' – hence, Aaron heard the Israelites proclaiming their gods and was so terrified they might assault him that he provided what they wanted. The modified reading appears in Pseudo-Philo (probably 2nd century AD) as "Aaron, fearful because the people were very strong ..." and subsequently in the *Samaritan Targum of Pentateuch* as "Aaron was afraid and built an altar in front of them ..." No longer a genuine idolater, was he merely a coward? – St Ephrem, in his 4th century *Commentary on Exodus*, managed to find a more positive hermeneutical spin: "[Aaron] cunningly ordered that they bring the earrings of their wives, it might come about that these would stop their husbands from making the calf so as to keep their earrings untouched". A case of 'divide and rule' perhaps?

In the 7th century Qur'an, with its fundamental emphasis upon monotheism and the rejection of any form of idolatry, the people's excuse that they were "burdened with the weight of people's jewellery" (Q 20.87) – and that it was after all Aaron's decision to "produce an image of a calf which made a lowing sound" – hardly held water. Yet Aaron is not rebuked here by Moses for anything he did, except his failure to fetch his brother back at once to sort things out. Sura 4.153 asserts his authority: "Even after clear revelations had come down to them, they took the calf as an object of worship, yet We pardoned this, and gave Moses clear authority." The emphasis is upon heeding God's prophet, whose mantle was now worn by Muhammad himself. We may note here that Moses' own destruction of the two stone tables he had just received from God himself is tactfully omitted from the Qur'an.

Yet whereas Muhammad's knowledge of the Hebrew Bible was probably an oral rather a written tradition, and so much more easily altered or elaborated, Jewish scribes were faced here with words "written by the finger of God" (Exodus 31.18). **Moses's** action could *not* be overlooked by them: surely his anger when he learnt of the Golden Calf fashioned in his absence should have been directed elsewhere? His defenders had a very simple answer. Pseudo-Philo wrote: "Moses hurried down and saw the calf. And he looked at the tables and saw the writing was gone, and he hurried to break them." Hence, no sacrilege was committed! A similar, if slightly more complicated, response was needed to explain the Deuteronomic version of the story:

> I took hold of the two tables, and cast them out of my two hands, and broke them before your eyes.

Why were they 'cast out'? – the rabbinic answer was that the divine writing relieved Moses of some of their weight, but once that had disappeared the tables became too heavy to hold any longer. So Moses, although displeased by what he found, was not uncontrollably furious; he was simply not strong enough.

Nevertheless, there remained one further episode which put him in a most unsatisfactory light. In their seemingly endless journey through the wilderness, the Israelites experienced many hardships, and from time to time complained bitterly.

> And the people spoke against God and against Moses, "Why have you brought us up out of Egypt to die in the wilderness? For there is no food and no water, and we loathe this

worthless food." Then the Lord sent fiery serpents among the people, and they bit the people, so that many people of Israel died. And the people came to Moses, and said, "We have sinned, for we have spoken against the Lord and against you; pray to the Lord, that he take away the serpents from us". So Moses prayed for the people. And the Lord said to Moses, "Make a fiery serpent, and set it on a pole; and everyone who is bitten, when he sees it, shall live". So Moses made a bronze serpent, and set it on a pole; and if a serpent bit any man, he would look at the bronze serpent and live.

This appears to be a clear infringement of the commandment forbidding graven images before which people might "bow down" or "serve". The escape clause was found to lie in the phrase "set it on a pole", which required the people to gaze upwards; *and if so gazing*, they were actually looking towards God himself, rather than the serpent. This explanation is found in the early (1st century AD?) *Targum Pseudo-Jonathan*, where we read "Moses made a bronze serpent and put it on an elevated place, and it happened that when a snake would bite a man, he would look upon the bronze serpent and direct his thoughts towards God and live". Or at least that's what he was supposed to be doing, but anyone with an ounce of common sense could see it was quite likely to remain but a pious aspiration. Fortunately a few hundred years later king Hezekiah did what was necessary, "he broke in pieces the bronze serpent that Moses had made, for until those days the people in Israel had burned incense to it" (2 Kings 18.4). There is an additional reference to Moses "lifting up the serpent" to be found in St John's Gospel, but this simply draws the reader's attention to Christ himself being "lifted up" – the significance of the serpent being irrelevant.

The early centuries after Christ saw the production of many 'apocryphal' writings which heightened the respect in which apostles and prophets (the biblical saints) were held by detailing heroic exploits and miracles not previously known. Some of these stories may have had a factual element, but in general they may be termed 'devotional fiction'. Nor was this development confined to Judaism and Christianity; in the Muslim world many legends came to be circulated about the Prophet himself; collectively these constitute the *Hadith,* whose status is similar to that of the church's own canon law. Although some of the qur'anic texts that feature biblical characters are also quite different from the original, there is one outstandingly contentious re-writing, namely, the denial that Jesus (or *Isa* as Muslims know and revere him) was ever crucified: "They did not kill him, nor did they crucify him, though it was made to appear like that to them" (Q 4.157). In later centuries even to dream otherwise was to court disaster. Jamal al-Din ibn Wasil, who died in 1298, told this story:

> Al-'Uris saw in his sleep Christ Jesus Son of Mary … [He] asked him, "Did the crucifixion really happen?" Jesus said, "Yes, the crucifixion really happened." Al-'Uris then related his dream to an interpreter, who said, "The man who saw this dream shall be crucified. For Jesus is infallible and can speak only the truth, yet the crucifixion he spoke of cannot refer to his own, because the Glorious Qur'an specifically states that Jesus was not crucified or killed. Accordingly, this must refer to the dreamer, and it is he who shall be crucified." The matter turned out as the interpreter said.

Over the centuries the sacred writings of every religion have been expounded and re-interpreted time and again. Since featured characters who serve as role models sometimes behave rather badly it is possible for their imitators to be led astray; religious authorities therefore often attempt, as illustrated above, to explain their errors away or to make additions that enhance their reputation; in the last resort they may even omit the disturbing passages altogether. The last of these options was liable to be practised when biblical texts were first translated into the vernacular. This happened in Anglo-Saxon times when monks prepared so-called Old English translations of the Old Testament from existing Latin versions. Study of the Old English Hexateuch, catalogued in the British Library as *Cotton Claudius B-iv*, reveals a whole series of omissions. Where patriarchal figures engaged in murder, rape, deceit or sexual licentiousness these incidents were edited out of existence if a satisfactory explanation could not be found. Thus, Lot does not offer his daughters to the Sodomites; Rachel's theft of Laban's household gods is omitted, nor does Jacob sleep with her servant; Esau has no second wife; Joseph does not practice divination utilising his silver cup ("Do you not know that such a man as I can indeed divine?"); Ruben has no affair with his father's concubine; and (naturally) both Aaron and Moses are cast in a better light by subtle changes to the text.

Jump forward eight hundred years to those Christian missionaries who took their Bible to places like Africa, where they observed similar cautionary measures. How else could they hope to promote the ideals of Christian morality in a polygamous culture if not by purging the Old Testament ancestors of their multiple wives?

Or jump back nearly as many centuries to the promiscuity found in the Roman world. Once the age of martyrs had passed, there was still a need for role models who appeared wholly committed to their faith: monks and virgins surely filled the gap? And indeed, the New Testament itself provided textual support – if read judicially. St Paul, himself not burdened by a wife on his travels (as he indicates that some other apostles were), exhorts the Corinthians not to get married if they can manage otherwise, since the Day of the Lord was imminent and marriage ties might prove too much of a distraction. Yet something of a challenge to this well-intentioned caution lay close at hand – within the Holy Family. Yes, Jesus himself was born of a pure virgin, but as he grew into adulthood we learn in the Gospels that Mary had apparently given birth later on to several siblings: "Is not this the carpenter, the son of Mary and brother of James and Joses and Judas and Simon, and are not his sisters here with us?" One of them indeed took a leading role in the early Church, as St Paul recalls in his Letter to the Galatians: when he visited Jerusalem, he "saw none of the other apostles except James the Lord's brother".

Nevertheless, there is uncertainty here: in many cultures the terms 'brother' and 'sister' do not necessarily refer to blood relatives, but merely to people of similar age belonging to the same tribe or living in the same village. In modern usage too a step-brother or step-sister might well be introduced as 'brother' or 'sister'. An influential writing dating from the later 2nd century, known as the *Protoevangelium of James*, claimed that Jesus' "brothers" and "sisters" were Joseph's children by a former marriage, and that before her birth Anna dedicated Mary to "serve the Lord all the days of her life" (PJ4.1), a promise usually interpreted in line with Hannah's dedication of the infant Samuel (1 Samuel 1.28). Can this be true, or is this a fake presentation? The latter seems likely, since the author displays ignorance both of Palestinian geography (such as the location of Bethlehem) and of Jewish customs, he also contradicts certain details of the canonical Gospels and gets in a muddle over names. It seems highly implausible and somewhat derogatory for him to suggest that when visiting Elizabeth, Mary had already *forgotten* "the mysteries which the archangel Gabriel had told her" (PJ 12.2)! St Jerome was certainly unimpressed with the author's thesis that James was Jesus' step-brother, and proposed that they were simply cousins, an explanation that met with papal approval. He also claimed (in *Against Helvidius*) that Joseph was a virgin:

Jerome did, however, leave Mary's virginal dedication to the Lord intact, which may well be appropriate, but – given the unreliability of the *Protoevangelium* – there is not a great deal of evidence, other than Jesus' commendation of his mother to the Beloved Disciple standing by the cross together with the fact that Joseph does seem to have been a man of more advanced years who disappears from the scene long before the time of Jesus' ministry. What is indisputable is that Mary certainly "served the Lord" all her days, but not in any narrowly defined religious setting.

Whether or not she was conceived 'immaculately' remained a controversial matter for many centuries. Ultimately it rested upon biblical texts which today would be interpreted rather differently. The key text was that of St Paul writing to the Romans: "Therefore as sin came into the world through one man and death through sin, and so death spread to all men because all men sinned – sin indeed was in the world before the law was given, but sin is not counted where there is no law." The concept that emerged from this was termed 'original sin', the sin deriving from our origin. Today the story of our human descent from Adam is not taken literally (except by Bible fundamentalists), nor is St Augustine's notion that male semen is the vehicle by which all of us are 'infected by sin' from our birth taken seriously. Adam's sin is better understood as the universal tendency to displace God by making ourselves the supreme authority which "knows good and evil" i.e. has total control over everything. Regarding Mary, it is surely better to 'accentuate the positive', and focus on the 'fullness of grace' that she received from God throughout her life. A person's sanctity is not defined by the absence of sin but by his or her response to God - a point made by Jesus himself:

> "When the unclean spirit has gone out of a man, he passes through waterless places seeking rest, but he finds none. Then he says, 'I will return to my house from which I came.' And when he comes he finds it empty, swept, and put in order. Then he goes and brings with him seven other spirits more evil than himself, and they enter and dwell there; and the last state of that man becomes worse than the first. So shall it be also with this evil generation." While he was still speaking to the people, behold, his mother and his brothers stood outside, asking to speak to him. But he replied to the man who told him, "Who is my mother, and who are my brothers?" And stretching out his hand toward his disciples, he said, "Here are my mother and my brothers! For whoever does the will of my Father in heaven is my brother, and sister, and mother".

A further citation of Christ's words highlights the innocence of young children:

> And calling to him a child, he put him in the midst of them, and said, "Truly, I say to you, unless you turn and become like children, you will never enter the kingdom of heaven. Whoever humbles himself like this child, he is the greatest in the kingdom of heaven".

If children were blighted from birth, as St Augustine argued, they could hardly serve as saintly role models. (Older children are a different matter: the present concern with safeguarding children – certainly of great importance – may overlook that communities sometimes need to be protected from their antisocial tendencies. Children don't necessarily remain innocent for long!)

One of Jesus' parables, the "wheat and the tares", highlights the folly of pre-judging as between saints and sinners. He urges instead, "Let both grow together until the harvest". Indeed, in his own ministry he strove to overcome the Judaical practice of separating 'clean' and 'unclean': he ate with "publicans and sinners" and at his crucifixion "the curtain of the temple was torn in two, from top to bottom": thus, as St Paul expressed it when writing to the Colossians, "God was pleased ... through him to reconcile to himself all things, whether on earth or in heaven, making peace by the blood of his cross"; or again, "there cannot be Greek and Jew, circumcised and uncircumcised, barbarian, Scythian, slave, free man, but Christ is all, and in all". Indeed, "he is our peace, who has made us both one, and has broken down the dividing wall of hostility" (Ephesians 2.14).

Christ's universal outreach can be seen above all on the occasion of the Last Supper. Among those who gathered with him was Judas Iscariot, whose evil mindset was already apparent to Jesus. It is highly unlikely that ordinary human beings would want to share such a special occasion with their most treacherous enemy, yet this is the sign given us by the Son of Man. St Paul urged the Thessalonians not to "repay evil for evil, but always to do good to one another and to all", echoing Jesus' words, "Love your enemies, do good to those who hate you".

An obvious implication is that *among Christians* there should be more opportunities for inter-communion. As St Augustine observed, whoever prays the *Our Father* ... is my brother or sister in Christ. Perhaps if doctrinal correctness intervenes, we should let Christian love prevail? And what of *other religious believers*, who live good and compassionate lives? In so far as they are doing God's will, they too are our brothers and sisters – certainly not to be treated as sinners beyond the pale.

On the site of a church torn down by East Germany's communist rulers, a new place of worship is set to rise that will bring Christians, Jews and Muslims under one roof. The foundation stone of the House of One in Berlin will be laid at a ceremony on 27 May 2021, marking the end of 10 years of planning and the beginning of an estimated four years of construction, and symbolising a new venture in interfaith cooperation and dialogue. The €47m building, designed by Berlin architects Kuehn Malvezzi, will incorporate a church, a mosque and a synagogue linked to a central meeting space. People of other faiths and denominations, and those of no faith, will be invited to events and discussions in the large hall.

"The idea is pretty simple," said Roland Stolte, a Christian theologian who helped start the project. "We wanted to build a house of prayer and learning, where these three religions could co-exist while each retaining their own identity. This is not a club for monotheistic religions – we want others to join us. East Berlin is a very secular place. Religious institutions have to find new language and ways to be relevant, and to make connections."

Andreas Nachama, a rabbi who is turning the vision into reality in partnership with a pastor and imam, said: "There are many different ways to God, and each is a good way." In the House of One, Christians, Muslims and Jews would worship separately, but would visit each other for religious holidays, commemorations and celebrations, he added. "It is more than a symbol. It is the start of a new era where we show there is no hate between us."

SHEEP SMELLS

On Holy Thursday 2015, Pope Francis urged Catholic bishops and priests to be close to their flocks and to know the people they serve like 'shepherds living with the smell of their sheep. God's grace comes alive and flourishes to the extent that clergy are among their flocks giving themselves and the gospel to others'.

The wolf found that shepherd's clothing works even better.

Some clergy exemplify this better than others. The same is true (and certainly more noticeable) among the higher clergy including the popes of Rome. Eamonn Duffy writes of the 'dark century' that followed Nicholas I who died in 867:

> The papacy became the possession of the great Roman families, a ticket to local dominance for which men were prepared to rape, murder and steal.

The reputation of many popes in this era left much to be desired. One of the nastiest was Stephen VI who in 897 put the mummified body of one of his predecessors on trial. The corpse was dressed in pontifical robes, and after being found guilty of crimes such as perjury had its fingers hacked off and was thrown into the Tiber. Stephen himself was soon afterwards deposed and strangled to death in prison. In the following century the then ruler of Rome, Alberic II, arranged for his 18 year old son Octavian to be elected as Pope John XII. He died in his twenties, apparently having suffered a stroke while in bed with his mistress.

Fortunately, this sad state of affairs has not been repeated too often and is counterbalanced by those in high office who have lived up to their saintly calling (and of course many of the early popes were martyred for their faith). Even so, intrigue has never disappeared altogether, one of the worst offenders in recent centuries being our own Cardinal Henry Manning who (according to Lytton Strachey's *Eminent Victorians*) regularly whispered his suggestions into the ears of influential officials in Rome. It is worth remembering that, despite his personal austerity, he was much less restrained in indulging his ideas and in seeking to impose them on others. He ruled his diocese, says Strachey, with 'despotic zeal'. He held a literal interpretation of the Last Things and identified the Antichrist as collectively the entire Jewish people – thus making today's antisemitism seem quite mild by comparison. Jews, in his book, were definitely wolves and not sheep.

In recent years there has been a welcome return to more inclusive teachings and to life styles more in keeping with the Gospel, even though the accoutrements of pomp and ceremony continue to obfuscate the message:

> The twentieth-century papacy began, as was appropriate in this century of the common man, with a peasant pope, the first for three centuries. Giuseppe Sarto, who took the name Pius X (1903-14), was the son of a village postman and a devout seamstress from northern Italy. He was chosen in deliberate contrast to the style of his predecessor, the remote and regal diplomat Leo XIII.

The French Cardinal Mathieu explained that the Conclave had sought a man 'who had grown old in the care of souls... who would be above all a father and a shepherd'. None of Sarto's predecessors in the previous century had ever been a parish priest, and although at the time of his election he was Patriarch of Venice he retained 'a gusty humanity', 'a strong emotional piety' and 'a personal approachability and warmth'. As pope he continued to conduct catechism classes every Sunday afternoon in a Vatican courtyard. He issued a stream of initiatives to encourage more frequent communion, which for him was 'a remedy for shortcomings, not the reward of perfection'. One of his unprecedented innovations was to reduce the age of First Communion from the early teens down to seven, an immensely popular move. James Morris records that 'he scorned convention, pretence and stuffiness':

> He once demonstrated to a lady, in private audience at the Vatican, the steps of a Venetian dance. When a nun asked for a pair of his old stockings, as a remedy for her rheumatism, and later pronounced herself entirely cured, the Pope declared it very odd – 'I wore them myself far longer than she did, and they never did me any good!'

Pius X was not, however, universally popular. While his peasant roots accorded well with the masses, they left him with a fierce anti-intellectual bias, quite out of sympathy with contemporary critical thought. Liberal Catholics, he had declared in Venice, 'are wolves in sheep's clothing' – hence later on as Pope he waged war on the Modernist movement (which certainly needed careful theological evaluation) to such an extent that public confidence in the integrity and freedom of Catholic academic standards was shattered for a generation.

Since his day there have been other popes with an appealing earthiness who have recognised also the need to temper some of the harsher teachings inherited from the past. John XXIII summoned the second Vatican Council specifically to consider the Church's possible *aggiornamento*. Like Pius X, his origins were humble: he was the fourth of fourteen children in a family of village sharecroppers. He initiated pastoral visits within his diocese of Rome, going to see children hospitalised with polio, and the next day inmates in a local prison – 'You couldn't come to me, so I came to you'. When he visited a reformatory school for juvenile delinquents he dropped the conventional papal 'we' and spoke informally in the first person singular. The media noticed this and reported that he talked to the youths 'in their own language'. His frequent habit of sneaking out of the Vatican late at night to walk the streets of the city of Rome earned him the nickname of Johnny Walker!

Pope Francis has continued in similar vein, indicating his preference for public transport, a small apartment, and meals shared with colleagues. He is also prone to use a mobile phone (not usually, however, during mass) to get in direct touch with needy people brought to his attention. The clergy too are often reminded to model a church that is 'poor and is for the poor': in line with this, 'the bishop of bling' (in the German town of Limburg) found himself dismissed from his charge in 2014 for spending £26 million on his own residence. 'Bishops should not live like princes', the Pope insisted.[6]

Times are certainly changing, and the contrast today between the residences of the hierarchy and those of the 'lesser' clergy is not so blatant as in centuries gone by. In England, Anglican parochial clergy have generally been poor by the standards of the educated and professional classes. For example, in Elizabethan times a country priest lived no better than the majority of his flock; in Kent there were perhaps a dozen rich livings, predominantly offered to relatives of the aristocratic patrons or to members of one of the cathedral chapters (Canterbury and Rochester). The creation of Queen Anne's Bounty in 1704 made a difference for some clergy, although curates remained poorly remunerated, especially in the days of pluralism when relatively prosperous incumbents hired them at minimal cost to look after one or other of their livings.

---

[6] Yet – lifestyles apart – in the Catholic Church there is still a significant gap between some of the hierarchy, who continue to think and breathe as if medieval expressions of faith and devotion must remain the touchstone of Christian life today, and the many who struggle with the complexities of the modern world, who may have never been exposed to medieval thought forms but nevertheless have a deep but relatively '*un*-philosophical' biblical faith – in other words, their thought mode is Hebrew rather than Greek.

By the early 19th century pluralism had reached scandalous proportions, as had the huge discrepancy between the income of bishops and that of typical parochial clergy – as of the mass of people, some of whom joined protest demonstrations (shades of the French revolution!). Attempts at reform took place in the 1830s, the first of which was defeated by the bishops in the House of Lords. This only inflamed the public anger: bishops were seen as corrupt, 'revelling in fashionable luxury at their palaces while they knew nothing of the labourer's cottage' at the cost of over half a million pounds each year. It was disclosed in the press that between them nineteen prelates held sixty-one pieces of preferment – for example, the Dean of Canterbury was also Bishop of Oxford and rector of a Staffordshire parish. 'What is the church', asked a speaker at a London rally, 'but one unvaried system of fraud and robbery?' It took several years before Parliament enacted corrective legislation, such as the pluralities act of 1836 limiting the number of benefices held by any one person to two. Yet the rapid growth of urban populations combined with the steady drift from rural parishes increasingly complicated the issue as the century progressed. By the start of the last century about one parish in two was supplementing the parson's income with a voluntary Easter offering.

Hence in 1925 Thomas Hardy could write in his poem *An East-end Curate*:

> A small blind street off East Commercial Road;
>   Window, door; window, door; every house like the one before,
> Is where the curate, Mr Dowle, has found a pinched abode.
> Spectacled, pale, moustache-coloured, and with a long thin face,
> Day or dark his lodgings' narrow doorstep does he pace.

A few years later he reflected on the contrasting fortunes, on the one hand, of the 'eloquent' orator who had become a bishop[7] and, on the other, the priest who was 'the sincerest of all; whose words, though unpicked, gave the essence of things', whose 'mind ran on charity and good will'. Where is he now? they *'whispered at the church-opening'* (the poem's title): 'He's but as he was, a vicar still'.

During my own years as an Anglican, proposals for change continued to be debated – and were sometimes implemented. I recall that all glebe land was nationalised in the late 1970s: in Irchester this therefore ceased to be my personal responsibility, its management and income having been transferred to the Church Commissioners. The diocesan secretary went the rounds of deanery chapter meetings

---

[7] Not all Anglican bishops were eloquent, least of all William Howley, Archbishop of Canterbury from 1828 to 1848. Making a speech at a girls' school, he struggled to get started: 'My dear young friends – my dear girls – my dear young catechumens – my dear Christian friends – my dear young female women'.

to explain the new system. My own concern was that no one would now ever check (as I used to do from time to time) whether the fields, hedges and ditches were being properly maintained. But another priest was so deeply troubled by the prospect of his fishing rights on the river Nene being taken away that he broke the habit of a lifetime – and actually attended the meeting. I never met him again, so presumed that he was generally to be found, if not actually lying down 'in pastures green', still meditating 'the quiet waters by'.

In a subsequent decade, a motion came before General Synod promoting parity of remuneration for all those in full-time ministry. Early speakers in the debate appeared to have the backing of scripture, such as the passage in Acts which described how the primitive Church held 'everything in common' and made distribution 'to each as any had need' (not to mention the parable of the vineyard, where all the workers were paid the same). We held our breath, wondering if and when one of the hierarchy would speak defensively (or otherwise) on their behalf. It was an archdeacon from the Midlands who first rose. Differentials of pay, he observed, are ubiquitous in our society. In some businesses they are unjustifiably extreme – and therefore it is the church's duty, not to abolish differentials, but to use them 'responsibly'. A palpable sigh of relief could be heard from the bishops' bench! At last someone had spoken sense, and synod could be gently steered away from its leftish, trendy twaddle. The Bishop of Chester then stood up to remind us what a hard life he and his episcopal colleagues had to endure (and by implication how much they deserved to be in a significantly higher income bracket than a vicar with a mere twenty thousand souls in his cure and probably a crumbling edifice to restore at the same time). He exhibited some of the trials of his daily life: 'We have frequently to entertain in the palace, and when everyone's gone home I have to tidy up and help with the washing up. But I don't mind – it's *all for Jesus*. Or my wife and I have to get in the car and go shopping, and I push a trolley round the supermarket. But I don't mind – *it's all for Jesus*'. After several such illustrations of his personal martyrdom, a few uncouth members of synod began to chime in with the chorus (*'it's all for Jesus'*). Suitably chastised by our elders and betters, the motion was thus lost, enabling ambitious clergy to dream on.

It is true that many of the sprawling rectories inherited from earlier centuries have been replaced by more modest dwellings, and that medieval palaces, if retained, now serve multiple purposes, with the bishop himself occupying perhaps only a flat for himself and his household. Yet whereas the norm for incumbents used to be a four bedroomed house, grander properties seem to be popping up again. In West Monkton there was quite a merry-go-round. First of all, the Bishop of Taunton decided to dispose of the possibly inconvenient Sherford Farm House in favour of a new luxury five bed-roomed house in the centre of our village (on a hillside previously occupied by sheep). This was not his (or her) abode for too long, as a house in Wells has latterly replaced it. His West Monkton residence has instead been taken over by the local Archdeacon, despite his having moved to a new house in Taunton not so long ago. To complete the confusion, the rectory we occupied – conveniently adjacent to the church, with a barn that served as a meeting room complete with its own kitchen and an accessible toilet – was sold in favour of another new five bed-roomed house on an estate in Bathpool, at least a mile from the church, and no nearer to any of the three parishes added recently to the benefice. It is admittedly closer to where some newer parishioners live, which may be what 'strategic planning' currently suggests; but my own experience would definitely argue in favour of living reasonably close to an active worship centre. In Wells itself this was also the view of many lay people a year or two ago when they strongly resisted plans to move the diocesan bishop from his historic base to an old vicarage several miles away. One assumes that previous experience as an estate agent is now an essential qualification for any aspiring bishop?

The African scene is different again, although human instincts remain the same. When we arrived in Malawi, our bishop lived near the diocesan centre at Malosa, about 10 miles east from Zomba. His predecessors seem to have fulfilled their responsibilities satisfactorily throughout Southern Malawi, but as James was more upwardly mobile he was increasingly finding himself – an articulate black African – in fashion with episcopalian dioceses in the eastern States, and as a result began to spend much more time on international committees. This prompted his plan to divide the diocese into two, of which he aimed to continue as bishop of the western half where a site for a house not too far from Blantyre airport was available. The eastern half, where we lived, became known as Upper Shire. The Archbishop, a Malawian who was finding life difficult in Northern Zambia, was keen to support James' plan since – having not long since failed in his bid to become Bishop of Northern Malawi – Upper Shire afforded him another chance whereby he could return to his homeland. This time no mistakes were to be made: the legalities were observed, but far too little attention was drawn to the nomination deadlines, and the inevitable anger boiled over when a significant group of lay Anglicans came to realise that the 'election' had effectively been rigged. Bishop James, it might be added, had become less popular with some of his clergy, who complained how readily he took off (sometimes with his wife) on transatlantic flights yet refused them a simple refund of minibus fares when they needed to attend the local mission hospital. Likewise Archbishop Bernard had come under suspicion in Zambia for his possible mishandling of money; there was little supporting evidence, but in Africa rumours travel far and fast. (It should also be remembered that qualified accountants are a rare and expensive breed, so diocesan treasurers are usually 'book-keepers' doing their best.) Whereas Bernard has long since retired, James has gained a well-paid teaching post in North America. He was a great loss to the country and to the diocese he once served.

The presence of expatriates in an African country tends to confuse the picture. Although missionary pay is about one quarter of an English stipend, and one's house a modest two – or at most three – bed-roomed bungalow, by African standards that is luxury. In Lesotho we had the use of a tough Toyota truck, which carried us over quite a few rocky terrains, not to mention fording the Orange river on one memorable occasion. In Malawi I bought a four seater Nissan truck, knowing how easy it would be to dispose of when we finally left the country (the charity known as Why Wait?, which promotes teaching programmes about personal relationships in many secondary schools, was glad to take it over). It wasn't unexpected, therefore, that one or two of our students demanded to be equally well provided when they reached ordination; nor that bishops aspired to the lifestyle of colleagues in wealthier provinces elsewhere. Bernard's successor was actually one of my own former students, who seemed to be doing well in his episcopal role until he flew to Kampala for a regional meeting of bishops. He was met at the airport, and the car that chauffeured him onwards was provided with a police escort. On his return to Malawi he announced, 'Now I know how bishops should be treated'.

Since returning to England we have lived in semi-detached houses which certainly leave one less 'isolated' than many a clergy dwelling. It takes us back to my curacy days in Northampton, and even earlier to memories of shared student lodgings. I recall my landlady at 13 Portugal Place in Cambridge, who struggled to bring up young children in the frequent absence of her American Airbase husband, whose return was invariably a rowdy one with midnight arguments on the stairs and plenty of smashed crockery. It was more peaceful at 5 Parkfield Avenue, the house that cost St Mary's Parish the unbelievably small sum of £4500 in 1971. Here an elderly couple lived on one side and guided us through some of the mysteries of domestic life. Mr Penna was a great gardener and kept us fully informed about what to plant and when (although unlike him we had access to limitless heaps of pig manure delivered free of charge by a bachelor farmer who was a colleague on the Infant School governing body: his only intervention as a governor occurred when kitchen waste was mentioned, which – as he invariably pointed out – he could usefully recycle). Mrs Penna was a kindly soul, whose knitted hot water bottle cover we still use.

Dominique and Lydia were our other neighbours, an Italian couple with three lively children; we learnt something of their inherited Catholic customs and rather more about the hot dog and ice cream trade which often took Dominique to sporting events at the other end of the country. We may have alarmed them at one stage when we looked after a teenager named David, thus freeing his parents to visit the Holy Land together. David stayed with us for more than a week. He was autistic, and his obsessive hobby was making sensational paper darts which he then took outside and fired with the aid of elastic bands. We have never seen the like: his missiles soared high above the roof tops, and then disappeared from view as they headed back to earth – across the street, in the next door garden, over the far side of a nearby house, it was impossible to predict. On the rare occasions when David was able to collect the debris, he conducted a funeral service by our dustbin, solemnly intoning his own burial chants.

Perhaps the greatest blessing of living where we did lay in knowing Cynthia, a wonderful West Indian friend who lived a few streets away; she was generosity personified. Her husband had abandoned her, so she survived with her three children on a very basic income. All her clothes came from charity shops, but she dressed like a queen. She showered us with multi-coloured home-baked cakes and sometimes her own home-grown vegetables. I once rebuked her for a rather sharp reaction to something that had upset her: 'Two blacks don't make a white', I said – and then wished I hadn't.

The most colourful neighbours we have ever had were probably those in Sherborne. Initially the adjoining property was occupied by an elderly lady, whose husband had won the Victoria Cross in the Second World War. Although she was active when we first knew her – playing tennis and visiting the races – her health steadily deteriorated; after a couple of fires were set off (one caused by an overheated electric blanket, the other by a faulty microwave) her family moved her into care. We missed her, despite being relieved that the threat of incineration and personal oblivion was no longer hanging over us.

Her successor, also a widow, was downsizing from a large country mansion; this left her with a considerable surplus of funds, which allowed her much scope in altering her new property. For the next two years, the noise of workman clattering and hammering throughout the day seldom ceased (nor did the piercing radio during the night). However, not everything was done to the highest standards – the rear gutters were fixed so badly, for example, that on a wet day the back door was quite unusable, while the new sun room faced north-east. Outside at the front, vans frequently cluttered up the courtyard and took over other residents' parking spaces. On one occasion a delivery lorry smashed into a neighbour's house; on another, a truck blocked all vehicular access precisely when we were expecting up to a dozen visitors for lunch. Although there were restrictive covenants which applied to all our properties, it was clear that they had never been studied. Then one day, I noticed a gardener attempting to dig into the surface of the parking area, obviously for the purposes of planting a climber to cover the adjacent stone wall. He explained that the lady of the house had so instructed him. I pointed out that, with only a limited area for parking, it was unlikely that other residents would sanction this action, which was legally necessary before he could proceed any further. At once he stopped work, brought her to the door and said firmly: 'Madam: until now you've lived in a large house in the country where you could do exactly what you wanted. You have to realise that things are different here – you've neighbours all around you who have their rights too. I'm not doing any more now until you've sorted this out with them'. So ended this little episode, thanks to one man's bravery, surely well up to VC standard. (The lady in question did, however, redeem herself! Her rural background enabled us to deter pestering pigeons with some success, and when we moved on she threw a farewell party for us. I believe that the climber was ultimately achieved somehow, so in the end sweetness and light prevailed – until perhaps another property within the courtyard changed hands?)

On our other side the house was rented out, at first on a three year lease to an American Catholic working at Westland Helicopters on a defence contract. He was easy and amiable. When he returned to the States our new neighbour was a retired Catholic priest Father D, who had lived elsewhere in the town until his landlord decided to use the property himself. We already knew him well, so were delighted to welcome him next door to us. On moving day we watched open-mouthed as more and more 'stuff' poured into the house, only a fraction of which could be unpacked in the time available. It was later on, when he needed an increasing amount of help, that I noticed still unopened boxes occupying a whole bedroom and more. Some contained pristine items of IT equipment – printers and the like – which he'd never got round to using. Downstairs the kitchen was equally crammed full, with a second refrigerator blocking the back door. At first he continued his ready hospitality, and we enjoyed more than one evening meal with his various guests. Wine was always in abundant supply, and the living room held his large 'cellar' (another bulky cabinet). We usually needed to assist him in the kitchen, because the one weakness of his cuisine was getting its components assembled simultaneously; quite often potatoes, or vegetables, or gravy, would have to make their way to the table a good ten or twenty minutes later.

Having blocked his back door meant that Father D never ventured into his small garden. This had repercussions, which became acutely problematic after a couple of years: weeds flourished where there had once been a flower bed and a lawn. They grew to a height of two or three feet, and scattered their seeds far and wide, not least in our own back garden and on to the graveled area used for parking. One day I plucked up courage and alerted him to the situation, offering – if he wished – to get a gardener in to help him. 'I can't see any weeds', he said. As it happened there were several growing on his very doorstep, so I plucked one of these and held it up to illustrate my point. Reluctantly he agreed to engage the gardener on an occasional basis.

By now he was growing frailer and needed hospitalisation more than once. This was not an experience he enjoyed. On the first occasion he managed to ring me up from the sister's office, begging me to get him 'out of this hell hole'. I could hear the sister remonstrating – he hadn't yet been discharged, his medicines weren't ready, and so on. When I reached the ward that evening, I murmured an apology – 'I hope he's not been too much trouble?' She replied somewhat wearily, 'We've known worse!' After this episode he came round a number of times for a meal, always good company, entertaining us with memories of life abroad in his army days (his was a late vocation, and he was proud to have been ordained by Pope Paul VI in the Sistine Chapel).

When Sarah's older sister, who was handicapped, came to stay, one highlight of her visit was always a cup of tea next door with Father D. Kind friends helped him with his shopping, which was probably preferable to his own expeditions abroad on market days given the hazards of the return journey. With a bag or two of his favourite delicacies he would ask for assistance crossing the street; the unwary would willingly give him a hand, not knowing that, once over, their task was not finished. On the far side it was never far from home (so Father D would explain), so the Good Samaritan would offer to see him safely all the way there. Although it might only be two hundred yards, it was no sprint – it could easily take another half hour, because Father D would shuffle a couple of steps and then each time converse for a couple of minutes. It took a real saint to come to his rescue a second time!

He now became adept at falling out of bed but was able to summon emergency help via his red button. This usually worked well, until one night at about 11 o'clock the paramedics arrived and couldn't gain admission – the spare key was blocked by the key he'd left in the lock on the inside. They tried all the windows of course, and finally decided to summon the police. The constable on duty seemed a little inexperienced – in his place, I would have broken the glass panel on the door allowing me to reach through and extract the obstructing key. But he evidently saw this as a golden opportunity to emulate his metropolitan colleagues who lived a more exciting life pursuing drug dealers and potential terrorists. He went back to the police station, donned a pair of heavy duty boots and proceeded with heavy kicks to smash the door down. Father D was then whisked off to hospital, and a little later (it was now well past one o'clock in the morning) a carpenter arrived to secure the premises. It took a further two months before a new front door was fitted, at a cost of £800. Shortly after this Father D went permanently into care, and died, a much loved priest, not long after celebrating his 40th jubilee.

Although he was one of the old school, inclined to be fierce with his congregations. Thus, he refused to allow any but the deaf even to glance at their missalettes during the reading of the Gospel and rebuked those who failed to conform to his regimented expectations of posture. He also rather upset the children at a prep school mass on one occasion: when it came to the offertory, sure enough bread, wine and water were presented to him, but that was not all and several children remained standing with other contributions. 'What have you got there?' he demanded. 'We've drawn some pictures, Father.' 'What of?' came his reply. 'They're pictures of Jesus', they answered a little timidly. 'Well, I don't want them. Take them away.' Unsurprisingly he was not invited to the school for any further visits. Older congregations, however, saw through his often crusty exterior. Once he forgot to turn off his radio mike when mass was over, and so broadcast to all and sundry his opinion muttered to the server in the sacristy afterwards: 'They're just like a flock of frightened sheep'. But the sheep took it well – it became one of their favourite anecdotes!

There are still, alas, too many priests who (to change the metaphor) "rule the roost" and intimidate colleagues and parishioners alike.

CONTEMPORARY CRISES

The Church's popularity has ever waxed and waned – and hence, so has the wealth at its disposal. I did, however, as a curate in the diocese of Peterborough once write an article for the monthly circular Cross Keys pointing out that the Church was generally a lot wealthier than was often appreciated. It is St Luke, describing the (possibly 'idealised') practice of the earliest Christians in the book of Acts, who makes this clear:

> The company of those who believed were of one heart and soul, and no one said that any of the things which he possessed was his own, but they had everything in common.

Quite evidently, therefore, most local churches can claim 'ownership' of not a few houses, cars, and bank accounts. Even an apparently struggling rural church, attended by a mere handful of parishioners, in this revised reckoning is worth a few millions!

The principle wasn't by any means a Christian novelty. Its roots are firmly embedded in the Jewish tradition of tithing, which understood that wealth was never to be hoarded privately but was a gift from God that he intended to be shared. There were several tithing ordinances: the first requirement was to give one tenth of one's own 'inheritance' to assist the ministry of Levites:

> To the Levites I have given every tithe in Israel for an inheritance, in return for their service that they do, their service in the tent of meeting.

Ten such tithes were presumably regarded as adequate for the support of a single Levitical priest (and his family). Later, when synagogues became widespread, it was ordained that a *minyan* of ten men over the age of 13 was a necessary quorum: although this Talmudic ruling is derived from different scriptural sources, it is based on the same idea of God's service as a communal responsibility. Other tithes extended this responsibility, for example, to the care of widows, orphans and the poor.

In my early years as an Anglican priest I was fortunate in having been appointed by the bishop to the Diocesan Stewardship Committee. This was run by a retired but still very energetic military man, Major Samson. Thanks to him, and his firm grasp of biblical teaching, parish finances throughout the diocese continued to respond favourably to the rising budgets and the ever-increasing expenditure needed for church repairs. Most remarkably, it was a parish in Corby around the time when British Steel, the main local employer, closed down that the average weekly giving to their church not only rose significantly but actually topped the diocesan league table. The figures were published each month in Cross Keys, so that churchgoers across the diocese could compare their own generosity – or lack of it – with what others were currently giving. Sammy's policy was for an 'every member' response, if at all possible. He recognised the value of the widow's mite just as much as the gold unloaded from the magi's camel. He appreciated that good communication and accountability were essential if parishioners were to understand the state of their local finances and to take proper responsibility for them.

Ever since then I have often followed his lead, challenging parishioners on a regular basis to face up to the needs of their church (and of the many missions and Christian charities operating in the wider world), and to revise their level of 'tithing' in line with their own personal finances. It is of course a good thing to raise awarenss too of the practical needs of a parish in terms of personal commitment and service, but Sammy suggested (correctly in my view) that to do this *within the same campaign* can divert attention from the financial challenge. People may salve their consciences by choosing, instead of giving 'sacrificially', to do something much less demanding; for example, to read a lesson in church just once in a while. Strangely, the option of volunteering to assist regularly with (say) the church youth group seldom proves such an attractive option!

Sammy's is not the only way to keep biblical principles alive. The aforementioned bishop Douglas used to suggest his own alternative: 'Get them to write out a cheque, and then persuade them to add an extra nought' (thus converting a donation of £10 into £100). In Lesotho a quite different system operates: in earlier years there was a standard annual charge, the *kabelo*, for regular worshippers; in 1901 it stood at 5/- for men and 3/- for women. By the 1980s circumstances had become more variable, especially regarding the many outstations. Each of these was in the care of a local catechist, who knew his flock extremely well, and could therefore judge the amount he reckoned each family could afford. They seem generally to have complied with such demands. The slightly surprising, indeed unorthodox, aspect to these transactions was that catechists in some places proceeded to deduct 25% of the takings for himself, to cover 'time and effort' expended, before handing over the funds. Apart from any such commission, the application of variable membership charges is not unknown in other parts of Africa – how else would local villagers know what was a reasonable level of support for the ongoing mission? Although, as St John Chrysostom put it, 'God wants golden hearts, not golden chalices', nevertheless the magi's gift of gold was probably useful on the flight to Egypt, while the much later mentioned 'alabaster jar of precious ointment' served a profoundly spiritual purpose.

Since becoming a Catholic I have come to realise that much is left to financial chance in my adopted Church, indeed that it is sometimes considered rather bad form to mention topics such as 'stewardship'. There is certainly much generosity in supporting worthy causes through a 'second collection' towards the end of mass, but the level of giving in the normal way of things seems lower than in the Church of England. A thorough statistical survey would be needed to establish the facts with some accuracy, but my impression (which may be completely wrong!) is that the average Anglican churchgoer in England contributes significantly more than the average Catholic. Currently I note that in a neighbouring Anglican parish (St Mary, Brook) there are 28 people registered on the electoral roll, and that the diocesan share levied on them (which covers among other things the cost of ministerial stipends) is over £12000 per annum. This amounts to over £8 each week for those on the roll – and much more if significant repairs are needed to the church fabric – although fund-raising efforts no doubt contribute as well. When I compare this with the still impressive Sunday mass turn-out within the Catholic parish of St Teresa, Ashford, I observe that weekly collections there are usually in the region of £1500, implying an average donation of (say) £3. Social and economic circumstances do of course vary widely, nevertheless the disparity is striking.

The culture is quite different as well. Control of finances in the Catholic Church is much more in the hands of the bishops and priests. Lay involvement (and accountability) is only slowly edging in and can still too easily be edged out again. In one parish where the finance committee had allocated £1500 for the support of a fledgling Third World seminary, the incoming parish priest simply commandeered these funds to redecorate his own presbytery. In another parish a priest built up his personal holiday funds by claiming expenses of office that he had not actually incurred. When tough decisions affecting the deployment of priests are needed, there are sometimes consultations by the relevant bishop with those likely to be affected, but there is (as I perceive it) seldom any great confidence that he will heed suggestions offered to him. Parish closures are high on the current agenda and may not always be sufficiently justified: lessons might well be learnt from the rather different structures of parishes in Africa, where multiple outstations flourish despite the limited number of priestly visits possible within any given month. Yet back over here, in the difficult financial situation faced by one diocese, several years of dialogue concerning the future of a highly regarded university chaplaincy resulted only in broken promises about 'decisions shortly to be made' and the eventual shocking news of its closure on the grounds that it did not offer 'value for money'.

Does that criterion, however, demean God's Church by applying secular commercial standards? There is a classic letter written by Hensley Henson in 1929 when he was the Anglican Bishop of Durham, demanding an explanation from one of his priests as to why only two girls from his parish were presented recently for confirmation when, according to the bishop's calculations, there must have been 'not less than 45 persons' in the same age group. His implied criticism was that the said priest was significantly under-performing (and therefore not worth keeping on the books?). There was certainly no hint of pastoral empathy on this occasion, and no obvious resonance with the shepherd extolled by our Lord who abandoned (if only temporarily) care of the larger group of ninety and nine in favour of seeking out and saving the one sheep who was lost. Thus, while financial prudence is not unimportant in the Church – as in the world – the gospel imperative is to put God's priorities (especially his concern for the weak and vulnerable) before all else. Perhaps too the parable of 'the pearl of great price' has some relevance? Jesus told of a man who gave everything in exchange for the one truly valuable prize, a clear indication that conventional assessments of 'worth' are liable to miss out. Thus, men (and women) are not ordained for the sake of an institution, but for a deeper purpose – to promote the well-being of all God's people. We need to remind ourselves of this priority, and sometimes need to nudge those who hold 'the keys' to uphold it within the Church:

> In the earliest period of my Oxford residence (so wrote Francis Newman in 1857) I fell into uneasy collision with him (his brother J H Newman) concerning Episcopal powers. I had on one occasion dropt something disrespectful against bishops or a bishop – something which, if it had been said about a clergyman, would have passed unnoticed: but my brother checked and reproved me – as I thought, very uninstructively – for 'wanting reverence towards Bishops'. I knew not then, and I know not now, why Bishops, as such, should be more reverenced than common clergymen; or Clergymen, as such, more than common men. In the World I expected pomp and vain show and formality and counterfeits: but of the Church, as Christ's own kingdom, I demanded reality.

Whether Christians have consistently demanded the same is sometimes in doubt, given the scandals that continue to emerge into the light of day. Plainly, however, 'reality' is what the public at large expects today. And, once again, it is still to be found in the pages of the New Testament. St Paul was refreshingly blunt. He told the Galatians:

> When Cephas came to Antioch I opposed him to his face, because he stood condemned.

Indeed, there is no attempt in any of the Gospels to conceal St Peter's earlier failings (including his three-fold denial of Christ at a critical moment) nor those of his fellow disciples (the ambition of James and John, the doubts of Thomas, the cowardice of those who ran off in the face of danger, not to mention their general 'slowness' in understanding). So undue deference to the hierarchy is certainly not inherent within the Christian tradition, even if in today's churches it tends (as Newman indicated to his younger brother) to be the norm. My only plea here is that Catholic leaders should be far more open about the finances of the Church, and much more direct in inviting the entirety of their flock to shoulder the necessary burden. When gospel priorities are clearly spelled out, the popular response can take one by surprise!

It is – unsurprisingly – St Paul who gives a clear lead, appealing more than once to the generosity of his converts:

> Now concerning the contribution for the saints: as I directed the churches of Galatia, so you also are to do. On the first day of every week, each of you is to put something aside and store it up, as he may prosper, so that contributions need not be made when I come.

Or again, following this up in his 2nd Letter to the Corinthians, St Paul gave the clearest teaching about Christian giving that can be found anywhere:

> We want you to know, brethren, about the grace of God which has been shown in the churches of Macedonia, for in a severe test of affliction, their abundance of joy and their extreme poverty have overflowed in a wealth of liberality on their part. For they gave according to their means, as I can testify, and beyond their means, of their own free will, begging us earnestly for the favour of taking part in the relief of the saints – and this, not as we expected, but first they gave themselves to the Lord and to us by the will of God. Accordingly we have urged Titus that as he had already made a beginning, he should also complete among you this gracious work. Now as you excel in everything – in faith, in utterance, in knowledge, in all earnestness, and in your love for us – see that you excel in this gracious work also. I say this not as a command, but to prove by the earnestness of others that your love also is genuine. For you know the grace of our Lord Jesus Christ, that though he was rich, yet for your sake he became poor, so that by his poverty you might become rich. And in this matter I give my advice: it is best for you now to complete what a year ago you began not only to do but to desire, so that your readiness in desiring it may be matched by your completing it out of what you have. For if the readiness is there, it is acceptable according to what a man has, not according to what he has not. I do not mean that others should be eased and you burdened, but that as a matter of equality your abundance at the present time should supply their want, so that their abundance may supply your want, that there may be equality. As it is written, "He who gathered much had nothing over, and he who gathered little had no lack".

French Revolutionaries helping to promote 'equality'

Equality of clergy pay has to a great extent been achieved within the Church of England. For forty years or more income received from celebrating the 'occasional offices' (baptisms, weddings, funerals), as well as from Easter offerings and other local resources has been pooled and (thanks to the steady rise in inflation) has by now eliminated the relatively few 'wealthy' postings. This happens to a lesser extent in the Catholic Church, where (for example) mass 'stipends' and direct receipts from members of the congregation can still result in significant variations between the income that priests receive. Sometimes, indeed, remuneration hovers on the brink of simony – the exchange of spiritual blessings for financial gain.

However, in terms of parish funding there can still be huge differences across every denomination, chiefly depending upon the population (for example, urban or rural) that is served, but reflecting too the parish's historic endowments. Since most congregations have been shrinking since the 1960s, it can certainly be a struggle to make ends meet, especially when major repair work to the fabric is deemed necessary. Here again Anglicans and Catholics tend to part company, not only because in Britain there are few medieval Catholic buildings but also because there is a sharp divide over the use of a sacred edifice for fund-raising (and for apparently *secular*) purposes.

In the earliest days of the Church there were no sacred edifices at all, so that domestic dwellings used for Christian worship would inevitably have been 'multi-purpose'. It was probably not until the later 2nd century that there were 'chambers' reserved exclusively for worship and only under Constantine in the 4th century that Christian temples came to be erected. The instinct to provide a holy space for prayer and sacrifice is, however, universal; within the human heart there is a yearning to reach out to what is divine, and without any special sanctuaries away from the mundane routines of daily life such yearnings can be inhibited. Although Christ prophesied that if any earthly temple was destroyed he could nevertheless 'build another, not made with hands', he was still glad to find his disciples gathered prayerfully together in Jerusalem's Upper Room.

The dilemma today is often how to raise the funds needed to maintain and repair inherited church buildings of considerable symbolic significance when those who use them for worship have seen their numbers so depleted. Local church members can of course sometimes be encouraged to roll up their sleeves and tackle what needs to be done themselves. At both Irchester and West Monkton the cost of internal redecoration was cut enormously by this means. In Africa too we found self-help to be the norm; this included molding bricks (50,000 or more might be needed), building walls, laying floors, and erecting roofs. Long before our time in Malawi this was commonplace in the pioneering ministry of the Presbyterian Scot, Dr Robert Laws, who established a widespread network of primary schools in the north of the country. One of his biographers, Michael King, wrote as follows:

> [Dr Laws] could see that human progress depended on the problem of ignorance being tackled first. Primary schooling for children had first priority in all his work. In 1905 the Church of Scotland could not understand why the total cost of running 200 schools was only £1300 per year. Laws himself went into the villages to build these simple mud and wattle schools, and the only equipment needed was a few alphabet boards and a slate and chalk for each child.

A typical outstation in mountainous Lesotho – in a rondavel

In other ways too the Church may need to practice 'the art of the possible'. The Anglican Bishop of Bloemfontein observed in 1921:

> Catholics, as a rule, think in terms of a resident priest and a church with a daily Eucharist just around the corner; but suppose you live at [*he named some remote places*] and have a celebration once a month. It is possible to be regular, but difficult to be permanently devout. This is why I think the sacramental religion of the Catholic must be supplemented by the domestic devoutness of the Evangelical [*Bible reading with private and family prayer*].

Both Anglican and Catholic expectations also need to be modified in Britain today, where there are fewer priests than in the past. Yet church expenses do inevitably arise and here by no means everything can be achieved by voluntary labour and perhaps not even by sacrificial giving. Extra sources of income are often very necessary. One avenue advised by the National Churches Trust in England is to rent out church buildings for community use, which no doubt sits comfortably with the fashionable (if still very strange and arguably unscriptural) Anglican practice known as 'messy church'. Their list of suggestions includes the following:

> Play groups, scouts and guides, women's and men's groups, keep fit, choirs, councilors surgeries, drop in centres, coffee morning and much more. In some areas they are also venues for vital services including school halls, libraries, cafes, health centres, training sessions, community shops, outreach post offices, food banks or a Citizens Advice Bureau.

Such initiatives are often backed by the observation that similar activities in Anglican churches were by no means unknown in earlier centuries. Thus, a will of 1544 ordered that on the Sunday following the testator's burial there should be provided 'two dozen of bread, a kilderkin of ale, two gammons of bacon, three shoulders of mutton and two pairs of rabbits', desiring 'all the parish, as well rich as poor, to take part thereof, and a table to be set in the middle of the church with everything necessary thereto'. In the 18th century it was customary for the squire's family to be provided with refreshments such as sherry and biscuits which could be consumed during the parson's no doubt tedious sermon, and sometimes the squire had letters and newspapers delivered to his pew. Smoking during services was not unknown! At other times, when divine worship was not being held, there are stories of farmers gathering around the altar, where they played cards and drank liberally.

A sad spectacle observed by J.M.W. Turner in 1795

Ewenny Priory in Wales, complete with chickens and farming implements

Catholics may have been more respectful of sacred edifices and less self-indulgent during their devotions, but even they debate where the line is to be drawn, as the following conversation illustrates:

> A Franciscan and a Jesuit were friends. They were both smokers who found it difficult to pray for a long period of time without having a cigarette. They decided to go to their superiors and ask permission to smoke. When they met again, the Franciscan was downcast. "I asked my superior if I could smoke while I pray and he said 'no'." The Jesuit smiled. "I asked if I could pray while I smoke. He said 'of course'."

Although such inclusive activities are sometimes promoted as fulfilling Jesus' intention to convey life 'in abundance', it is not accidental that their organized counterparts today (a summer ball, a bazaar, an auction, a village cafe, a parish dinner, a cinema club, a skate park, a concert, to name but a few) are in most instances held to the pecuniary advantage of the church – or at times, to be fair, of some worthy charity. This may be less so across the Atlantic, however, where motives can apparently be purely theological. Here Aaron Millar describes the new religion lighting up Denver, Colorado, where the 'elevationists' of the International Church of Cannabis were in session:

> As the service begins we are encouraged to get to know each other: people spark up joints and pass them around. Long wisps of smoke float to the ceiling and cover the congregation in a flowery shroud; splutterings of coughs and giggles, the sharp intake of breath on all sides.
>
> Lee, a former Bible quiz champion, raised in a strict evangelical Christian home, has the credentials of a preacher if not the look: bushy hipster beard and long messy hair, dark bags under his eyes and the whiff of old smoke on his shirt. Then he starts to speak.
>
> "Being an elevationist means being an explorer. Our spiritual journey is one of self-discovery, not one of dogma. We believe there is no one-path solution to life's big questions. This is simply a supportive place for each one of us to find a pathway to our own spirituality. Think of it like the pick 'n' mix of belief. There is no doctrine, no creed, no scripture or book. Simply choose bits of whatever world religions work for you, or make something up yourself, mix it all together, and see if it tastes good."

In fact, cannabis use has long been part of religion, from ancient Chinese shamans to modern-day Rastafarians: inducing altered states of consciousness has been a cornerstone of belief since time immemorial. And even without drugs, whether it's spinning Sufi dancers or drumming voodoo priests, or just simple meditation, taking the mind to a higher plane has always been a road to the divine, however that may be conceived. If that is a key aim of any church, then perhaps the elevationists have a claim to be more on track than the ballroom dancers or the coffee drinkers (or indeed than many a 'messy church')? The church fathers tended to disagree on such points: thus, whereas St Basil of Caesarea considered dancing to be the noblest activity of the angels (and therefore worthy to be emulated on earth), St Augustine of Hippo thought it far too licentious. As regards tobacco (and, for that matter, cannabis), it wasn't yet known to either of them – but surely they couldn't argue with the prophet Malachi when he foretold the day when

> From the rising of the sun to its setting my name will be great among all nations, and in every place *incense* will be offered to my name, and a pure offering.

Smoking or non-smoking?

'And God said, Let the earth bring forth grass, and the earth brought forth grass, and the Rastafarians smoked it.' (Genesis 1.8, according to Spike Milligan)

We may still ask, however, 'what should be the goal of a Christian church'? Some at least of the 'fresh expressions' currently being marketed look suspiciously indulgent and may give rise to a diminution, rather than a strengthening, of Christian mission – perhaps too inducing a degree of self-deception? Christ's words recorded faithfully in the gospels instruct his followers to '*do this* (the breaking of the bread and the sharing of the cup) in remembrance of him', and for two thousand years this teaching has been central to the practice of the Catholic Church. It doesn't necessarily require elaborate ritual or the splendour of Gothic architecture, nor does it need a vast outlay of expenditure, nor the presence of a numerous congregation. (And Moses after all managed with a portable tent for quite a long time!) An Anglican archdeacon on trek in 1923 to visit missions in the east of Basutoland (as it was then known) recorded the following episode in his report:

> At 6 am after a wash in the river, I rigged up an altar by means of a writing pad on a stone, covered with a purificator, and we offered the Holy Sacrifice before the sun was up. In the middle of the service a herd boy rode up and sat on his horse silently looking at what must to him have been a strange sight in these regions.

A little later he added:

Here is almost the roughest part of the country — enormous mountains and gorges with threadlike tracks that make one's head swim to look at, and yet here and there are a few Christians who appear from hidden villages when they hear a priest is passing. They rarely if ever get a service, and it is quite impossible to reach these parts with any regularity. Their religion consists in wearing a cross round their necks and holding prayers together in a hut; how they remain as loyal as they do passes human, though, presumably, not divine comprehension.

I myself have said mass by the roadside on a pilgrimage in France, in a restaurant on a cruise liner while acting as ship's chaplain, in a parishioner's front room, in a hospital ward, outdoors in Africa by a missionary's grave, in a hotel bedroom in Tito's Yugoslavia — as well as in more conventional settings. ('The hour is coming', said Jesus, 'when neither on this mountain nor in Jerusalem will you worship the Father', which seems somewhat to expand one's liturgical scope?) I hope thereby that, as well as those who gather in consecrated buildings, at least a few others may have encountered the mystery of Christ himself — whether in 'the streets and lanes of the city' or among 'the highways and hedges'.

A fellow missionary in Malawi once noted (cf. the above painting by Turner of a decaying church, which in his day seems to have been given over entirely to a brood of hens) that chickens were running around the church during divine worship — and felt that this augmented the sense of God's all-embracing presence. But does it also help to have chocolate drops offered to children as an alternative to the Blessed Sacrament; to have multi-coloured lighting in a cathedral so that it resembles a night club; or to board over the nave of an abbey for skating purposes, however beneficial this may be for physical exercise? Should we not recall that 'the gate is narrow and the way is hard, that leads to life, and those who find it are few'?

??? JESUS RAVES

QUIRKY CUSTOMERS

Gallia est omnis divisa in partes tres, wrote Julius Caesar. A similar observation might be made about parish life: there are *regular services* which require organisation, *pastoral situations* which often demand immediate attention, and, if time and energy permit, various *new initiatives* may be needed. So the priest finds himself engaged first with his *worshipping congregation*, then through the occasional offices with others perhaps *on the fringes*, and hopefully in the end with *the wider community*. The balance obviously depends upon factors such as population and geography and physical resources, which sometimes leave little room for manoeuvre. When a priest moved from St Paul's Cathedral to ministry in a dour inner city parish, he reported a vastly smaller congregation, where little outside interest was shown in special events or even the festivals of the Christian year; but there were still a few babies to baptise, the odd couple who wanted to get married, and inevitably a few deaths that kept him busy.

Occasional offices provide the opportunity for getting to know a wide variety of people. There's only one downside, so far as I'm concerned. Whether it's a christening, a wedding or a funeral it's *de rigeur* to mention the names of those involved, and my living nightmare is that sooner or later I'll get a name wrong. In my early days as a priest I was once at Milton Crematorium on the outskirts of our Northampton parish. We were often called upon to do duty there for folk from further afield, and it was never the easiest thing to minister to people whom one hadn't met in advance of the service. Here, as usual, I was just given the essential details on a card by the undertaker minutes before we started. At the committal I used the Christian name as typed before me. Afterwards all hell broke loose: it was not the deceased's name. Of course, I gave my utmost apologies, but the buck stopped with the funeral director. He too was abject and explained it was solely a scribal error in his office. It took a very long time to persuade the relatives that no other mistakes had been made, and to reassure them that their loved one had indeed been in the coffin. My own doubts remain to this day...

To avoid making any similar howlers myself, I now resort to those wonderfully simple post-it stickers, on which I can record whatever names I need. Impossible feats are no longer required of my increasingly geriatric memory. Yet it's surprising how often at a funeral the given name or names need careful adjustment. The deceased may have been (say) John Charles, but you learn that he wasn't known as John nor as Charles; to family and friends he was Fred, to his workmates he may even have been Popeye.

Nicknames do sometimes take over, and names do get altered. I wonder if you've heard the story of a rather deaf old priest who was performing a baptism? The little baby girl in question was called Lucy, but her mother was rather timid and had a lisp. When asked to prompt the priest with her baby's name, she barely whispered, 'Luthy, thir'. 'Lucifer!' he bellowed indignantly, 'I shall call him no such name. He shall be called John'. The naming of children often features too in (irreverent) cartoons, with captions such as 'We're calling him Bill, because he came at the end of the month', or (a really modern and entirely plausible response from the priest) 'I'm afraid the name Sally is taken, but Sally2018### is still available.

I learnt from my predecessor in Zomba that during the 1980s there were two seminarians with unexpected names in the very same class at the theological college. Their parents, like all Malawian parents, retained a belief that a baptismal label had a vocational bearing and a potency for future achievement – hence, if you heard tell of a great man in the world, you appropriated that same name to work wonders for your own flesh and blood. The names chosen for the aforementioned students were a pair of the most renowned men of the 20th century: one was called Stalin (but let us not forget that he was once described in an evangelical book dated 1944 as 'an inspirational example for the Christian'), while the other was named Hitler. When Fr Hitler, as he became known, started to use his second name, matters were not much improved: born in the month of May, that was his other option, but Fr May sounded confusingly bisexual. More to my taste was a lad who had certainly fulfilled his parents' ambitions, a high-flying scholar aptly called Cogitator. In complete contrast was a no-hoper, doomed from birth as Lastboy. One understands that his mother had some ten children already and really didn't want any more, but I did think she might have considered her son's prospects too. If she'd called him Goodluck, for example, he might have risen to be President, as happened with Mr and Mrs Jonathan's son in Nigeria. I heard tell of another youth called Skeleton, but this may have been a joke, as he was apparently rather plump. Girls often seem to have less startling names: Mercy and Charity are still popular in Africa (as they were for Dickens, who reduced them to Merry and Cherry). Although the first name may have Christian resonances (and Immaculata was a favourite for girls, at least among Catholics), it is customary in some districts of Malawi for a middle name to be the first word spoken by the mother after giving birth, which has led to children even being called Chidongo ('a scrap of mud') or Matikenia ('jiggers').

In passing, it's worth noting that to this day African businesses, buses, shops, restaurants also have names that are much more evocative than those found in European settings. Thus, I recall 'Tarmac View' pharmacy (paved highways are in short supply, and cherished when they materialise), 'God Help Us' minibus (presumably because either there were no brakes or the steering was faulty), 'No Money No Friends' maize mill (a blunt refusal to offer credit), and perplexingly the 'You're Not Going To Be Happy' restaurant. When asked by a friend if this last fascia board didn't rather deter customers, the proprietor explained: 'No, no, not at all – the name tells people outside what they're missing if they don't come in'.

I think I've only once queried the choice of a proposed baptismal name. This happened in younger days in the UK, and I ended up with egg on my face. The parents wanted to call their son (I think) Hadadezer. It didn't altogether surprise me because people have increasingly fanciful ideas these days, but when I asked where the name came from, the answer was – the Bible. Hadadezer, in case a reminder is necessary, was king of Zobah, and was defeated in battle by king David. I guess David's an easier name to remember, but I forbore to suggest this, neither did I mention that throughout his life young Hadadezer might find his name misspelt rather frequently. I note that Parson Kilvert's diary records how he once baptised a girl as Mahalah:

> Which Mrs Jones declared to be the name of one of Cain's wives, on the authority of a book she had read called the Life of Abel. She called her elder daughter Thirza, which she says was the name of Cain's other wife. Not a happy allusion.

Do names make a difference? P.G. Wodehouse (whose surname curiously derives from the Anglo-Saxon *wudewasa* – the wild man with shaggy hair and irrational impulses) was convinced that they did in his case:

> If you ask me frankly if I like the names Pelham Grenville, I must confess that I do not. I have my dark moods when they seem to me about as low as you can get. At the font I remember protesting vigorously when the clergyman uttered them, but he stuck to his point. 'Be that as it may,' he said firmly, having waited for a lull, 'I name thee Pelham Grenville' ... I little knew how the frightful label was going to pay off thirty-four years later'.

Maybe research is needed to see if the Hadadezers of this world have been conspicuously more or less successful than the tribe of Davids (although a British PM named Hadadezer Cameron sounds unlikely at present; perhaps now that Cameron has been exposed as rather a bad PM he'll change his name to Hadadezer anyway?). Church registers, however, would seem to indicate that it's more often the surname that gives an indication of a person's future career. Typically I once spotted a Mr Batters who'd graduated as a panel-beater, on the very same page as a Mr Carver who described himself as a stone mason. And I dare say it was inevitable that, when a Mr Chips came to see me to organise his wedding, his fiancée was a Miss Fish. Quite recently I helped to prepare a Mr Pope for reception into the Catholic Church. I was certainly aware of a Mr Priest who was ordained, as well as a Mr Bishop – even though the latter never quite achieved his full promise. Years ago I had a colleague called Fr Saint, and more recently a convert from the world of rock bands took on the name Mr Holy – and became a vicar. By contrast, I once knew a Mr Swindell who came to auction our harvest produce each year; he ran a firm of estate agents called Swindell, Swindell, Swindell and Swindell. I think, however, that the story of the Mr and Mrs Peace who chose the name Warren for their son is apocryphal.

In these multi-ethnic times a priest is sometimes required to tackle unpronounceable Polish or Nigerian or Venezuelan names; and in the Catholic church there are Gaelic names (with many apparently redundant vowels) still preferred by parishioners with Irish roots. Another challenge is the sheer proliferation of names at a mass baptism. In Northamptonshire our parish incorporated the official county gypsy site, and every so often a lorry would arrive at the vicarage, where granny (it was always granny) would explain that baptism was now required for her grandchildren. Once there were ten of these, ranging in age from a few months up to about sixteen years old. I'd get out the diary and say, 'How far ahead are we planning? Roughly when would you hope to hold the service?' The answer was always the same: 'This afternoon, please – we're on the road in three days' time'. I could usually persuade granny to opt for the coming Sunday, but that was the limit. Yet it's fair to say, they were more reverent than most congregations. This was not a mere social ritual for them, but a profound religious ceremony. And if many of the adults were illiterate, they were superbly able to make their responses a split second after those few who could read. Only once did I have a flicker of misgiving when, as the father of a large brood was the last one leaving the church, he looked longingly at the organ pipes, and remarked, 'Nice bit of metal you've got there'.

A couple of decades later in Malawi, in addition to my appointment as a lecturer, disputes in the diocese led to the archbishop asking me to take on the parish as well; this, despite the assistance of a Malawian colleague studying at the university, inevitably included the celebration of occasional offices. The main church was St George's, but there were about two dozen village congregations, many of them in remote areas inaccessible during the rainy season. On my first rural safari, when the rains were over, I went to say mass in a small village (plunging through a rushing stream to get there, the bridge having been washed away), and was about to leave for the return journey. 'You can't go yet', they said, 'you haven't finished. Since we last had a priest here three months ago, fifteen babies have been born. Their families have all come this morning expecting baptisms'. So we organised a production line, and the font (which may shock those more familiar with medieval stoneware) was a blue plastic beaker. The seminarian assisting me gave them all a pep talk, and the ceremonies ended with a dance down the track to where the truck was parked a hundred yards away.

Gypsies and Africans follow more traditional ways, but in the UK it's obvious that in recent years there's been a sea change in people's expectations of these rites of passage. What tipped the balance in favour of customer demand was, I think, Princess Di's funeral in 1997. Here in Westminster Abbey was a high profile disregard of the traditional Anglican funeral liturgy. It was followed rather more freely than the rubrics permitted; it featured Earl Spencer's tirade from the pulpit, while of course giving Elton John the real number one spot. Not long afterwards a church conference was convened in London to review an even more important royal ceremony, the coronation. Questions were discussed: What is really needed in a service to enthrone a monarch of the realm? Is there just one essential element? A wit on the back row called out, 'No question at all – it has to be Elton John'.

The perception of what had happened at Di's funeral was widespread. It encouraged the populace to think, 'If the royal family can tailor a service to their own requirements and incorporate their favourite singers, so can we'. It wasn't a novel idea, and most clergy have always tried to accommodate personal requests – but usually within reason. Long ago crematoria started to introduce music centres, so that, even if a versatile live organist was present, some people would insist on using their own tapes and CDs. I had my own advice, and a rule of thumb. I'd say: 'You've asked for a Christian priest to be here, so what happens should be in keeping with our Christian faith, and ideally be a positive witness to it. If there's anything that strikes a different note, keep it separate so that our service retains its Christian integrity'. This is much easier said than done with those whose religious ideas may be somewhat nebulous. Other priests are obviously less old-fashioned or restrictive than I am myself, to the extent of wearing Elvis Presley costumes for the occasion if so requested and rejoicing in totally non-religious funerals being held within their precincts. In London I believe there are Free Church ministers who use the side-cars of motor-bikes as hearses, and no doubt plenty of others who daringly meet ever-changing cultures (and, increasingly, agnostic sons and daughters of the deceased) more than halfway.

One curious choice of music once greeted me as we processed in: it was simply the sound of bees humming. I asked afterwards why that tape had been played. The funeral director explained that the deceased's favourite song had been 'I love you, honey', but as the family couldn't find any recording of it they'd settled for a background hum as the next best thing. In parenthesis, I should explain that funeral directors are usually very helpful in humouring clients and elucidating such quirky choices. Once I was standing next to the undertaker while wreaths were being unloaded from the hearse. 'Do you see that big purple wreath?' he muttered. 'Yes, what about it?' 'Do you know who it's from?' 'No', I said, 'tell me'. 'It's from the dog'. 'O really?' 'Yes, and do you know why it's purple?' 'All right – go on'. 'That's the colour of the front gate where the dog waited each day for his master to come home from work. Quite possibly he used it for other purposes too'. I think you'll agree that's a touching story, illustrating that odd requests may well reflect deeply personal memories, including those of our dumb friends.

It's at weddings and funerals, much more than at baptisms, that a firm hand[8] – or rather, the voice of long experience – is particularly needed to curb personal excesses. The difficulty often lies in the way people copy what their friends have been allowed to do elsewhere. It's not uncommon for a couple to propose writing their own version of the wedding vows (which would of course then be invalid), nor is it unusual in some churches for everything apart from the vows to be drawn from secular sources. After all, the point of a wedding is to enjoy the life of a celebrity for half a day (documented exhaustively – undoubtedly *le mot juste* in the circumstances – by a *prima donna* photographer, if not a team of cameramen), and to indulge one's fantasies. As a teenager I used to deputise for our church organist whenever there was a West Indian wedding. He was not in the least bit racist but had his ironmonger's stores to run – and couldn't spare the extra time needed for our Caribbean friends. When they booked a wedding at (say) 3 pm, that was actually the time of the bride's appointment in a hair salon. I might then need to play the organ for a good hour until she finally arrived in all her glory at the church door.

Another out-of-the-ordinary example was a girl who came to book a wedding with me for the following year. I said, 'This is just pencilled in for now. It can only be provisional until I've met with your fiancé as well. What's his name, by the way?' It wasn't quite the answer I was expecting. 'I'm not sure yet', she said, 'I haven't quite decided which one to go for'. Bridegrooms can indeed be less enthusiastic participants, aware that they're simply to do as they're told. This commonly includes handing over the fees when prompted by the bride. The most imaginative initiative undertaken by a groom in my experience was the young man who put a small jar of grease in his pocket, and immediately prior to the blessing and exchange of rings smeared some of it on the fourth finger of his left hand.

---

[8] Never so firm, however, as that which Parson James Woodforde recorded in his diary on November 22, 1768: 'I married Tom Burge of Ansford to Charity Andrews of C. Cary by License this morning. The Parish of Cary made him marry her, and he came *handbolted* to Church for fear of running away'.

In Lesotho no weddings ever came my way, chiefly because elopement across the border into South Africa was more common there, allowing the groom to avoid paying what was often a hefty bride price to her family. On my introduction to weddings in Malawi, though, I rapidly discovered that rituals were different. First, the engagement had to be approved by both families, with maternal uncles usually acting as the go-betweens. This might seem cumbersome, but it had the advantage that, if later on the marital relationship was under strain, the same uncles were called upon to discuss the situation and advise the couple accordingly. Then, although the bulk of the marriage service was similar to practice in the UK, the entry of the principal parties was far more elaborate. At my first rehearsal, I outlined the usual routines for coming in, only to be met with the response, 'But that's not how we do it here'. In fact, there can be a superabundance of ushers and bridesmaids (at one wedding, six wearing yellow, six in green, six in pink, and six in cream) who come in pairs to dance slowly down the central aisle. Any following pair has to wait until the previous pair has reached the front, so that this grand entry can take twenty or thirty minutes. Preceding the bride herself are the little page boy who carries a prayer book, and the page girl who scatters petals.

Once in progress though, the useful thing about church weddings – whatever the local customs, and with whatever motivation for the occasion – is that the priest has a captive audience with whom he can share a few tips about marriage and family life. The down-side is the amount of litter remaining behind. Confetti is now occasionally 'green', but the same is not true of cigarette ends: my record count of those picked up was one hundred and twenty eight. The advent of the digital camera now thankfully spares us from all the Kodak film wrappings thoughtfully donated as collector's items. Their place has been taken, so I am told, by empty plastic water bottles.

Part of today's problem is that communal singing, which used to bond congregations together, using tried and tested words, is now a thing of the past. Football crowds still unite in song, but their repertoire (including 'You'll never walk alone') isn't necessarily suitable for a church service. I daresay the present repertoire of universally known hymns is little more than the *National Anthem*, *Abide with me*, and *All things b and b* – plus *Shine Jesus shine* if you're under 25.

Because music can at times say more than words, people obviously like to include it. Live musicians would be everyone's first choice, and that's fine if you're wealthy or the royal family; but otherwise only the local organist is likely to be available. So CDs are increasingly preferred, although at a wedding there are times when friends who are singers or instrumentalists are enlisted to perform. What these kind folk may not realise is that their apparent audience may be less inclined to listen: congregations these days have a distinct tendency to talk during musical interludes. This in turn makes it much harder for the bride and groom to regain attention on their re-entry after signing the register.

Mind you, I recall once having to postpone this dramatic moment, with everyone on the edge of their seats, while a search was conducted in the churchyard for the organist. He was a chain-smoker who invariably took time out for a puff and a drag during the couple's vows: on this occasion he'd forgotten to come back and was meditating on a tomb stone. There was another wedding (which I attended as a guest) where the bride had brought along all her female operatic friends, each of whom had been allocated a slot in the programme. So enraptured was the priest by this musical feast that he jumped a page and was about to conclude the service before the legalities had been completed.

Although I can't now remember marrying this couple!

Joking apart, given the present insistence upon individual choice, this scenario could possibly come about within a generation – no doubt in America. When I first encountered a 'gender change' in England, it concerned a man in his 50s, married for 30 years and with 2 adult daughters (the younger one, who was shortly to be married herself, said that she would refuse to walk down the aisle on her father's arm if he was wearing a dress and high heels). Despite pleas from his family he was determined to become a woman, for – as he was advised by his NHS psychiatrist – 'if you think you're a woman, then you are a woman'. Would the same logic apply if I thought I was a sheep? Is this what Descartes anticipated when he wrote his famous 'Cogito ergo sum'?

The funeral service has also evolved in recent years. It tends to be no longer an awesome preparation for whatever lies beyond death, but the celebration of a person's life. This can leave those most affected by the bereavement rather isolated in their grief. I remember one appalling tribute that dwelt at length on what a lad his father used to be, with an eye for all the girls and a large appetite for drink, despite the fact that his widowed mother was sitting there listening. At other times, however, it can be very moving to hear (for example) a couple of grandchildren speaking of their fond memories.

The modern generation often likes to find out more about its ancestry, and the advent of the internet has certainly facilitated this, with genealogical searches quite high on the usage chart. In my earlier days as an Anglican vicar, however, it was more common to receive requests to inspect the parish registers (many of which have since gone into the more professional care of county record offices, where digitalization continues apace). The main problem with visitors searching the registers in person was the need to stay with them lest they secretly ripped out a few pages to take home. But even written requests could be very time-consuming, as with the man who wanted to know more about his grandfather, apparently 'surnamed Smith who lived in the parish during the 19th century'. I recall finding the burial details requested by another enquirer, and duly reported that his forebear was interred on the north side of the church 'as a common criminal' (so the marginal note explained). Strangely, he inquired no further!

The vestry at a crematorium, where one hears relayed proceedings from the chapel, is another educational experience. All too common is the new secular mode of saying farewell. Two or three people pay a tribute (or, as they call it, a eulogy), evocative music is played, someone reads a poem, and the leader concludes by saying, 'We've so appreciated knowing you, Emily, Sue, Charlie or Fred. We really miss you'. Fine, I suppose, if Emily, Sue, Charlie or Fred is listening: in which case, I wonder, doesn't something further need to be said or done? Strangely, although such services are apparently non-religious, there is often a prayer or two slipped in.

Such a ceremony may yet be a more honest way of proceeding than some of the more sentimental send-offs that exaggerate the virtues of the deceased to the nth degree. As a young priest my eyes were opened when I took the funeral of an elderly lady living near the church. She had four sons, all of whom gushed with poetic emotion in the Birth, Marriages and Deaths section of the local newspaper. They outbid each other in heartfelt grief. As I'd been visiting their mother for some time, I knew that her main sadness had lain in the fact that none of the sons had been near her for years or had even written. Yet who knows? Perhaps there were postmortem regrets and a little genuine sorrow? Or perhaps their mum's mind was failing – not long afterwards I visited a care home where on the stairs I passed the family of another parishioner on their way out. 'Thank goodness you've come,' was the greeting that met me two seconds later, 'I've not had a visitor for two weeks now'.

Memories certainly get less reliable as we get older, and appearances too are not always what they seem. Yet I have never met 'mourners' quite as vindictive as the Parson Williams who is mentioned in Kilvert's diary: he 'was to preach a funeral sermon for a farmer with whom he had quarrelled. He chose this text, Isaiah 14.9: 'Hell from beneath is moved for thee, to meet thee at thy coming'.

At this point I'd like to introduce my great uncle Edwin, who was a church organist in Lancashire for many years, and whose hobby in retirement was searching churchyards for unusual epitaphs. Even where his first reaction might be one of amusement, he commented:

> Then our better nature asserts itself; for the churchyard is not the fit and proper place for humour or ludicrous doggerel … The stone, which should have added sacredness to the few feet of ground around which it stood, can become the object of ridicule, a monument of ignorance, frivolity and irreverence … Grave stones are often great liars.

Insincerities and distortions of the truth, he noted, are actually quite commonplace, though I rather like this self-correction:

> Here lies the body of Mary Jones
> Who met her death through cherry stones;
> Her name was Lord, it was not Jones
> But Jones was put to rhyme with stones.

Sometimes punctuation is ambiguous: 'To James Silvey, accidentally shot by his brother as a mark of affection'. Biblical quotations were quite often added for piety's sake, but occasionally exposed the deceased to hidden meanings – and eternal mockery: 'Here lieth the body of James Robinson and of Ruth his Wife: Their warfare is accomplished'. One isn't quite sure about the expectations of a certain Jane: 'Erected by Jane, To the memory of her husband John. Him that cometh unto me I will in no wise cast out'.

But plainer speaking can also be found:

> Here lie the bones of Robert Lowe:
> Where he has gone to I don't know;
> If to the realms of light and love,
> Farewell to happiness above;
> If haply to a lower level
> I can't congratulate the devil.

And this next epitaph breathes a huge sigh of relief:

> Beneath this silent stone is laid
> A noisy antiquated maid:
> Who from her cradle talked till death,
> And ne'er before was out of breath.

She may not, however, have been such a gossip as Arabella:

> Here lies returned to clay
> Miss Arabella Young,
> Who on the first of May
> Began to hold her tongue.

Yet some tributes are subtly sympathetic:

> She was married twenty four years
> And in all that time never once
> Banged the door.

One senses considerable provocation in the background. This is on a par with a memorial plaque in my own Somerset church; it recorded a devoted wife and mother of six children, who had evidently been quite a handful between them. It said very simply, 'She did what she could' – a tribute which I sometimes mention on Mothering Sunday, and which I daresay is the highest compliment you can pay to anyone on God's earth.

In his notebook Edwin also records several epitaphs that include blatant advertisements:

- Here lies Jane Smith, Wife of Thomas Smith, Marble Cutter.
  This monument was erected by her husband
  as a tribute to her memory and a specimen of his work.
  Monuments of this style £50.

- Here lies Mrs Nuttall, wife of Wm Nuttall, Master Blacksmith.
  The railing around this tomb was manufactured by her husband.

- Beneath this Stone, in hopes of Zion,
  Doth lie the landlord of the Lion.
  His Son keeps on the business still,
  Resigned unto the Heavenly Will.

However, James Williams 'who came to this city and died for the benefit of his health' might have been a more effective advertisement for the spa in question if advice had been taken about the wording!

EXTRACTS from 'In the hour of Death' (1969)

Reminiscences of William Russ aged sixty-one

Gravedigger of Akenfield in Suffolk

So far as funerals are concerned, we've gone from one extreme to the other. Bodies used to be kept in the house for twelve days. Everyone kept the body at home for as long as they could then; they didn't care to part with it, you see. Now they can't get it out quick enough. They didn't like hurrying about anything when I was young, particularly about death. They were afraid that the corpse might still be alive - that was the real reason for hanging on to it. People have a post-mortem now and it's all settled in a minute, but there's no doubt that years ago them were a rare lot of folk who got buried alive. When a sick man passed on, the doctor was told, but he never came to look at the corpse. Ho just wrote out the death certificate. People always made a point of leaving an instruction in their wills to have a vein cut. Just to be on the safe side.

There was an old man near Framlingham, old Micah Hibble, he was laid out for dead three times. The last time he was actually in his coffin and waiting for the funeral to begin. When I asked, 'Anymore for a last look before he's screwed down?' there was the usual nuisance pushing his way through the mourners and saying, 'Yes, I do!' Trust somebody to get you fiddling about and making the funeral late. The bell was going, so you know how late it was. Anyway, when this man looked in the coffin he saw that Micah had moved. Well do you know, he recovered! And what's more, he is supposed to have written a book about what he saw, although I've never set eyes on it. He reckoned he saw Heaven and Hell but he wouldn't say what he saw in Hell; he thought it would be too much for Framlingham. He lived for years after this.

I've dug for all denominations, from Catholic to Plymouth Brethren. The chapel people are the worst. First of all, they're a good three-quarters of an hour in the chapel while the preacher spouts about the dead man and estimates whether he's saved, and then, when they get to the grave, on it goes again. There's no end to it. They forget we all knew the corpse. And then, when they're none too sure about the saving, you should hear them then! There was Jed's funeral - well we don't need any telling about Jed! Well Jed might have been a bad lot but he wasn't a bad sort. You know. I mean he was Jed, wasn't he? Well, this chapel preacher stood there by the hole I had got ready for Jed and was as near as damn-it saying that Jed wasn't saved although he *hoped* he was. So after the funeral I went up to him and said, 'My God, you've had some talk about Jed, haven't you? I know you're here to say a few words - but you've said too much!' I said, 'Do you reckon that you are saved?' He said, 'I hope so'. 'Very well then,' I said, 'but do you remember when you get in front of your Maker he won't ask you what Jed has done - he'll ask what you've been up to.' You could see he didn't like it.

The parsons aren't much better. But there, you don't find many *parsons* now. Only men who have done their life's work serving as a colonel or a schoolmaster and then get themselves ordained. I don't really call these people parsons. I don't mince my words with them. When you bury between 180-200 people a year you can afford to be honest.

It is usually the case that, while some people sketch out ideas for their funeral service, they leave the memorial stone, if any, to their next of kin. In a graveyard the ground certainly needs to settle before any permanent monument can be put in place, which allows plenty of time to agree on its wording. I was surprised therefore one Sunday in West Monkton to be approached by a member of the congregation who bore, not only instructions for his own requiem, but the actual plaque intended for the site where his ashes were to be interred; moreover, the latter was already engraved with his name, date of birth and a verse from the Bible[9]. All that was missing was the date of his death, which, he kindly explained, was not yet determined. (Our grandson Samuel at the age of 4, asked his Granny: 'How old will you be when Grandfather is dead?' which is a very good question, whose answer still remains unclear to me.)

> John Palfreyman who is buried here,
> Was aged four and twenty year:
> And near this place his Mother lies,
> Likewise his Father, when he dies.

But let's not anticipate the outcome, as the lady did who copied words from Purcell's gravestone ('He has gone to the one place where his works are excelled'). Unfortunately, her husband had been not a musician but a firework manufacturer.

Skull and cross-bones don't usually indicate a pirate's burial!
In the medieval view, they comprised the essential remains
for the deceased to be able to rise from the dead.

On the whole, I think I'd rather not have my own remains deposited anywhere at all: there's a real chance that neglect would eventually obliterate the grave, that archaeologists would dig it up in centuries yet to come, or that bulldozers would demolish it anyway.

---

[9] Poetic lines might sometimes be an acceptable alternative, but today's home-made doggerel is seldom so entrancing as the verses recorded by my great uncle Edwin. Brevity is still the soul of wit! I like the epitaph to a one-time waiter, which read 'God finally caught his eye'.

CHANGING KEY

Change of key – and a change of mood – by Brahms

For the first twenty-five years of our marriage Sarah and I owned a Dolmetsch spinet, purchased by means of generous wedding gifts. We took it with us to Lesotho in 1984, which proved disastrous climatically but also somewhat unnecessary, since a neighbour (Alan, the Canadian chemistry professor and a devout Quaker) on the campus at Roma offered us the loan of his upright piano in return for hosting and conducting the small choir of expatriates which he had recently formed. We gave the occasional concert, and at Christmas toured the wards of the local mission hospital with supposedly 'familiar' carols of which only one or two actually resonated with the African patients.

Back in England I inherited a church organist who had just suffered a break-up of her marriage and who felt unable to commit herself beyond playing for Sunday services. Once again, and quite unexpectedly, I found myself looking after regular Friday evening choir practices (the junior choir went from strength to strength under Sarah's direction on a separate occasion). We met in our drawing room, with accompaniment provided, not on the spinet, but on our upright piano. But the sopranos were by and large ladies 'of a certain age' who didn't always find it easy to reach the top notes. After several years coaxing them along, a different solution occurred to me. The spinet had needed frequent tuning ever since its disastrous sub-tropical years, and with a busy working schedule there was only limited time to sit down and play it, even if it hadn't needed much TLC. The opportunity came to sell it, and to replace it by an Italian organ keyboard (with digitally sampled real time organ stops) along with a specially commissioned oak stand and lid. This was versatile in more ways than one: it occupied much less space than the spinet; it could easily be carried by hand and moved elsewhere; it operated off batteries as well as mains electricity; and above all – for singing purposes – it had a *traspositore* lever that could raise or lower the pitch by up to two tones. Our choir ladies could now learn their melodies more comfortably in a lower key, after which little by little they were able to climb up imperceptibly towards the designated pitch!

Latterly the keyboard served a related purpose on several visits to Ashford Rotary Club's Christmas dinner. The meal was invariably followed by several male Rotarians (we were merely guests) providing lively entertainment – carols, stories and songs, the favourites being those of Tom Lehrer or from Gilbert and Sullivan. More often than not, the request was made to myself as the accompanist to play it 'a tone or two lower, please', which could of course be miraculously effected in a trice. Publishers of sheet music ought actually to be more aware that they too often exaggerate the upper reach of adult male voices; the same is true of settings in many a hymn book. We overcome that in our (usually unaccompanied) b singing at St Ambrose Church in Wye by pitching the note ourselves, and so accommodating both ladies and gentlemen much more comfortably. This often prompts visitors to comment on the robustness of our singing. When other clergy bemoan the difficulty of finding a regular organist, my usual suggestion is that they too may well be better off without one (especially any whose playing is ponderous): there are few organs in Africa, yet the singing far surpasses that of a typical English congregation, and frequently breaks into harmony as well.

'Tempering the music to the voices' is also a metaphor for effective pastoral practice and for Christian outreach generally. The goal is spelt out succinctly in St Paul's Letter to the Romans:

> Do not be conformed to this world but be transformed by the renewal of your mind, that you may prove what is the will of God, what is good and acceptable and perfect.

Occasionally dramatic results may be possible, but too often in the past the Church has expected the desired transformation to be accomplished 'in the twinkling of an eye'. This was not Jesus' own approach: the best example is probably found in his final exchange with St Peter [Jn 21.15ff]. Three times he asks him about the depth of his love – twice he uses the root word *agape*, but Peter affirms his loyalty in terms of the somewhat weaker word *philo*. So the third time Jesus himself takes up Peter's own terminology, which expresses affection and friendship; yet he goes on to point beyond it to Peter's coming death when love (*agape*) in its fullness will at last be realised. Again, Jesus' teaching of God's ultimate intentions – such as the ideal of lifelong marriage, or the readiness to embrace poverty for the sake of God's kingdom – does not depict them as imposed decrees but rather as true wisdom, which individuals will need to appropriate for themselves as they grow in the spirit. The Samaritan woman at the well, for example, has led a most irregular domestic life, but is now offered 'living water' by the Lord despite her matrimonial status. (In line with this, the early Church was prone to look upon the Eucharist as 'medicine' or 'viaticum' – 'food for the journey'.) There is again a man who longs for eternal life: 'Jesus looking upon him loved him, and said to him, "You lack one thing"', and tailors his advice to his questioner's spiritual condition – he should sell all his possessions and give to the poor. This is not necessarily demanded of other disciples whose journey of faith is different. Using the phrase of an Asian theologian, Jesus is a 'three mile an hour' God, who travels at the speed of the slowest.

St Paul evidently understood the need for a flexibility of approach in his own mission. His policy was to become 'all things to all men', if he could thereby save a few. While there were obvious clashes between Christianity and certain pagan beliefs and practices, as the centuries unfolded it was generally realised that there was also a good deal in pagan life that could be affirmed, indeed that could be seen as *preparatio evangelica* – ready to be fulfilled with true Christian import. Missionary strategy often became one of 'inculturation', whereby the Christian religion was not imposed exclusively in (for example) European mode but accommodated the local language and culture whenever possible. The musical analogy fits in here; one might say that there are those who sing a tune in perhaps a slightly different rhythm or key from the song that Christians know, so an appropriate modulation is needed – sometimes 'connecting chords' can facilitate the necessary change.

In my student days the professor of moral theology at Oxford was fond of a different analogy: he suggested that Christian mission might be likened to a veterinary doctor administering a pill to an ailing horse, blowing it down a tube into the animal's throat. The only trouble, he pointed out, is that sometimes the horse blows first! One famous example occurred in New Spain, the former Aztec empire, where the Franciscans introduced the cult of saints as a way of replacing the existing idols. Some natives developed a fervent devotion to St James, who was usually depicted as a knight on a steed, trampling down the enemies of Christ. Or so they thought at first; in fact, it proved to be not 'Santiago' who was adored, but the horse he was riding, since this resonated strongly with an existing local deity. A later example occurred in Malawi, where the Montfort Fathers arrived in 1901. Father Bourget selected the most imposing baobab tree in Nsanje, placed a medallion of Mary on its trunk and offered a prayer entrusting the whole country to Our Lady. He and his colleagues then received a tremendous welcome from the villagers, who were overjoyed to see these foreigners making an offering to the spirits of the land, as they did themselves!   The policy of inculturation therefore entailed the risks both of misunderstanding and of 'watering down' the gospel, opening the door to much controversy within the Church (as, for example, in the 17th century clash between Jesuits in China who sought to blend Christian and Confucian wisdom and the other religious orders who regarded this approach as heretical). R.P. Carroll once noted:

> If the religious community seeks to evangelise the culture, it must also be aware that it is being evangelised by the culture.

This is particularly liable to happen with the use of signs and symbols, or more generally with what has been called the 'sacramental economy'. As bridges (or 'connecting chords') between the material and the spiritual world, they are necessarily somewhat ambiguous, being open to more than one interpretation. Even the outstanding Fathers of the Church seem to have lapsed at times: St Gregory Nazianzen wrote approvingly of his sister Gorgonia's 'pious' act in rubbing her entire body with Eucharistic bread intincted with wine as a means of healing an injury (so what price 'take and eat'?); or again, St Augustine recommended sleeping with John's Gospel under one's pillow as a means of curing a headache (but who knows? perhaps it really works). Are these examples so very different from the response of the crowds as recorded in the book of Acts, who 'even carried out the sick into the street, and laid them on beds and pallets, that as Peter came by at least his shadow might fall on some of them'? When we read in St Jerome's *Life of Saint Hilarion* that in a chariot-race in Gaza the saint was persuaded to sprinkle the 'horses, charioteers, carriage, and even the bars of the starting stalls' with holy water, we begin to wonder if he should not have been reported to the appropriate Olympic committee for cheating?[10] Nevertheless, we are told that one of his blessed horses won and 'became the occasion of faith for a great many'. Am I the only one who doubts the depth and cogency of that faith? I suspect that Jean Gerson, chancellor of the University of Paris at the turn of the 15th century, would have agreed. He wrote:

> There are many things introduced under the appearance of religion among simple Christians which it would have been more holy to have omitted.

If in the past the Church has sought to confirm rather than to condemn existing ideas and practices – as Clement of Alexandria did when he called Homer 'an unwilling prophet', as Augustine did in referring to Virgil as 'a prophet unaware', and in the widespread acceptance of the greatest classical philosophers as 'Christians before Christ' – the challenge today is also to identify those elements of the Church's own life which resonate most with the needs of the world beyond its borders. These 'connecting

---

[10] He might, however, have been lucky with his assessors, as was a friend of mine sitting his final Schools at Oxford. Before the exam started he placed several relics on his desk. The invigilator noticed these and inquired what they were. On being told that they were saintly relics, he – being a non-believer – allowed them to remain. Had he been a devout Catholic, however, he would most certainly have insisted on their removal. In the event my friend gained a very respectable degree. Discuss!

chords' surely need to be amplified, as Pope Benedict XVI expressed it in an interview he gave in 2001:

> The Church must tap all her creativity so that the living force of the Gospel will not be extinguished... What is most important, in my opinion, is to look at the 'essence', to use an expression of Romano Guardini. It is necessary... to concentrate on the essential, which later might find new ways of incarnating itself.

St Augustine would have endorsed this encouragement to make vital links:

> An individual will be moved to action if what you promise is what he likes... if your recommendations are in harmony with what he embraces... if he rejoices over what you claim is a reason for joy.

In October 2013 I was privileged to be in central Portugal to engage in an exercise of such discernment. For three weeks Sarah and I shared in a 'residency', partially funded by the EU, with our daughter Trish and her husband Dan (a sound artist), and of course with Samuel then aged 21 months. It was a remote area facing abandonment or at least creeping extinction. There is little employment here apart from forestry and goat herding, few children or youngsters are left, elderly people easily find themselves isolated, communal activities are under threat, and the church is a shadow of its former self, but now in the care of an imported Brazilian priest. Each year the project known as Binaural has proposed a theme to attract visitors to look at some particular aspect of the local culture – maybe traditional agriculture, legend or folklore, but for us focusing on the religious scene as it continues to evolve. The theme in 2013 was *Divina Sonus Ruris* – 'the sound of the divine in the rural setting'. Several other sound artists from different parts of the world had been invited as well; we met with them every day at lunch in a mountain café. The sounds they recorded tended to be taken from the natural environment and from the harvesting activities currently under way, but they also reflected the great attraction of the isolated terrain for prayer and for pilgrimage. Our attention was largely given to meeting local people, several of whom (*marked here with an**) I interviewed (always through an interpreter!) in order to appreciate their particular concerns and contributions: the 'divine' addresses us through nature, yes, but even more so through the people who are dear to God. One such interview was later broadcast on Portuguese radio.

In these mountains of Gralheira south of the Douro river there are people still searching for God, even though many no longer identify themselves so readily with the community of faith. Long ago one such pilgrim was the legendary St Macarios, about whom little is known beyond his life as a hermit doing penance (for the murder of his wife, whom he is supposed to have caught in the act of adultery); he lived on the top of stony slopes above the ancient village of Macieira. Like others before him – Moses,

Elijah, indeed at times Christ himself – he found himself closer to God in a place far removed from the everyday grind. His chapel finds itself today between two radio masts, designed to relay signals from afar – as he did once himself. The streams flowing down the mountain side symbolise this process even more vividly: we discovered that the waters in the valley where we were lodged in an old mill complex are so highly regarded that an EU agency tests them every six months to check that their purity is maintained.

Macarios' example continues to inspire pilgrims to climb to the summit named after him. They believe his intercession will bring healing to themselves and to those for whom they pray – especially if they suffer mental problems or skin diseases – and so they offer *ex voto* wax images of the limbs where their ailments are or were located. In reality the relief they seek may often be denied, not because their prayers are unheard but because a deeper spiritual healing must take place. How is this to be fostered? There are some for whom the way ahead is not apparently within the ongoing life of the church. One such man is the *stone carver of Macieira, whose personal quest is expressed in his artistry. As his life on earth draws to a close, his aim is to complete a sanctuary where others visiting the mountain can find both silence and solace in the Christian images so beautifully created in his intimate chapels. His inspiration may be summarised in a verse of St Luke's Gospel: 'Jesus said, I tell you, if these disciples keep silence *the stones will cry out'*.

Of course, not all who worship regularly appreciate his distinctive calling, which is perhaps akin to that of Macarios himself. It may be that the traditional liturgies of the church suffice for them, although without necessarily deepening their faith nor provoking recognition of what others outside the church may be seeking. When, for example, a loyal *sacristan was asked what blessings a new priest might bring to his parish he could only suggest that the statues needed repainting and the finances managing better. Thus, maintaining the status quo, rather than promoting any enrichment of faith, was his priority. The challenge, in *Bishop Ilidio's view, is for parishes to embrace the *aggiornamento* envisaged in the teachings of Vatican 2: in other words, to face their need to change, in order to respond better to the outreach of faith. How this is to be done was the subject of the *inquérito* then being conducted throughout his diocese. (We met the bishop in the cathedral town of Viseu: although I was dressed as a priest, the others looked rather more casual and might easily have been mistaken for a motley bunch of reporters hell-bent on discovering some new scandal among his clergy. It took at least ten minutes for his suspicions to be allayed, and even than he spoke with considerable caution.)

There was no doubt that many local parishioners already accept that an outreach of care is an essential part of their calling. One excellent example may be seen in the partnership between church and civil society in the well-established social centre of St Martinho just beyond the mountain. Here trained *helpers go out each day of the week to provide some thirty elderly people in the surrounding villages with support in their homes along with cooked meals. We learnt that their role embraces whatever is needed on a day-to-day basis, for example, cleaning or dressing or simply listening, as well as relaying specific needs back to the centre (and keeping the priest informed).

In a similar way most churches in the area broadcast their masses over speakers so that the housebound can feel part of the worshipping community. This took me by surprise when I joined *Padre Lindoval at the altar in Sul; unexpectedly he pointed his finger to the place in the altar missal where I was invited to continue the prayer. For the first time in my life, I read haltingly out loud in Portuguese, knowing that my efforts would echo around the neighbourhood far beyond the confines of the church itself. At least it made the congregation prick up their ears, with the kindly comment offered afterwards, 'Well, it sounded Portuguese'.

Further questions remained: what was being done to respond to the spiritual needs of others, not least of the younger people who, though fewer in number these days and in any case likely to be more indifferent to the practice of faith, are nevertheless not without their own problems. An appropriate text for Christian communities may be that in the 1st letter of St Peter: 'Christ is the living stone, rejected by men but chosen by God; *set yourself close to him, so that you may be living stones making a spiritual house'*. Sometimes it is the young people themselves who contribute the necessary life and vigour to this transformation. The parish of Sul is fortunate in that Padre Lindoval is young and energetic, and coming from the South American continent finds himself already familiar with new ways of reaching out to the whole community. We were impressed by the youth activities he had fostered, of which the guitar-playing ensemble we heard one evening was but one.

Perhaps his example, and those of others like him, will inspire more vocations to the priesthood? In earlier (pre-Vatican 2) days, seminaries often provided the only chance for impoverished families to find an education for one or more of their sons. As a result there was a steady flow of candidates for the priesthood. The *forester, who owned the mill where we were staying and lived there as a child with his widowed mother, began this route himself but the harsh atmosphere he then encountered failed to inspire him to continue. Now, employing twenty others (an achievement of paramount importance in retaining younger men in this area, as *Jose Pedro the local political leader emphasised to us) he surely makes an equally valid contribution to God's work in the world – especially with his commitment to restoring a proper balance in the natural environment.

Times have certainly changed and continue to do so. It is not easy for an older generation to adapt. Some regret the passing of old certainties, and the loss of more self-supportive rural communities that were once largely isolated from the outside world. An *emigré who made his fortune in South Africa before returning to end his days in his home village (where he built his own palace!) is disillusioned about these changes and finds today's church very different from the one he knew long ago, when it was much more the life blood of a flourishing community: he sees the church now as 'a business'. In so far as it is bound up more in its own affairs than in its pastoral and spiritual outreach, maybe the criticism needs to be heeded? God has many ways, including voices beyond the church, to remind us of the directions we should take and the responsibilities we have for each other. Yet equally the church remains God's chosen repository of truth to inform and inspire the world to which it belongs. Sometimes secularity can intrude too much upon the spiritual quest, as it has done in recent years at the annual pilgrimage of St Macarios (which had begun to resemble a summer pop festival); so we were heartened to learn of Bishop Ilidio's recent resolve to lead others to the chapel there in a more authentic Christian way.

We were moved too by the presentations made by *fellow artists on the final day of this Sound Art residency. These were young people from several different countries whose art was not in opposition to their faith but bore the hallmarks of sensitive spiritual insight. Rodrigo and Ana (from Porto) recorded five women praying the rosary together in the church at Macieira; as we listened they seemed to be joined by the saints themselves, represented by the resonating glass reliquaries on the altar. The recital of the rosary was the theme that also illuminated Mary and Monique's earthy recordings from the 'goat' village of Covas do Monte. Its steady repetition was echoed by the rhythmical round of rural life – in the early autumn by the harvesting of maize (an activity in which we shared one afternoon; the close proximity to so many goats alas! gave us multiple flea bites, which took a couple of weeks to clear), and in the daily herding routines, which thus became prayerful activities in themselves. The tapestry of everyday sounds made by (Uruguayan) Ana in the village of Sequeiros was heard too as a meditation on words found in the Catholic mass: 'You give life to all things and make them holy'. The divine, in other words, had not abandoned this tract of land, even if it was now struggling to survive.

Capela de S Macario de Cima

Finally, *Christoph (a Franciscan lay brother from Germany) took us back to St Macarios' chapel. His was a meditation on different limbs of the body, which collectively embraced the entire range of human experience. Using a trio of languages, we prayed in turn for the whole of ourselves and for all humanity.

And here I was reminded of St Paul's imagery about 'the body of Christ' of which all Christians are 'members' or particular organs, each called to fulfil a special role or function. Thus, one person is 'a hand' with a practical gift to share, another is 'a listening ear', another is 'a compelling voice', many will have 'a heart of compassion', and so on. No one member, says St Paul, is more important than another, and each is needed if the Church is to fulfil her mission. In the end it's not our own inclinations that matter; it's the Holy Spirit who prompts our sphere of service. I recall my early upbringing as a Methodist, when each New Year we held what was known as the Covenant Service, when those present were invited to renew their Christian commitment. Its original version dates back to 1755 when John Wesley incorporated words from *Vindiciae Pietatis* (1663), a Puritan text by Richard Alleine. Those which struck me most ran as follows (here in the modern version):

> Christ has many services to be done. Some are more easy and honourable, others are more difficult and disgraceful. Some are suitable to our inclinations and interests, others are contrary to both. In some we may please Christ and please ourselves. But then there are *other works where we cannot please Christ except by denying ourselves*.

A Christian vocation doesn't, therefore, necessarily correspond to one's own inclinations nor may it immediately offer any assurance of personal fulfilment (although it may well!); it may not even be the exercise of a charism that others recognise within us. On occasion we may face the same challenge as Isaiah – 'Whom shall I send, and who will go for us?' – to which he responded positively when he realized there was no-one but himself to answer the call.

In the modern world life is constantly changing and throwing up new challenges. *Lumen Gentium*, one of the documents that emerged from the 2nd Vatican Council, put it like this:

> The Church, which the Spirit guides in way of all truth and which he unified in communion and in works of ministry, he both equips and directs with hierarchical and charismatic gifts and adorns with his fruits. By the power of the Gospel he makes the Church keep the freshness of youth ... It is not only through the sacraments and the ministries of the Church that the Holy Spirit sanctifies and leads the people of God and enriches it with virtues, but, allotting his gifts to everyone according as He wills, He distributes special graces among the faithful of every rank.

There is a reference here both to 'hierarchical' and to 'charismatic' gifts. An impressive example of an innovative ministry has recently developed in Zimbabwe, where a significant proportion of the population now suffer from stress, depression and mental illness, and find the 'friendship bench' an invaluable help: the voluntary counsellors are local African grandmothers. Another (global) initiative has been the calling of young people to serve in areas of conflict and unrest as peace agents, promoting not only reconciliation but inner spiritual peace. They are intended to be Christlike models, who bring hope and healing and the message that restraint, forgiveness and dialogue are the best – and usually the only – way to end a situation of hatred and strife. So historic developments of Christian ministry do not necessarily bind today's Church to reproducing only the models that have served well in the past – and it is worth recalling, given the shortage of priests in some areas of the world, that there have been times when 'lay' celebration of the Eucharist might have been feasible. John Moschos recorded in the late 6th century that at Choziba Monastery near Jerusalem a lay brother 'bringing the oblations recited the holy prayer of offering on the way' and 'an angel of the Lord' declared them thereby to have been 'consecrated and made perfect' – but Abba John (later a bishop) stepped in to rule against this happening again (nobody was to learn the prayer unless he had been ordained!).

Young people in Britain sometimes have the opportunity of having a 'gap' year following a course of study in which they can discover more of the wider world and hopefully discover where their own future might lie within it. The Isaianic response is to seek out the 'gaps' – those areas of life which receive insufficient attention from others, but where Christian service (irrespective of its 'sacred' or 'secular' nature) might begin to make a positive difference. The question of vocation is not primarily about being a priest or about entering the religious life (which too often is the exclusive focus of the Church's appeal to young people), but whether we can in some way 'preach good news to the poor, heal the brokenhearted, bring deliverance to the captives, give sight to the blind, or set at liberty them that are bruised'. Jesus proposes that same agenda[11] for himself as well for all the clergy and for every baptized Christian. And let's not forget that, after his youthful years of learning, he worked as a carpenter to support his mother Mary for a decade or more before finally reaching the climactic three years or so of itinerant ministry.

---

[11] In a distinct change of key! In her *Village Diary* (1957) 'Miss Read' recorded the following:

> A new chant to the psalms had us all bogged down, at church today, and I enjoyed watching the different methods of attack. My neighbour in the pew, Mr Lamb from the Post Office, preserved an affronted silence. Mrs Willet gobbled up three-quarters of each phrase on one uniform and neutral note, and then dragged out the last quarter in a nasal whine, somewhere near the printed notes. Mrs Pringle mooed slowly and heavily, a few beats behind the rest but with an awful ponderous emphasis in the wrong places; while the vicar, with a sublime disregard for the organist's accompaniment, sang an entirely different chant altogether, and did it very well.

SCHOLASTIC SHOCKS

An Anglican curacy is intended to set one up for life, and to expose a raw recruit to the stark realities of a parish. This was certainly achieved in Far Cotton, where I served as one of the curates at St Mary's. Very early on I was assigned two unfamiliar duties: the more congenial was to keep an eye on the church bowling club, a group of mainly retired men whose devotion to their outdoor game left them little energy for indoor activities such as church worship (I rapidly discovered that by rolling a long jack I could easily emulate their bowling performance, since few of them had the strength to dispatch their woods to the far end of the green); the other eye-opener was to be a governor at the local infant school, in addition to taking assemblies there and at two other schools in the parish.

Nigel Molesworth at St Custard's

It was at the infant school that I discovered the hazards of attempting to teach young children, who these days if they know anything at all it is their own rights and privileges. A classroom assistant, a kindly middle-aged lady, reported that she had spent some considerable time assisting a recalcitrant five year old boy to spell out words and improve his reading. She said to him: 'Now it's your turn. I've been looking at your book with you for the last twenty minutes, so I'd like you to try reading this page back to me for a change'. 'I shan't', said the boy. 'Well, if you're not going to cooperate at all', came back the helper, 'I shall have to give you a smack'. 'You lay a finger on me', he replied, 'and I'll have the law on you'.

Another report that came before the governors concerned the school's broken television set. This had been smashed by one of the older pupils when he fell through a skylight above it. He had been climbing on the roof with his friends out of hours when this accident occurred, but – fortunately – apart from cuts and bruises had incurred no broken limbs. The headteacher explained to us that, while interviewing the boy's parents she had raised the possibility of legal action being taken against them, only to meet with the riposte that they themselves intended to sue the school for damages to their child on the grounds of negligence in safeguarding against access to the roof. Such is the blame culture of the contemporary world!

A couple of years later, my responsibilities were extended when I was asked to partially take over the timetable of the RE specialist teacher at Mereway Comprehensive School, who was away on a sabbatical for a term in the north of England. Two different classes were involved; the one where the children were approaching 15 years of age proved the more challenging. The problems of inattentiveness were not helped by the modern open-plan lay-out of the school, which had only just been built with special government funds to replace the decaying secondary school much nearer the church. Whereas more traditional classrooms would doubtless have been provided with doors accessed from a corridor, there were virtually no doors at Mereway. Pupils who needed to visit the school office or elsewhere in the building during lesson time were obliged to traverse other classrooms on their way. As they passed through, they would naturally wave to any friends they might see – or even exchange a few words. Equally, those who sat close to the thoroughfare could also look into the classroom beyond, where occasionally a film or a slideshow might be projected. The only mitigating factor was that all classrooms were carpeted, which did help to dampen the tramp of feet and the sounds in adjacent rooms.

There was no serious indiscipline, but an over-relaxed atmosphere not particularly conducive to study. The only student in my more difficult class who paid no attention to distractions was a single-minded Jewess, who was determined to work hard and master every topic. At the opposite extreme was a lad who never even brought a writing implement with him to school; in the end, I called on his father at home and enquired if family circumstances prevented compliance with Mereway's stated requirements. 'O no', he responded, 'look on the mantelpiece. I've a whole jar of biros there what I've nicked from work. He could easily take one of those with him to school'. When I suggested to another lazy pupil that if he didn't gain any qualifications he might find it much harder to get a job on leaving school, his reply was instant: 'My dad never passed any exams. He's a scaffolder and he earns a lot more than what you do'.

A couple of weeks into the term I inquired of the year head what sanctions might be applied to 'under-performing' students. 'Not very much at all, I'm afraid', came his reply. 'You could keep them in for extra work after school, perhaps – but then, they probably wouldn't turn up'. So it was obviously classroom discipline that counted, and here my chief target was by now a boy of Caribbean background with whom I'd thus far avoided any confrontation (not wishing to appear racist). He was generally idle but overstepped the mark one morning by flicking a paper pellet across the room. I checked him very sharply and for some time he concentrated on his work. Towards the end of the lesson, however, he repeated his misdemeanour: I stalked round behind him, calmly reminding him of what I had said earlier. The moment he dropped his defences I clipped him round the head – shame on me! – no doubt a seriously chargeable offence? He immediately jumped to his feet, knocking his desk over in the process and waving his fists in Cassius Clay fashion. 'I'll kill you', he said. The rest of the class perked up and left off whatever they were doing to enjoy the drama. It lasted, however, less than a couple of minutes because as soon as the bell rang for break-time, they abandoned the room and hurtled outside to gain the freedom of the playground. The protest was thus entirely defused – without an audience all resistance was pointless. For the rest of the term, I had no further trouble from this source, and the entire class behaved much better themselves. It also gave them pause for thought: in the next session we had together, I was challenged by another boy. 'I thought vicars weren't supposed to hit people', he said. 'Is that in the Bible?' I asked him. 'Why don't you all open your Bibles and see if you can find a verse that says so?' It was the one and only time that the entire class buried their heads in the Good Book; for five or ten minutes they scanned its pages as they had never done before. Perhaps there is a moral to be drawn from the episode?

The real problem facing this age group, I came to realise, was the fact that their reading ability had declined rather badly since primary school years, when no doubt much encouragement was given by teachers and parents alike to improve their reading skills. Yet having in some degree once 'mastered' the art of reading, they had now effectively stopped reading, and so could really only cope with a few sentences at a time. Hardly any of the class could answer comprehension questions beyond the first paragraph of any text. I suspect similar difficulties might have arisen from declining numeracy as well: thus, in my previous experience as a teacher of mathematics it was not uncommon for pupils to grasp that 'x times x is x squared' but to be quite baffled by '9x times 3x' – simply because they didn't know that '9 times 3 is 27'. (Not long ago, the UK government announced new targets for learning multiplication tables: up to the 12 times table should be mastered by all pupils by the age of eleven. This was supposedly to improve educational standards, but I recalled that in the early 1950s we were meant to reach the same level by the time we left infant school at the age of seven.)

There was only one modification that I made in the programme left behind by the teacher on sabbatical leave. He had provided work sheets on a variety of world religions, but alongside Hinduism, Buddhism, Jainism etc he had included 'cannibalism'. I removed this option for the term, feeling that both the class and myself had enough on our plate already without worrying about whether or not we should eat each other.

When I moved to my first parish as incumbent, it proved easy to establish a pattern of ecumenical involvement in the schools similar to the tried and tested cooperation experienced in Far Cotton. In Irchester, however, there was no comparable secondary school; instead a small residential school for 'girls in need of care' occupied a large old property on the outskirts of the village. The standards of care were certainly very high there; yet although the girls were generally well on the way towards rebuilding their lives in a secure environment, again and again they expressed many fears about the future. It was in fact the height of the Cold War when the prospect of nuclear conflagration was very much in the news. Indeed, it was around this time (in 1980) that the Home Office issued a booklet offering advice on how civilians might best respond to a nuclear attack. In addition, environmental concerns were surfacing and predictions were all too common that very soon natural resources such as oil might run dry. Nor was it only these teenage girls whose anxieties needed addressing; a few doors away from the Vicarage a boy of similar age would often come round and talk through the very same issues.

There was one other unusual facet of educational provision in the same parish. Irchester contained the county council's only official site for gypsies, who included quite a few families with children, hardly any of whom had ever received any formal schooling. The decision was made that they should be sent to schools in the locality; since for most of them this meant starting from scratch, the LEA judged it appropriate that even the nine and ten year olds should attend the first year at the infants school. Hardly surprisingly, problems arose regarding their integration, not least in playground activities where the new arrivals introduced a level of noise and energy that was deemed distinctly intimidating to the existing pupils. By the end of the first term plans were rapidly revised, and a peripatetic teacher was sent to look after the gypsy children in a mobile caravan on their own site.

Some years later we had a very different experience of schools, this time in Lesotho. Discipline wasn't necessarily any easier, as Sarah found when she was engaged part-time to teach music. What disconcerted her most was the way the audience of mothers talked non-stop through the children's performance of songs. Gabriel spent a term in the campus primary school, but we soon felt that the emphasis – all too common in Africa – on rote learning was not really helping him. It came to a head when we found him required to memorise geological terminology that meant absolutely nothing to him, at which point we began our own much more successful 'home school' under the guidance of the Worldwide Educational Service (WES) based in London. Having heard of a visiting missionary who quizzed pupils on their basic biblical knowledge only to be told that 'the disciples crucified Jesus', 'Joseph was the same as God' and 'Jesus worked in God's shop because God was a carpenter', I am rather glad not to have been involved in the religious education programme at the primary school. I did, however, help outdoors: once a week I took a group of youngsters for cricket. They showed considerable aptitude for both batting and bowling but were almost totally uninterested in the idea of fielding. So in the end the programme was discontinued – there were seldom sufficient balls retrieved to make a game possible.

The main eye-opener in Africa concerned children's out-of-school activities. The blunt reality is that most children do not possess manufactured toys, and – except perhaps in certain supermarkets found in the largest towns and cities – there are no shops that sell them. Playthings are therefore predominantly homemade, using whatever raw materials present themselves. In Roma we lived next door to two small African boys and their slightly older sister. Initially we were shocked to find that our waste bin, put out once a week on the university campus to be emptied, was raided by these neighbouring children. They often left debris scattered around on the ground; but it was not necessarily strewn at random, as we came to realise – the spread of tin cans or plastic bottles was sometimes the remnant of some imaginative game. Many children in fact could also work marvels of construction with scraps of wood or metal, which in England might well take pride of place in an end-of-term school display. Woe betide anyone who erected a wire fence in Lesotho – it tended to disappear rather rapidly before re-emerging in multiple model cars or motor bikes, or sometimes as the skeletal form of an animal. Once we purchased the remarkable figure of a boy who pedalled his bicycle as he was pushed along by a steering handle. I recall too a racing car with an impressive sprung chassis, which had likewise been painstakingly put together by an eight year old. So, if schooling for these children had certain limitations, there was certainly no shortage of talent.

In fact, by no means all children were enrolled in schools, whose distribution in a mountainous country was patchy. The lowlands (where Roma was located) were much better served, but elsewhere much depended upon the different Christian missions. In any case, boys of primary school age were liable to be seasonally employed looking after the family's flock of sheep far from home. Even those as young as five or six might find themselves up in the mountain pastures during the summer months, with a sack of maize meal to feed themselves, the shelter of simple huts, and the company of other herdboys. They would of course supplement their diet by catching mice and small birds, and were adept at firing catapults for this purpose. A tragic side-effect was the steady erosion of wild-life, which along with the growing population's reliance upon trees and shrubs for their fuel led to increasing barrenness of the landscape. In turn, the decimation of mountainous vegetation meant that when it rained torrentially (as it often did), the waters would descend rapidly to flood the lowland valleys and wash away more of the topsoil, leaving only eroded 'dongas' no longer capable of supporting the rich harvests of earlier years when the region was known as 'the bread basket' of South Africa. And alas! the dongas steadily accumulated the detritus of modern civilisation viz. the multitude of plastic wrappings and containers that seem to be unavoidable in the Age of Shopping. Subsistence farmers such as the Basotho needed much help in adjusting to the new ways of the world. It was the womenfolk especially who bore most of their impact, since many of the men worked away from home in the South African mines. Apart from the contribution that better education might make, we sometimes wondered why the university in Roma failed to offer courses that might promote or enhance employment opportunities within the kingdom of Lesotho itself – where, by contrast, even though every year a dozen or more students graduated in chemistry, only one or two lucky ones might then find a job, usually in a local brewery.

When we returned to England, to the parish of West Monkton in Somerset, our African experiences certainly broadened the scope of school assemblies to which I contributed. We had a church primary school and also a large comprehensive school (both situated in the same cul-de-sac, which resulted in much traffic congestion at the start and finish of each school day). Geoff Bowling was the warm-hearted Methodist in charge of the primary school, whose gifts as a teacher became steadily overshadowed by the daily deluge of paperwork issued by the Department of Education. He retired early from the post and died soon afterwards – but not before we had shared his delight in country dancing, and his annual maypole celebration. The latter engaged all the children in slowly encircling the pole with their ribbons, which they wove in and out;

it was not really a spectator sport until one of the infants made a false move, at which point the entanglements became hilariously engrossing to all of us who looked on.

At the secondary school, we covered a wide range of topics in assemblies, including the drug scene, consumerism, career choices, Third World realities, and even more ambitiously plumbed the mysteries of the universe; as the staff took a relaxed approach to these gatherings (unlike the regimentation at the Anglican-R.C. St Augustine's School further towards town which I visited regularly) the students were generally attentive and receptive. In my role as Director of Ordinands I also attended other secondary schools across the county to engage in their annual career conferences. I learnt very early on that the church stall needed to be in the main arena, and not shut away in a separate classroom; the best location was next to the usually crowded army display, since pressure of numbers there often led to interesting conversations with those awaiting their turn with the military. As always, my intent was to stretch people's ideas and to broaden their horizons; the purpose was not to recruit vicars per se, but to suggest that experiences such as a gap year working in Africa or Asia with a reputable agency might prove extremely valuable, if not actually life-changing. In fact, we had several who subsequently offered to serve in Christian ministry as a result of time spent in this way. It was quite common for pupils in their GCSE year to complete a questionnaire about their personal abilities and leanings, which would then be returned by a careers agency offering ideas for their individual futures. Anyone who indicated that they 'liked working with people' would invariably be pointed to a career as a psychologist (no mention of Christian ministry ever appeared): was it a mere coincidence that the agency was run by a team of psychologists?

Back in Africa, the four years spent teaching in Malawi didn't include any time working in schools at all. We heard regular reports, however, from a missionary colleague Anne who had travelled out with us on the same flight from England to teach RE in the diocese's leading secondary school at Malosa, where she was in effect the school chaplain as well. We learnt that the President of Malawi, Bakili Maluzi, who had succeeded the long-time dictator Hastings Banda, had been educated at Malosa. When he took office, his school record would naturally have attracted considerable media attention; but his agents got there first – they insisted on removing Bakili's every trace from the school files. Could one conclude that he was a less than satisfactory pupil? We were never quite sure about Anne herself, and whether some of the difficulties she described might not have been of her own making. On the journey out, before we even left Heathrow, she disappeared from the departure lounge to buy a coffee and stayed away so long that she nearly missed the flight. When we reached Lilongwe, where we needed to change planes for the internal flight down to Blantyre, she performed a similar trick; this time she craved a bottle of Fanta but had to change money into the local kwachas first. By the time her thirst was assuaged, the second leg of the journey was fully booked, necessitating her further wait in the airport before another flight was available. Again, after a couple of years she had a new cooker installed in her bungalow at school and decided to throw a party to mark the occasion. It went off with quite a bang – that is, she had thought her cooker was all-electric, whereas the oven itself worked off gas; after being turned on, supposedly to heat some mince pies, it was not actually lit, and eventually exploded with such force that poor Anne was knocked to the ground. We seldom visited her school ourselves but did observe a mountain of uneaten cooked maizemeal steadily accumulating just outside its kitchen quarters: this must surely have attracted rodents by the score. For the first time in my life I began to think that stringent health and safety regulations might not be such a bad idea after all.

The friend we admired most in Zomba was Diane, a young Presbyterian from Northern Ireland, who began by working with our theological students' families and later branched north where she set up a chain of 'early education schooling opportunities'. After ten years' devoted work in Malawi, she then transferred to continue this work in Zambia. We were indeed aware of much greater enthusiasm for education in Central Africa than was often exhibited in England. The one item for which children badgered passers-by in the street was a pencil or a biro (seldom money) so that they could continue their school work. Exam successes meant a lot, unfortunately to the extent that – as our near neighbour Mike Nkhoma, who worked for the Malawi Examination Board often reminded us – cheating in one form or another was all too rife. There was a related risk too with a minority of our own students: while it is true that a period of formation is an opportunity for testing one's vocation, sometimes resulting in a few (for good reason) abandoning their course altogether, there were occasionally others who, after accepting the free education offered by the churches, would acquire a diploma or a degree and then plunge straight into a secular occupation as soon as they had graduated.

After leaving Malawi I also left the Anglican Church, although it was not the easiest of options. On becoming a Catholic, I faced the prospect of at least a year's unemployment before (hopefully) I could be ordained into the Catholic priesthood. I was fortunate therefore in securing successive temporary posts to teach RE, firstly for two terms at Sherborne School, followed by another two at Sherborne Girls' School. There were marked differences between these establishments, which may be summarised as follows:

- In the staff common room at Sherborne School there was always a wide variety of tea, coffee, spring water, biscuits, sometimes fruit; whereas at the Girls' School, very limited supplies appeared on a Monday morning, and were supposed to last for the entire week (very often they were hidden away in a locker, and invariably the biscuits ran out).
- A similar contrast was noticeable in the classrooms. IT equipment, including projectors, was installed in most of the classrooms at Sherborne School, but was woefully inadequate at the Girls' School. Boys, but certainly not girls at that stage, were allowed to bring their own laptops into class. (This was a mixed blessing, since some boys viewed rather undesirable material of their own choosing during lessons unless strict vigilance was exercised: when their computer screens started to attract wider attention, it was obvious what was going on!)
- The majority of boys were late in handing in their work; when challenged, they would proffer excuses such as 'the house printer broke down' or 'surely you got my email attachment?' For the first two weeks I was inclined to believe them, but thereafter I knew they were lying to their back teeth and hadn't even started the assignment. By contrast, nearly every girl was punctilious in delivering her work; those who failed seemed genuinely heart-broken and wept profusely.
- All this changed dramatically, however, in the sixth form. Boys perked up and showed immense interest in the broad sweep of world affairs and were generally keen to engage with big issues of the day. Girls were quite different; they switched off from studies such as RE which were non-examination subjects to focus almost exclusively on their personal appearance. Not being equipped to discuss the latest fashions or hairstyles, I lost their attention.
- Staff attitudes were far more relaxed among male teachers. There was, for example, discussion in Sherborne School about who should become the new head of the RE department. The obvious choice was a zealous lady who wanted to turn things around and re-organise the curriculum, but her male colleagues frankly preferred their existing laid-back, less demanding habits and opted for one of their own kind who would keep things just as they were. In the Girls' School I had an end-of-term report returned to me which failed to meet the high standards of grammar required by the headmistress (I had begun a sentence with the word 'But'). There was also an embarrassing occasion during an overhead thunderstorm when the girls I was teaching at

the time begged to be allowed shelter under their desks. Naturally I concurred; but, just as they had taken refuge, in walked the headmistress, who looked distinctly unimpressed.

- Broadly speaking, the boys would leave school with a mere smattering of notions to do with comparative religion. The girls would be much better grounded in Christian principles, with a working knowledge of at least one Gospel and maybe a little moral idealism. (I recall one boy who could never grasp why Jesus never featured in the Old Testament, and many – indoctrinated by Dan Brown [12] – who were convinced that the New Testament was a fabric of lies.)

Upon ordination the bishop specifically charged me to maintain good links with all the schools in and around Sherborne, which was very much an educational centre: apart from the two schools already mentioned, there was a Church of England secondary school and a Catholic boarding school. Every other year I steered a confirmation group from each of the schools where I had taught. We met in the library at Sherborne School, and in the upstairs drawing room of the one of the boarding houses at the Girls' School. It was at the latter that I sinned yet again. Our earlier

---

[12] Dan Brown opened up a can of worms that infected many others as well. Not only did he excite widespread interest in Mary Magdalene, but managed to create the illusion that later apocryphal gospels and similar writings were full of genuine historical reminiscences. A free-for-all culture spread which retold 'the true story' of Jesus and his followers. In recent years I have received copies of publications from amateur exegetes (whose names coincidentally began with the same letter B – indicating a **B**rownian virus?) as follows: (1) Mary Magdalene spent the rest of her life living in a cave in Provence, where eventually she was tracked down by St Mark. Having learnt what really happened from this authentic witness, he then composed the Fourth Gospel. MM appears in it in more than one guise – she was the bride at Cana of Galilee, but then worked her way through several husbands to become the woman at the well in Samaria. (2) Contrary to the general opinion that MM came from Magdala, there is actually no such place; the word 'Magdalene' derives from a Hebrew root suggesting a tower or pillar of strength. As such she was unpopular with male chauvinists like SS Paul and Luke, the latter denigrating her reputation by mentioning her psychiatric disorder (an infestation by seven demons). Since in much later texts (although the Gospel of Mary is dated from the "early 1st century") Mary, the mother of Jesus, is highly exalted and seen as a tower of strength, it follows that MM is actually the same person – the BVM or (as the author prefers) "the Great Mary". I was a little puzzled as to why St Luke should rate her so highly in his birth narrative, but later disclose her severe mental disorder? (3) Much more simply, my last correspondent was proud to have discovered that the Beloved Disciple in St John's Gospel was none other than the anonymous owner of the Upper Room in Jerusalem, scene of the Last Supper, and the true author of that Gospel. Clearly a dark horse, he seems to have been previously unknown to the other disciples, whose clue to finding him was "a man carrying a jar of water", but he was modest enough not to mention that the famous meal took place on his own premises.

meetings had taken place in the late winter, but as the days lengthened it was possible to catch a glimpse outside while I waited for the girls to assemble. A door gave access to a platform whence I could view the garden. As I stood there, bells rang out and pupils streamed out into the garden. This struck me as slightly odd until I realised that a fire drill was in motion. Two or three minutes later the horrid truth dawned that it was I who had set it off – the door by which I had emerged was in truth a fire door giving access to an emergency flight of steps. I recall that my group of Catholic girls then rallied in my defence, so all was not lost. In fact, they – as indeed every other confirmation group I led in the school – were invited to present a morning assembly, which they did very creditably.

As for the Catholic school at Lewiston, I did spend a little time teaching there one term when staff were in short supply. It was quite different from the hi-tech experience of Sherborne School and the zealous mindset at the Girls' School. Most problematic of all was gaining access to the buildings in a regime ruled by keypads and yet more CRB checks. Yet when I functioned there later as their 'visiting chaplain', relationships were much easier and staff proved to be very helpful. (There was, however, a continuing problem with gaining access. Unlike schooldays, when one of the secretaries would open the main door for me, on Sunday mornings they were not on duty. Instead, I usually had to go round to the back of the kitchens, knock on a window, and then beg to be admitted. Otherwise it was impossible to prepare the chapel in time.)

As chaplain I had the full support of the new head of music, who was a fine musician keen to develop worship on both Sundays and weekdays. My regular weekday talk inevitably had to be different in style from the Sunday homily (attended by parents and other visitors as well), so I often looked then to the lives of individual saints for inspiration. The one bizarre moment of each year came during the Speech Day mass, when outgoing prefects stripped off their black gowns which their successors then took up. 'Stripped off' says it all, as underneath the gowns the leavers were dressed in all their finery, which was (shall we discreetly say) 'minimalist'.

Only once was I invited to the Anglican secondary school (The Gryphon), for an assembly in Christian Aid week when they hoped I would speak about life in Africa. I duly reported to the school office, who gave me a visitor's badge and asked me to wait in a small room nearby until a member of staff came to collect me. Some minutes passed, and it became clear that children were flocking into the school hall. Then all went quiet, and I prepared to be summoned. But nothing happened – so I quickly returned to the office to check that I hadn't misunderstood my instructions. They reassured me that very soon someone would appear. Time continued to pass as I waited, and then I heard the sound of many children re-emerging from the hall. As the assembly was clearly over, I sought further advice in the office. They promised someone would ring up later in the day. And that evening the call came through, from the teacher who had invited me. She had been away at a clinic during the day, leaving the assembly in the capable hands (as she thought) of a colleague. He had not been fully in the picture, however, as to whom he might expect as speaker. When the children were with him in the hall, a minister from Yeovil had burst upon the stage ready to give his talk, so naturally all seemed to fit into place. It was only afterwards when the office reported my bewilderment that checks were made. The intrusive speaker was apparently an Elim Pentecostalist who had visited the school on a previous occasion and was shortly due to go there again – only he had muddled his dates. Rushing into the school at the last minute, he had omitted the formalities required of visitors and had gone straight to the hall. The apologies I received were profuse: I was assured another invitation would be forthcoming (but it never was). The best laid plans of mice and men, as Robbie Burns once put it…

So much for safeguarding procedures!

Home-schooling Samuel *aged 8*

Why do you think the author (of The Wind in the Willows) repeats "scraped and scratched and scrabbled"?

Samuel's 1st answer:
I reckon the author probably repeated this phrase be cause his wife had just told him dinner was ready, so he thought he'd annoy her by being slow and re-writing what he'd just written.

Samuel's 2nd answer:
OK I'll write what the teacher wants me to write … Because Mole was doing it for longer.

CHRISTIAN COACHLOADS

*Little Bo-Peep has lost her sheep,
and cannot tell where to find them.*

One of the apparent perks of being a parish priest is being able to disappear from the scene for two or three weeks at a time, and *not* call it a holiday. The secret is, to lead a pilgrimage. Although this may take one to far-off desirable destinations, the spiritual nature of the exercise enables it to be seen as work rather than leisure. And indeed so it is, if one is responsible for the well-being of maybe twenty, thirty or forty pilgrims no longer as young as they used to be, some of whom are likely to have well-formed, if not dogmatic, views about their own needs and priorities.

The first time I led a party abroad was to Oberammagau in 1980. Disaster nearly struck when we arrived at Ostend in the early hours of the morning. Our Belgian coach failed to meet us. The ferry terminal cafe was closed, as was our tour company's office back in England. Fortunately the weather was dry so I led 45 people for a short stroll on the beach to enjoy the breaking dawn, reassuring them all the time that we were on the early side. I had no other plan in mind except to pray for a divine rescue operation. This of course is where it pays for the tour leader to be in holy orders: my prayers were answered within the hour. The coach driver was apologetic. He'd stopped in a lay-by and fallen asleep, which was obviously much better than having a nap later while cruising at 70 mph on an autobahn with passengers onboard. So, all was well, allowing us to reach Ulm for a scheduled overnight stop.

Now Ulm has a wonderful Gothic minster with the highest spire in the world, but the driver's own must-see recommendation was a shop down a side street offering amazing discounts on cigarettes and chocolates. Judging by some of the items members of our group took home later, I suspect the coach driver knew his customers better than I did. Here in Ulm two hitherto unnoticed pilgrims first made their mark. They were elderly ladies travelling together, known as Minnie and Mona. Mona's parents had evidently consulted a clairvoyant about her name, and the evidence suggested she was spot on. Mona amply lived up to her name, with Minnie giving her whatever support was needed. Their principal concern was the size, shape, location, amenities and outlook of their hotel accommodation. A large en-suite room was required near the lift, with air-conditioning, a view over the garden, no kitchen smells, and no noise from elsewhere in the building or from the street outside – and it must certainly be in no way inferior to anyone else's room. I managed to pacify the two of them in Ulm, while remaining blissfully ignorant of the battles yet to come over their dining arrangements, heated plates, size of portions and speed of service.

These two, by the way, also claimed to have weak bladders, and so demanded rather more comfort stops on the journey than had been allocated. For example, on our return trip through Germany we had to pull in at a service station solely for their benefit. I specified five minutes in which to do the necessary, hoping that we might on our way again after perhaps ten. When nearly half an hour had elapsed, a search party set out. They were discovered sitting in a dining area enjoying the first course of a meal, with more to come. The news was not popular, and the challenge now was to persuade the other passengers not to abandon them to their fate. We should take to heart the message of the Passion Play, I suggested, and try to curb our baser instincts. And be back on the coach within 20 minutes, or else.

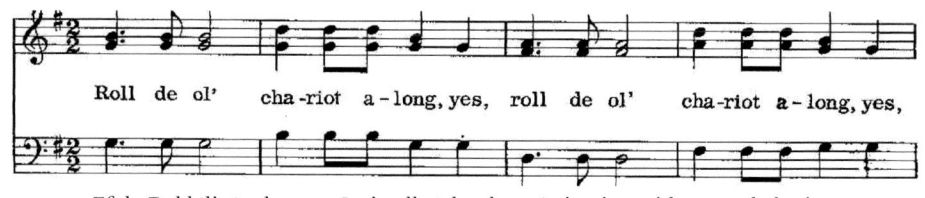

Roll de ol' cha-riot a-long, yes, roll de ol' cha-riot a-long, yes,
Ef de Debbil's in de way, Jus' roll right ober, An' yo' mus' hang on behin'.

Two years later came a visit to the Holy Land – Galilee first, then further south. There was quite a contrast between the Israeli run hotel in Tiberias – efficient but impersonal – and the warm friendly Arab establishment in East Jerusalem where not quite everything worked. The difficulty here was that there were no spare rooms, so when complaints started to mount up, the ever-helpful management had only one option – to re-allocate those already in use. This proved remarkably successful. Thus, the person with a room where the toilet didn't flush very well was more than happy to go to another room with a functioning toilet but an inferior view. The person they displaced there found themselves with a lovely view but a wardrobe whose door kept falling off. Despite this being a standard-sized room, its previous occupant was pleased with the smaller room where she now found herself because of its vastly superior wardrobe. Whereas the person in the small room now got a much bigger room and didn't at all mind the air conditioning not working very effectively. Whereas there was yet another complainant for whom good air conditioning was essential, but (being a man on his own) who couldn't care less about the toilet flush.

I retain fond memories of the genial and ever-obliging Arab manager who had mastered the difficult art of keeping everyone happy. He'd have made an excellent parish priest. He was also very good to me, because with every complaint he offered me a free drink, hence so I well-compensated for the various rumblings and grumblings, indeed I came to see them in a more positive light. On our last evening he approached me during dinner and told me that the wine at our table was 'on the house'. I was puzzled because I wasn't aware that anything had gone wrong: surely a catch somewhere? After dinner the manager had a further word in my ear: 'I wonder if you could do me a little favour?' 'Well, of course,' I said, 'if I can'. 'Would you like to write a little testimonial for this hotel'. I thought rapidly: we've enjoyed our time here, the staff are helpful, the cuisine is superb – why spoil it for anyone else? So I said, 'What kind of wording would be appropriate, do you think?' Once again he was on the ball. 'Something like this perhaps: I thoroughly recommend this excellent establishment, with its first-rate cooking, comfortable rooms, and every attention given to the residents'. 'You write it,' I said, 'I'll sign it'.

The year was then 1982, and tourists weren't over-abundant because of the political tensions. As we pulled up outside the Old City for the first time there was the sound of gunfire. Alarm and despondency rippled through the coach. 'I think they are just practising,' announced our Israeli state guide. The driver muttered a different opinion as I passed him getting off: 'I think this means trouble'. Sure enough, two days later we narrowly missed a bomb attack on the conical hill (the Herodian) near Bethlehem. In any case, we didn't by now regard our guide too highly, since his fund of knowledge had obvious limitations. He applied a basic formula to many of the sites we visited. 'This is where the Holy Family stayed,' he said, 'on their way from A to B,' displaying considerable ingenuity filling in the blanks each time. I have to say, on a return visit 10 years later we had a guide who was incredibly well informed.

One doesn't, of course, want a guide who tells you everything (including the exact dimensions of buildings, which one can see for oneself), or boredom can set in. On a visit to Althorp House, long before Princess D appeared on the scene, group tours were *de rigueur* and in the Long Gallery - containing nothing but portraits of all the Earls Spencer since the time of Adam - we were inflicted with a detailed biography of each and every one of them. When we'd reached something like the 15th Earl I tried to escape to the tea room but was severely rebuked for my audacity.

At least on foreign soil some amusement can be gained by listening to curious English pronunciations, such as a French guide's repeated reference to a leading character named Wiggly who once resided in Avignon's Papal Palace. Eventually I realised that this was her version of Gregory, better known as a Pope, and it struck me then that if a Pope of our own day were to take the name Wiggly it might work wonders for the Catholic church.

It was in the later 80s and in the 90s that I was recruited by InterChurch Travel as a brochure leader every couple of years. Initially they were a subsidiary of Thomas Cook, but were then taken over by Saga, who had a slightly different approach. When I led an ICT group in 1988 to Medjugorje in what was then pre-war Yugoslavia, we met up at Heathrow, and I introduced myself and discovered who everyone was (mainly Catholics from Sunderland). Having said what a wonderful time lay ahead, I was then required to ask each person the following: 'In the unforeseen event of your death on this trip, would you like to be buried abroad or would you prefer to have your body brought back to the UK?' I never felt this was altogether the best way to foster a happy band of pilgrims, so I was relieved that Saga later dropped the procedure. It did however nearly come into its own just before the end of that 1988 tour (ever the leader's care-free holiday!). I was getting ready for bed, when there was a knock on the door, and I was told that Mrs So-and-so had died in the lift. It was a State Registered Nurse in the party who'd attended to her, so the report sounded quite authoritative. However, by the time I got to the lift, Mrs So-and-so had miraculously risen from the dead, which was a great relief, and the diagnosis had changed to an acute stomach pain (which eventually subsided). Had it been more serious, arrangements for Mrs So-and-so to stay on and get home later would have been necessary; as it was, a communist lady doctor examined her and threatened me with detention if I interrupted her a second time!

Having already raised our spiritual composure in Medjugorje itself, we surmounted this set-back with equanimity. Compared with difficulties experienced earlier it seemed a minor affair. Our guest house in Medjugorje may or may not have been unique, but it probably wouldn't have passed a building inspection in the UK – and it certainly tested our faith to the limit. For example, when one of our party opened their bedroom window, it disappeared entirely from view and was never seen again: it crashed to the ground below. In my room, there was a water closet immediately adjacent to the bed; this was very convenient; but I could only afford to flush it once a day, as it then flooded the entire bedroom floor. However, the fact that none of the party complained should really have been reported to the Vatican, because it lends considerable weight to the spiritual validity of the whole Medjugorje experience, offsetting sceptical views that it is now but a commercial enterprise promoted by those with financial stakes in its success.

Our heightened faith also gave us the confidence collectively to tackle a later problem in Dubrovnik, where the communist authorities refused to allow any religious activity on hotel premises, other than in one's bedroom. Mine seemed a small room; but it was larger than a standard British telephone kiosk into which a record 22 people once fitted. Even so I hadn't anticipated twice that number actually being accommodated there for our early morning service, including a group of Americans staying in the same hotel. It was indeed a crowning triumph of faith, hope and charity, in which we felt a common bond with persecuted Christians down the ages. My bedroom was at once a catacomb, a desert cave and a priest's hiding hole.

When Saga soon afterwards took control of the company, their main input was a more professional annual training day for tour leaders. We met in Swindon one year with the Saga claims manager, who advised us chiefly on what not to do. 'Someone in the party's cut their finger, you offer a piece of elastoplast – well, don't,' he said. 'They may be allergic to plasters, they get ill, they sue the company – you don't believe me? – I'm the claims manager, I see it every day'. Or, 'someone's got a headache, you give them an aspirin – well, don't – they may be allergic to aspirin, they get have a reaction, they sue the company, I'm the claims manager, believe me I see it every day'. Or, most unChristianly of all, 'they're getting off the coach, you stand by the exit and give them a hand down – don't,' he said, 'they may stumble a bit, they may even fall, they blame you, they sue the company, I'm the claims manager, I know what the consequences can be, I see it every day'. So, someone then popped the question, 'What about the Good Samaritan?' 'In my book,' says the claims manager, 'it was the priest and the Levite passing by on the other side who did exactly the right thing'.

Nevertheless, the tour leader does try to be helpful. I remember visiting Mont St Michael in Brittany with a group one year when I climbed up the stairs in advance to get the tickets. I then stood facing down the stairwell with the visitors streaming up towards me and thus was able to hand tickets to the members of our party as they arrived. A Japanese lady not in our group must have thought I was an official of some kind and asked me if this was where people had to pay. 'Yes', I said, 'it's ten francs each at the booth just there, and half-price for your little girl'. (There was a tiny person standing alongside her.) This proved to be one of the more embarrassing moments in my life, because she then said, 'That's not my little girl, that's my husband'.

The other particularly untoward event on that tour to Abbeys and Cathedrals of Northern France was getting mugged on the metro in Paris. But there's always a silver lining in the cloud: I now know from reporting the event that police stations in central Paris are virtually indistinguishable from taxi cab offices and that French policemen have adopted a casual dress code and the habit of lolling on duty with their feet on the counter. They have a wonderful sense of humour too; when I reported losing 400 euros, the immediate response was non-stop hilarity. I learnt the same evening that two other members of the party had also been assaulted by purse snatchers, whom one suspects may even have been off-duty policemen anyway. A day later a lady was left behind at a chateau in the Loire valley when I miscounted numbers getting on the coach, and she probably found that particularly memorable; what rankled most was that no one had missed her. We were actually lucky never to lose an elderly gent called Francis, who invariably wandered off on his own and forgot when and where we were meeting up. In the end, my wife became his chaperone, which just shows how useful a clergy spouse can be on these occasions. Francis was one of those slightly annoying people who've made a minute study of all the guide books and knows of (say) a little chapel just off the route which is 'well worth a detour'. He never appreciated that the itinerary is invariably the subject of a detailed contract between the coach company and the tour operator, leaving little scope for ad hoc improvements. Nor did he appreciate that the first duty of a guide is to keep his party entertained, which allows him (or her) a certain poetic licence. A guide likes to be free to embroider his account now and again, and doesn't care for pedantic students to interrupt his (or her) flow with factual corrections.

Every tour party, like every church congregation, has its Monas and its Francises; but I hadn't bargained to be in France with a young couple called Dave and Susan. They were really nice people, but they were *vegetarians*. Now, some of my best friends (as they say) are vegetarians and it's an excellent thing to be. But not, please, in France. They don't understand the concept. At every hotel I had to explain what this meant, and evidently my French wasn't quite up to it. Even after lengthy requests and explanations the waiters would still bring Dave and Susan plates groaning with meat, and they would then have to use vivid body language to wave it away. The plates would disappear into the kitchen and return – with a large vacant space where the meat had been. Only once did a hotel establishment manage to come up with an alternative vegetarian dish.

In complete contrast was a genial American called Ray, a retired Methodist minister from Kansas City. Ray had one object, and one only, in mind. The Holy Grail for which he searched the length and breadth of Northern France was a *hamburger* as good as those he enjoyed in Kansas City. He went home a disappointed man, but as one of his fellow-citizens put it, 'What kind of guy crosses the Atlantic for the sake of a hamburger?' The only compensation he had was in Laon, where he cut out the Gothic cathedral in favour of a large knickerbocker glory at a market café.

Most people do of course pursue their own quests on these pilgrimages. There were a few who came to Oberammagau in 1980 chiefly to buy Bavarian wood-carvings, of which there is a more than ample supply (I don't think shops sell anything else). The first time I went to Lourdes back in 1965 I confess it was really to buy toothpaste, which I then discovered is simply not to be had anywhere near the central zone. I had to settle for a bottle of holy water, which was probably just as good, if not better. On a visit to the seven churches of Asia Minor in the mid-1990s we had a youngish lady (Sylvia) who had the more laudable aim of walking in the very footsteps of the saints who've gone before. She took this to extremes by running a circuit of the stadium in Colossae (or was it Laodicea?), simply to identify herself with St Paul who 'fought the good fight', who 'finished the race', and who 'kept the faith'.

As a one-time civilian naval chaplain I know too that the annual services pilgrimage to Lourdes has a huge impact on at least some of those who go there. It's the companionship en route, the aura of faith and the entire reversal of human values when you arrive that makes a lasting impression. At Lourdes, the first are last and the last first. The sick and the handicapped are always at the front, with the fit and healthy ministering to them. And alongside all those who go on pilgrimages and tours for a holiday, there are some who are searching for God and some who unexpectedly find him. There was a Yorkshire TV cameraman called Geoff who came with us to Medjugorje who'd failed (as it seemed to him) to find God in his local church, and he thought he might find him in a very special place where others had communed with him. I think his quest was fruitful, and it made it personally rewarding for me to have led him there.

For myself, I still treasure a small lump of rock I once collected from the shores of the Sea of Galilee. You can buy packets of Holy Land soil in the souks of Jerusalem, and probably bottles of Holy Land air; but this was the real thing and it was free. I like to think that maybe Jesus himself once stepped ashore on this stone –and even if he didn't, my faith is re-awakened each morning when I see it. So I believe such spiritual adventures (or pilgrimages), which enable different expressions of devotion to be experienced, can often be helpful. Rowan Williams once described the priest as 'a traveller', whose task is to discover the varied traditions of the church over the two thousand years of its history, to learn too of the rich treasures of contemporary

Christian communities wherever in the world they may be based, and then to share these gifts and insights with his own people.

As a chaplain for the Apostleship of the Sea, I learnt that P&O Cruises have espoused a related philosophy. In the immortal words of Loretta, one of their tour managers, 'What you're all looking for is probably somethin' a lil' bit dif'rent'. Churches, however, weren't seriously on her agenda: 'We'll see a few as we drive along, but I know you can 'ave too much of that sort of thing, so we'll just tell you on the coach what's inside. That way we'll get to the viewpoint an' the coffee shop a bi' quicker. As you know, it's the cakes an' the pastries I look forward to – an' on this trip we might even get a wine-tasting!' The less mobile at any rate were well served, although Francis Kilvert might not have approved:

> If there is one thing more hateful than another it is being told what to admire and having objects pointed out to one with a stick. Of all noxious animals too the most noxious is a tourist. And of all tourists the most vulgar, illbred, offensive and loathsome is the British tourist.

So in terms of my own outings abroad, I suppose I could say, '*They* are tourists and *you* perhaps are visitors, but *we* are pilgrims'. Yet I still confess to a weakness for Loretta's cakes and coffee shops… and it is quite fun buying oriental rugs for timid elderly ladies in Eastern souks… Once I even bought a rug for myself. On entering the shop on the eve of our departure, I laid my cards on the table and said: 'I've just fifty pounds left to spend'. I was told that the rug I admired was priced at 300 dollars – 'But I'm English, not American', I protested. 'O then it's just 100 pounds to you'. 'I've only got half that'. 'Let's say we make it sixty – my father was once in the British army, you see'. 'No good, that's still too much'. 'Then I give it to you', he said. He then wrapped it and handed it over; but as I reached the door I thought it prudent to verify it really was a gift. 'OK. I take your fifty', came the swift reply – taken to the wire, one might say!

Outings back home are not nearly such fun. And here a final caveat is appropriate: beware of sitting on a coach with nine year old Brownies – they have a repertoire of songs that would shock even a coachload of drunken rugby fans. Equally, never attempt to find out what children enjoyed most – after visiting Coventry Cathedral and Warwick Castle, the favourite spectacle nevertheless turned out to be 'going round and round in the multi-storey carpark'.

SINK or SWIM

A few months after moving to my first parish, the local undertaker asked me how I was settling in and how I liked it there. He'd been in residence for decades, doubling up as a cabinet maker. There wasn't much he didn't know about the village, and he was generally helpful in alerting me to the intricate marital web that seemed to connect more than half the population with each other. Thus, one had to guard one's tongue, as gossip travelled with the speed of light. So I replied cautiously, 'Yes, we're fine. The people here seem very nice'. His response was unexpected, although on reflection it perhaps bore the hallmark of truth. 'They're not, you know', he said. I didn't press for details, but little by little discovered he was quite a wise old bird.

I also came to realise that my predecessor hadn't always got on with his parishioners; indeed, it was reported that some folk crossed the road when they saw him coming. Surprisingly, his wife (Diana) was also avoided; and we heard reports that sometimes she herself avoided callers at the vicarage door by crawling out of her front room and down the hall passage on hands and knees, in order to escape being seen. She was unaware that this mode of transport left her bottom bobbing up and down within the caller's line of sight.

We soon discovered ourselves from the condition of the vicarage that she was a lady with idiosyncratic ideas. The kitchen, for example, was entirely covered with bright blue paint, which she explained as the ultimate deterrent to all forms of insect life. Upstairs she had insisted (when the house was built in the 1960s) that bedrooms should be equipped with fireplaces and chimneys. This was not, we gathered, for the homely lighting of fires: indeed, none of them had ever been used. Rather, it was to provide a form of bedroom ventilation that avoided the opening of any windows, presumably to keep any flies from entering. The garden was almost entirely neglected (as was the church itself, with rusting lawn-mowers, battered chicken-wire, chipped flower vases, spider-infested watering cans, crumbling oasis, and yellowing magazines lurking on and under pews and filling the base of the tower). Its redeeming feature was a small bed of choice roses, which had been planted in an area covered with blue plastic; this no doubt inhibited both weeds and aphids simultaneously.

We found it necessary to invest initially in a couple of goats, whose task was to eat their way through the remaining undergrowth, although we discovered they had distinct preferences. Top of their list were the vegetables we had planted, then roses and other flowers in bloom, grass if all else failed, but certainly not any weeds. As we were newcomers to the village, their simultaneous advent made us even more newsworthy, attracting children on their way home from school to look over the garden wall. Diana had hardly set out to woo the public any more than her husband had. It was said of her that she would never take her place in any village shopping queue, because, as the first lady of the parish, she expected deference from everyone else, and would go at once to the counter to demand immediate attention.

I recall here the advice I heard from the Mothers Union worker in Lesotho, who was asked by our seminarians what was expected of their wives. 'She's an intermediary', was the reply. 'For example, someone comes to the rectory door and asks to see the priest. His wife might need to say, "O maybe tomorrow would be better – he won't be in such a bad mood by then."' If only Diana had spent time in Africa, she might have gained a humbler appreciation of her own status. A retired bishop of Mashonaland once spoke of an incident when his land-rover had become engulfed in mud half a mile from the church he was visiting. Word of his delay spread rapidly, and soon an army of uniformed Mothers Union members came marching to his rescue. They were traditionally-built ladies and had no difficulty in hoisting the vehicle out of the mud and bearing it triumphantly aloft in procession to the church. They insisted the bishop resumed his seat inside – but when his wife attempted to clamber in as well, she was firmly told to get out and walk. Even Mrs Proudie would have met her match here.

Diana's husband Ambrose had forthright views of his own. His major clash seems to have been with the bingo hall just beyond the church, at a time when bingo was seemingly a much more popular attraction. Ambrose viewed it as a rival temple, and matters were made worse by the fact that its proprietor lived immediately next door to the church in a house with gold bath taps. When I first saw the seemingly oriental name of this dwelling, I thought the family must be Asians, until I discovered that 'Chrispatjan' was merely a curious amalgam of the three daughters' names. (It was a more imaginative name than a parishioner's house elsewhere labelled 'Ivahome', not to mention the many variations I encountered on the theme 'Pleasant View', whose very profusion must at times confuse the postman. The African proclivity for 'Tarmac View' has at least some originality.) Despite the lucrative returns on bingo, the psalmist himself would not have been deceived: 'Though the wicked sprout like grass', he said, 'and all evildoers flourish, they are doomed to destruction for ever'. This was Ambrose's own opinion, which he didn't hesitate to make public. A headline appeared in the local paper: 'Vicar says, Bingo is a game for morons'. I don't suggest that's entirely incorrect in its assessment (the occasional game can be fun), but maybe it's a little unwise to advertise one's opinions so freely?

I can't be sure how soon I made contact with the bingo merchant's family, but I think it was on my first visit to their house that one of the daughters indicated she would like to be married in church. In the course of our preparation I discovered that she had never been baptised, and after suitable discussion she started to attend church. She was actually keen to be confirmed as well, which meant no less than three ceremonies were in view. To my surprise her father attended all of them. To my delight he also made a handsome donation each time, placing a large denomination bank note (£50) in the collection plate. I brushed aside the thought that such gifts might be considered ill-gotten gains (or at least exploitation of the feeble-minded) and fantasized instead about the possibility of a further ceremony. Perhaps this same daughter could become some sort of deaconess one day?

It soon transpired that the demand for organised bingo was rapidly decreasing, and it was not long before the hall in which it was held opened its doors for the last time. Eventually it found alternative use as the centre for a thriving youth club, thanks (curiously) to a community service order. An estate agent had been convicted of fraud, and on being handed a hundred hours of unpaid work within the village he threw himself wholeheartedly into starting a village youth club from scratch. He actually continued helping it long after his service order had been spent.

In marked contrast, there were a couple of times when I accepted teenagers for community service in the churchyard: once in a supervised group, and subsequently an isolated individual whom I had to supervise myself. The latter was docile enough but usually managed to avoid doing the job assigned to him. He did his own thing if he could, because – in his own words – 'it was a lot easier' than what he'd been asked to do. As for the group, it didn't last even a month. The person in charge had limited influence with the lads, who squatted down behind the gravestones and smoked. One of them was particularly candid: 'Catch me working in a b_____ churchyard? I'd rather serve me time behind bars' – which is where by his own choice he ended up.

Undaunted by this experience, I plunged naively into partnership with the then government's flagship scheme for giving school-leavers a taste of employment. We needed a toilet constructed at church, which was at one end of the village, isolated from any such amenities apart from those in private dwellings. There was ample room at the rear of the south aisle, with a short distance outside to connect to the nearest sewage drain. The wood of several redundant oak benches was available to allow the alterations to be finished in keeping with a grade 2 listed church. The key person in this Youth Opportunity Programme would necessarily be a well-qualified supervisor, and a man was appointed who came with glowing references. There were several youngsters still registered with the Job Centre; the latter pointed out that the better motivated candidates had already been snapped up, but nevertheless provided six lads to work for us. The idea was that they'd learn simple construction skills – basic carpentry, some skills in plumbing, tiling and plastering, electrics and so on.

It rapidly became clear that most of these sixteen year olds needed much more help even to get them started. They'd never previously used a tape measure, they'd never handled a saw, let alone a screwdriver or a drill. I was shocked to see how a simple exercise – to measure off a length of timber and to cut it square – could result in such hopeless deformation of the wood. There was one exception, a boy very keen to get a permanent job, whose determination was soon rewarded – so we soon lost him. A more forceful supervisor might have made progress with those who remained, but ours (alas) tolerated shoddiness. We also discovered that his references had much exaggerated his own abilities. The moment of truth came when we found that his wastepipe was installed in defiance of Isaac Newton's great discovery: it pointed uphill. What actually halted the scheme altogether was the boys' snowball fight in church during one lunch break, which resulted in the irreparable damage of an altar cross. And then what I found most surprising was that one lad never re-appeared to collect his outstanding pay.

Subsequently, my hands-on churchwarden came to the rescue. He was an experienced, self-employed builder, who offered to complete the work under a similar scheme for adults. Just one assistant would be adequate, he reckoned, so we advertised once more through the Job Centre and selected two candidates for interview. The first turned out to be an Irishman, whose Catholic allegiance, if any, must surely have lapsed: he was thirty minutes late and entered the church smoking. We prayed for more encouraging signs from his rival. These were amply forthcoming, apart from the discovery that he'd just been released from prison. I rang the Job Centre to report our good impressions and raised but a single point. Without unearthing his criminal record, what was he in prison for? 'O, homicide', was the answer, 'he killed his wife'. Although that was in some ways reassuring, enabling us to go ahead with his appointment, I was careful never to cross his path. In fact, the work was well done, and the scheme was extended to give us a new church floor as well. Hopefully our assistant gained a new start in life too.

One task remained within the church: its entire redecoration, as the whitewashed walls had long since been shades of grey or even black. Since we needed considerable funding to mend the magnificent landmark spire on the church's exterior, we decided to do the work ourselves. Being very much an artisan parish, people were willing to roll up their sleeves. We were fortunate again in having a professional decorator in the congregation who agreed to be responsible for any work needing use of high ladders. Volunteers who proved inept at painting were rapidly redeployed to essential tea-making or cleaning duties.

My own first task had been to drive to a lime kiln in Buckinghamshire to collect the lump lime, which then had to be slaked in a large dustbin. When it was loaded into the boot of my car, there was a cheery send-off: 'I expect it'll be all right'. 'What are you suggesting might happen?' I asked a little nervously. 'Well, just occasionally this stuff explodes if it's jolted'. I drove home very carefully indeed. The slaking of the lumps was the most hazardous activity, rather like making porridge on a large scale. Nothing happens for a while, and then suddenly the mixture starts to bubble violently, at which point – standing well clear – you wish you hadn't added quite so much water. We actually spread the work over three successive summers: a week each for the chancel, for the nave and tower, and for the side aisles. It was always a messy business because you never knew in advance how many coats of lime-wash would be needed; two or three with luck, but maybe four or five. Cheating with emulsion paint doesn't work, because the walls have to breathe, and sooner or later emulsion starts to bubble and flake. As we honed our technique, word spread across the diocese and I became the (unofficial) diocesan lime-wash adviser.

The initial work in the chancel had a more immediate spin-off in the parish: the long-awaited replacement of our other churchwarden. This was cloak-and-dagger stuff. Ron had occupied the post for many years and regarded this as his natural right as owner of the vast old rectory and tithe barn standing next to the church. He would have endorsed the poet William Cowper's earlier assessment of parochial life:

> There is still a greater man belonging to the church, than either the parson or the clerk himself. The person I mean is the Squire; who, like the King, may be styled Head of the Church in his own parish.

Ron was possibly the only gentleman farmer left in the county – in other words, he supervised a couple of labourers. Apart from his unmistakably weighty presence on a Sunday, his contribution to church life was hard to detect. He was, however, related to the farming family who'd once been locally prominent, so caution was needed.

This family had in fact once developed a pork pie factory in the village, of which the now defunct bingo hall had been the social centre. Their present matriarch still lived nearby, and she told me that making pork pies had accidentally come about through the proximity of the Midland Railway. Hungry construction workers would walk across the fields to the farmhouse, where pies were baked to feed them. 'So the first pork pie was made by your grandmother?' I suggested. 'I don't suppose so at all', came the slightly haughty response, 'it would have been her cook'.

Ron was in this line of tradition. One could imagine him eating pies, but not in baking them. One evening we'd been hard at work limewashing and were feeling exhausted. Sid was still up his ladder in the chancel. It was only a matter of waiting a few minutes for him to finish – so would Ron, who'd just come into church to inspect us, stay with him and lock up? 'No', he said, 'I must be getting back for a programme on television that I don't want to miss'. That for me was the moment of truth, undoubtedly marking the beginning of his end. An energetic Geordie salesman was keen to serve in his place, and the following April put up for election. He gained more votes than Ron, who took some months to recover from the shock. (One of the more futile debates during my time on General Synod was an attempt to restrict the number of years a churchwarden could continuously hold office. After hours of discussion it was decided that he or she should be limited to – I think – five years at most, 'unless the church council should decide otherwise'. It is in any case an annual election!) Later on, one of Ron's relatives became our treasurer and was subsequently elected as our first female churchwarden.

His immediate successor in office was keen to read the lesson in church. I had to point out that, without benefit of Pentecostal enlightenment, hardly a soul would understand his accent. He graciously turned his attention instead to the still overgrown churchyard. In a short time he tamed it with a ride-on mower, but with one casualty: a headstone cracked and fell to the ground after a glancing touch from the mower. It belonged to the Austin family who'd emigrated to Connecticut in 1889 (where they set up a still-flourishing organ company) but had remained generous donors to our church. I had to compose a grovelling letter of explanation and apology, half-expecting a law-suit. To my astonishment, they simply gave instructions that we should replace the stone at their expense, and enclosed an unsolicited extra donation of a thousand dollars, quite sufficient to cover the cost of our scheme of redecoration. After this I was inclined to incite John to drive the mower ever more recklessly. When the stone mason came, I enjoyed a fascinating tour of all the headstones, most of which had been cut by members of his family. He instantly recognised the distinctive style of his father, his uncle, his brother and so on.

It is of course a headache keeping a graveyard presentable. There are churchyard rules laid down by each diocese which are then adapted locally, although – at least in the immediate aftermath of a burial – relatives are inclined to ignore them. Typically, the grave will be tended almost daily at first, then weekly, then monthly, but eventually perhaps only once a year, by which time not everyone can recall exactly where to find the family plot. (I was once accused of having demolished the headstone and obliterated the grave, but fortunately was able to point them out some 50 yards away from where this particular visitor claimed it had always been). Quite commonly, after ten or twenty years the family, who have died out or moved far away, may no longer visit at all. So the church has to take a much longer view, knowing that it will be in their care for centuries to come. This is why larger plants such as shrubs are unwelcome if positioned thoughtlessly. Suppose a rose bush is planted inconveniently: two choices present themselves: to confront the relatives as tactfully as possible (risking a headline in the Daily Express about unChristian vicars) or to apply judicious doses of weed-killer under cover of darkness. I refrain from discussing which of the two approaches I preferred.

However, in time a churchyard may become full, and then another possibility arises – to hand over maintenance to the local authority, recognising that they are never likely to do it as well as a band of dedicated volunteers (usually retired gentlemen who seek any opportunity to get quietly away from their wives). The vital secret here is not to extend the churchyard contiguously, or the law will argue that the churchyard is not actually full. I was once advised that a strip of land one yard wide needs to separate any newly consecrated ground from the old if any transference of maintenance of the latter is to be successful. How do you prove that a churchyard is full? 'Easy', said our canny Archdeacon Len, 'you tell them you wouldn't have opened up space elsewhere if it hadn't been'.

It was also necessary to seek advice from the registrar on another occasion about the extent of land actually consecrated for future use, only part of which had been fenced separately from the surrounding glebeland. An elderly farmer still remembered the day of consecration when the bishop came. He was a choir boy at the time, and so I asked him about the route taken by the procession to mark out the new boundaries. His sole recollection was that the choirmaster had pitched the note of the processional hymn uncomfortably high! When I reported this to the registrar, he replied that it didn't matter in the slightest what the bishop had said or done, or where he had been, at the actual ceremony. All that counted was the plan on the legal document that had been signed afterwards.

In discussing this (on a long train journey to York) with yet another archdeacon, he said it reminded him of the first wedding he'd ever conducted. In his nervousness he'd omitted to ask the bride to make her vows, and he was too embarrassed later to recall her to this (apparently) essential task. The registrar's advice received subsequently was that, provided both parties had signed the wedding registers, the marriage was fully legal. So – if you want to be spared the expense of wedding dresses, bridesmaids, flowers, organists and ceremony – to keep it short and simple, just sign the book. (Yet I doubt whether it is really quite so plainsailing …)

There was just one occasion when I contemplated legal action myself (it will, however, take some time to get to the point!). Our church in Somerset shared a twisting driveway with the large property adjacent to it that had once been the Rectory. For our first few years it was occupied by a widowed lady who was a generous supporter of the church; every year, for example, she would allow her field of daffodils to be raided to make scores of Mothering Sunday bouquets for distribution to the children. We regularly played on her tennis court too (and learnt that the young Crown Prince of Lesotho had once played there). She herself was revered as a legend in her Liverpool school, where she was the only girl ever to have hit a six through the chapel window. Even in her eighties she still rode occasionally to hounds, and once a year had the local meet foregather in her daffodil field. I recall once starting a large bonfire in the churchyard when the inevitable happened – the wind changed direction and smoke engulfed her house. I went at once to apologise. Her housekeeper opened the door and explained that her ladyship was resting upstairs. The next thing I knew was her ladyship standing at the top of the long flight of stairs brushing aside my apology, simply declaring, 'O you have to expect that kind of thing if you live in the country'.

We learnt more about country manners on a subsequent visit to lunch, where we were joined by two of her elderly (county) neighbours. One of them had married and buried three rich men in turn and now lived in a lofty ground floor apartment nearby; she was sufficiently hardy not to need any central heating, never locked her door when she went out (despite having a large portrait of one of her ancestors by Sir Joshua Reynolds hanging on display) and drove a red sports car around the lanes until her daughter confiscated the keys. The other lived in a residential home (until the grand old age of 102) where she usually employed an ear trumpet to converse with any visitors. At pudding time, our hostess announced that she'd just bought some Greek yoghurt from Sainsbury's; this was quite new to her, and she asked us to give our opinion on it. Sarah and I were first in the field and offered politely favourable comments. Then there was an explosion from the more elderly of our companions: 'it's absolutely ghastly,' she exclaimed.

It taught me at least that her ladyship appreciated frankness, so when – annoyed by our teenage son nearly mowing her down on the driveway riding his bicycle – she unilaterally arranged for a casual Irish labourer to construct a series of so-called sleeping policemen ('to be sure, done much better than British Standard', he assured me), I had to remind her that our congregation was legally entitled to 'free and unimpeded access' to the church at all times, and that if nothing were done about these mini-hillocks I should have to take recourse to the law. This was in fact bluff, as one of her sons was a solicitor in Liverpool, the other a law lord. Initially she let me narrow each of the bumps sufficiently for pedestrians and cyclists not to be tripped. I did this so thoroughly that even a car could drive through without being too jolted, at which point she threw in her hand and had the bumps removed completely, leaving just a notice about speed restrictions at the entrance. When she died not long afterwards, I expressed regret to her daughter about this confrontation. 'Don't worry in the least', came the reply, 'it was the sort of thing that mother relished – gave her something to live for!'

In recent years the heavy hand of government bureaucracy has made life more tedious for the local church. Much of it seems to derive from legislation on health and safety, which in turn is motivated by a blame culture in which injured parties are ever ready to claim damages for their own misfortune (or carelessness?). This forces insurance companies to insist that a church guards itself against every eventuality and displays warning notices throughout church premises (usually so long and detailed that no one is ever likely to read them). A few years ago it even became mandatory to put up No Smoking signs; but although this Blair-inspired legislation is presumably still in force, most churches seem to have discreetly removed the signs. (From the outset I hid our sign behind a display rack of CAFOD leaflets!) At one point I remember simply refusing to have the church plastered with green arrows pointing to the exit. I argued that if people had entered by the door, they could probably remember whereabouts it was, and with a modest ration of commonsense would realise this was the most likely way out as well. Those who couldn't remember would surely be assisted by parishioners with more active brains. As yet, this hazardous assumption has not been tested, since the building has not been struck by earthquake, fire, tempest or any other act of God.

Here in Wye a health and safety check is carried out each year during the month of March (being Lent, it is a suitable time for amendment of life). The visiting fire officer always looks for some improvement: thus, the edge of an outside step is now marked with white paint and a first aid box has been acquired for the sacristy. His most recent concern was the position of a fire blanket on the floor not far from a votive candle stand. He felt that in an emergency someone might pick it up rather hastily, allowing their hair to catch on fire from one of the candles – so he advised that the blanket should be suspended from a hook placed on the wall. My first thought was that we might achieve even better results if we insisted that anyone entering the church should be required to have a haircut. On reflection I realized this might not be very practical; so a brainwave then occurred to me – why not move the blanket elsewhere, well away from the candles, thus avoiding the need for a hook? I recall that thirty years ago I climbed up and down high ladders to change light bulbs in church, and nearly twenty years ago our teenage son Gabriel shinned up the pole on the corner of our 90 feet high church tower in order to bring down the weathercock for re-gilding, replacing it there afterwards. Neither of these self-help enterprises would be allowed today in our risk-averse society. I don't suppose either that we could save money by having a couple of school-leavers (our son and his friend) rebuild part of the churchyard wall and redecorate the church both inside and out. Long gone, it seems, are the days when we could make our own prudential judgments.

I have to confess to one or two slights of hand in the past, in order to escape occasionally from archidiaconal control. It's right and proper that there is external accountability regarding repairs or improvements to the fabric of an historic building. Normally this takes the form of planning permission, but the Church of England is exempt from much of this, provided its own faculty procedures are observed. These can be irksome in respect of very minor details or where moveable furnishings are involved. I use the word 'irksome' because forms have to be filled in and sufficient time allowed for various committees to consider any application. Sometimes, if the work is urgent, faculties can be issued retrospectively. But I usually had a rule of thumb: if, on his next visit to our church, the archdeacon wouldn't notice what we'd done, we probably wouldn't need to take up his valuable time in seeking his permission. Instead, we'd consult locally and take the best advice offered by competent and experienced craftsmen instead.

As for furnishings, the problem here is that a committee can actually display rather poor taste and can possibly turn an attractive new fitment down on aesthetic grounds – this happened once to a beautifully carved Bavarian crucifix that was donated to the church. On a separate occasion, when we'd commissioned a woven wall hanging as a reredos, with the design complementing the modern stained glass windows above (the aforementioned Ambrose's great achievement) I arranged for the assistant bishop to dedicate it without delay, thus hijacking any decision from the faculty jurisdiction committee.

If pressed, I would have cited the precedent of a much younger Mervyn Stockwood. During his ministry in Bristol, the diocesan authorities turned a blind eye to his blatant disregard of faculty procedures. The bishop himself is said to have remarked on a parish visit, 'I always have to play Nelson here'. My favourite role model, though, is the 12th century St Hildegard of Bingen, who clashed with the archbishop of Mainz over a burial which she had permitted. His argument was that, as one who had been excommunicated, the man should not have been interred in consecrated ground. She maintained that, as he had received the last rites of the church, his reconciliation had been effected. When the archbishop persisted in his demands for the body to be removed, she invited him to come over and 'dig him up yourself'! (He ignored the invitation.) Since she is now a Doctor of the Catholic Church, her action possibly constitutes an authoritative precedent.

A formidable lady depicted in Hildegard's *Scivias Domini*
('Know the Lord's Way')

Rule-bound folk are hard to escape altogether, and this is where disaffected parishioners, who are not numerous, can make life hard for a priest. Fortunately I've escaped better than some of my colleagues. One complaint came from a woman attending a burial one summer when I was away. She'd fallen on the edge of the churchyard path, and it transpired that she'd broken her ankle. The priest who substituted for me was not told of the incident. It was *eight* months later, when presumably the ankle had mended, that her legal adviser demanded the payment of damages. Her claim was that the grass was slightly too long – a charge which failed to make any headway, because (by good fortune) that particular section of the path belonged to a neighbouring property owned by a top London solicitor, who dealt very firmly with her demands.

Again, a feminist in the parish, frustrated that parishioners were less enthusiastic than herself to see a woman as my successor, wrote to the bishop after I'd left that I'd purloined the office computer. This was the result of my having observed to the church council that, while I'd always provided my own word-processor and photocopier (not to mention items such as hymnbooks for the congregation and psalters for the choir), it might now be a good idea if they themselves equipped the parish with a computer ready for my successor.

This coincided with a not-unexpected clash with our outgoing parish treasurer, who had necessarily been replaced because of his refusal to comply with the clear financial decisions of the parochial church council; there had also been several complaints from those who 'covenanted' their regular donations that he reckoned not to have received some of these. Nor had his predecessor been much easier to deal with; in particular he refused to sign any cheques destined to help missions or charities working in Africa, claiming that Africa was totally corrupt and hence any aid sent there would be squandered (this may be true of funds passing through government hands, but Christian churches and agencies are usually much more trustworthy). I had therefore circumvented his objections by using a discretionary fund, whose other beneficiaries were local people facing personal crises and 'gentlemen of the road' who periodically called at the Rectory. With a couple of these donations our auditor agreed that it was in order not to request receipts since this would reduce the mission's administrative costs. This, of course, gave any disaffected parishioners (such as our rebellious treasurer) scope to lodge complaints. Quite a few years later when we met again, he offered a fulsome apology.

The handling of money is rightly subject to close scrutiny, but inevitably, with unprofessional volunteers, the paperwork can sometimes let one down. An issue in our Catholic parish of Sherborne related to the payment of legal fees on behalf of a Zimbabwean mother of two, whose presence in this country had depended on her husband's work permit. When he left her, she was faced with a deportation order. After consultation with the bishop I took her to the appeal hearing; this was successful but necessitated the payment of around £500 for court fees and the solicitor's expenses. Receipts for these were lost somewhere between the parish and the diocesan office, whose auditors seemed to imply that our visit to Newport was a carefree joy ride. In fact, the lady was a pillar of the church youth group and had a steady full-time secretarial job of her own. When her teenage son was invited by the judge to address the court, he was asked to indicate if he had any career of his own in mind. 'Yes,' he said, 'I'd like to be a judge.' There ensued much laughter in court!

A final case concerned the timing of a funeral, when an aggrieved family complained directly to the bishop. The deceased lady had for a number of years been largely shunned by her family in London, on account of her friendship with a man of whom they disapproved. When she died, they were annoyed to learn that he and a local solicitor had been appointed her executors, and that her estate had been left almost entirely to him. They were anxious – for whatever reason – not to miss her funeral, and indeed the date was rearranged to suit their convenience. Before it happened, there was a widespread fall of snow, particularly bad in the London area. They demanded a further postponement of the funeral by at least a week or two, vainly imagining that the weather in the following month would necessarily be better. The executors decided that as snow had already disappeared from most of southern England – with trains and coaches running from London as normal – there was no need to change the date yet again (which would surely have confused her many friends in the area). The funeral director offered to provide free transport from the station should they choose to come by train. The day itself was clear and sunny, and a couple of kindlier relatives drove down from Essex. I reported on the service afterwards to the non-attendees, but this well-intentioned gesture seemed only to infuriate them further. They sent a strongly worded letter to the bishop, telling him how I had single-handedly frustrated their fondest hopes and was the most despicable priest they'd ever encountered. While not denying the latter assertion, I think I may have pointed out to the bishop that, when she was dying, their deep affection had been less in evidence, indeed insufficient to prompt any visits at all.

Not that the deceased herself was always easy to deal with during those weeks: on Christmas Eve she discovered that she would be on her own for a few days and demanded that a member of our congregation should go there the next day to cook her a special Christmas dinner. At such short notice, that of course was an unrealistic request, so I did my best to stock her up with festive fare from a local specialist called Pudding and Pies. This was not quite the same as the roast turkey she expected; so half an hour after I had left her, she rang up the nearby Anglican vicar to complain that the Catholic church had now entirely abandoned her.

Sometimes one can't win! I think of a lady who stopped coming to church: I went to see her, and she said, 'I left because you didn't speak to me at the door'. 'But I invariably go there after a service and talk to people coming out'. 'I know,' she said, 'and when I saw you already talking to someone else, I walked straight past you and came home'. I'm reminded too of early days as a curate, when dressed in a long black cassock I paid hospital visits to sick parishioners. 'You know, doctor,' complained one elderly lady, 'I do think it's about time the priest came to see me'. So, what did she say when the doctor made his rounds? That, I guess, is another story. Doctors, one imagines, have their own tales to tell!

QUACKS AND CURES

> Mr Pilgrim looked with great tolerance on all shades of religious opinion that did not include a belief in cures by miracle. On this point he had the concurrence of Mr Pratt, the only other medical man of the same standing in Milby. Otherwise, it was remarkable how strongly these two clever men were contrasted ... Pratt elegantly referred all diseases to debility, and with a proper contempt for symptomatic treatment, went to the root of the matter with port wine and bark; Pilgrim was persuaded that the evil principle in the human system was plethora, and he made war against it with cupping, blistering, and cathartics.

So wrote George Eliot in her fictional account *Scenes of Clerical Life* in the mid-19th century. In earlier times clerics often administered potions when medicine men were not to be found. Medieval pilgrims would head for shrines in the hope of a miraculous cure, but the monks who were the custodians there would also have maintained a physic garden with herbs and other plants used for a wide variety of healing remedies. The 17th century priest George Herbert followed in their steps, advising that the parson should 'be all to his Parish, and not onely a Pasteur, but a Lawyer also, and a Phisician'.

> Home-bred medecines are both more easie for the Parsons purse, and more familiar for all mens bodyes.

The sort of remedies he might have used may be illustrated by the following near-contemporary examples.

- Whoseuer eateth two Walnuts, two Fygs, twentie leaues of Rew, and one Graine of Salt, all stampt and mixt together, fasting: shall be safe from pyson and plague that daye. (Thomas Lupton, *A Thousand Notable Things*, 1579)
- A speedy Remedy for Fits of Vomiting. Take a large Nutmeg, grate off one half of it, and toast the flat side of the other, till the Oily part begin to ouze or sweat out, then clap it to the Pit of the Patient's Stomach as hot as he can well endure it, and let him keep it on whilst it continues warm, and then if need be put on another. (Robert Boyle, *Medicinal Experiments*, 1693)

Two centuries later Sydney Smith was still at it. He used one room at his Foston rectory in North Yorkshire as a dispensary. On its shelves were his concoctions, labelled imaginatively as *Heart's Delight* — *the comfort of all the old women in the village*; *Rub-a-dub* — *a capital embrocation*; *Dead Stop* — *settles the matter at once*; *Up-with-it-then*. These were no doubt popular with his parishioners, as one of his rhyming couplets seems to imply:

> I know all drugs, all simples and all pills:
> I cure diseases, and *I send no bills*.

> Keep out of reach and sight of children
> TAKE 2 TABLETS DAILY In Blind Faith
> BENEFITS: Unknown
> SIDE EFECTS: Unknown

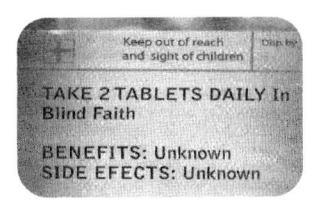

It was later said of James Murrell, a renowned early 19th century herbalist, that his clients (unlike ourselves?) were 'ignorant, credulous, and superstitious'.

Medical science in the UK has moved on a little bit since then – or has it? Forty years ago I consulted our GP, a real family doctor who called on his patients without being summoned, to see how they were. My particular ailment was a frequent recurrence of debilitating headaches, possibly the outcome of a rugby injury (a shoulder and neck dislocation) that resulted from a crash tackle by the master in charge of our practice game. He downplayed the likelihood of any such connection, so I suggested to him instead that perhaps they were an allergic reaction to something I was eating. 'I don't suppose so', he said. 'But isn't my body an organism of biochemical tissues and cells, which might interact with the substances I ingest? Isn't the practice of medicine based on scientific principles?' I protested. 'To some degree', he admitted, 'but put it like this: I've known patients sleep with a dead mouse under their pillow, and it's worked wonders'. He didn't on that occasion prescribe any mice, dead or alive, but nothing else was on offer at the time.

He could, of course, have suggested one of the many remedies we discovered during our time in Africa. This one is for hearing difficulties, rather than headaches, but – who knows? – it might have been worth trying:

> Take banana water from its rotten tree, mix this with little petrol, egg and a few gun powder, and read Psalm 16 to it three times with the holy name Eliala pronounced fifty times.

In urban settings particularly, African healers experiment and innovate all the time: the market for new medicines is insatiable. Traditional recipes may be the starting point, but other substances now get added – synthetic animal fats, over-the-counter pharmaceuticals, patent medicines, industrial chemicals, you name it. The resulting mixtures are so powerful that sometimes only the fittest survive.

But even if all this seems haphazard, like random guesswork, there is an objective behind it, more ambitious than in most Western laboratories:

> A medicine is not, as in the West, simply a substance imbued with natural powers for healing. It is anything that activates the visible and invisible forces, and enables human beings to deal with them for good or for ill.

The point is that while misfortune of any kind, including ill health, may have a proximate cause (for example, an *anopheles* mosquito bit me and infected me with malaria) the question of its ultimate cause still needs to be resolved (why did the mosquito choose to attack *me*, rather than someone else?). Thus, even if disease can be diagnosed in scientific terms, to the African there's usually a deeper personal or spiritual explanation: a malevolent neighbour or a hostile spirit is to blame and therefore needs to be subdued. Diviners, spirit mediums, and witch finders can then all too easily accentuate and exploit the climate so frequently generated of fear and suspicion. They know that retaliation and revenge are likely to be considered as a necessary part of the cure. Even if not, herbalists will claim that their medicines need help from the spirits to be effective. Hence, when graveyard soil, crushed bones or pubic hair are added to the mix, the medicine is perceived by the patient to be more potent.

Positively, one has to accept that traditional healers may be the only accessible source of help and counselling, and may actually have a better grasp of social or psychosomatic problems than their Western counterparts. A typical Xhosa therapy would be fourfold:

> Firstly there are the songs, the words of which instil faith and confidence. These are accompanied by the sustained action of clapping, the beat of drums, and dancing, all of which stimulate the nervous system in a type of convulsive therapy that results in physiological changes that relax the mind and body. Thus the patients are helped daily to dance away their tensions. Thirdly their psychosis is controlled through the use of sedatives – herbal extracts and snuffs being administered as tranquillizers. But the final recovery rests on the patient's complete confidence in the infallibility of the higher powers vested in his *igqirha*.

The *amagqirha* aren't novices. They have a lengthy apprenticeship, in which they acquire a huge knowledge of indigenous plants and their properties: in botanical terms they may be at least as expert as some medieval monks. Considering that one of the most successful methods of discovering new drugs has been through the study of plants used by people closely in touch with their natural environment, the *amagquira* need to be seen as partners, not as rivals, to more orthodox medical practitioners – with the proviso that in some areas such as childbirth their practices can be positively harmful. It's also fair to note that such healers don't claim to cure every ailment, and for some decades have sometimes referred cases to hospitals.

Surprisingly perhaps, the reverse has also been known to take place, even if (as yet) government hospitals aren't wholly reliable in knowing when alternative treatment is likely to be helpful. An example reported by a charity running several African schools was of a pupil who died of what was almost certainly a fairly treatable seizure, yet was diagnosed by the hospital as being demonically possessed. He was sent to a witch doctor, but failed to survive the journey.

I once met Tambulani, in all but name a witch doctor, but calling herself a Christian healer on account of her membership of the Lutheran church. She claimed that her powers came directly from God. She was actually a 'spirit medium', who communed with ancestral spirits. It was from them, she reckoned, that her understanding of sickness and the particular client's problems was gifted to her:

> I dance to diagnose such cases as high blood pressure, fever, epilepsy, madness, pneumonia, venereal diseases, food poisoning and barrenness, and to establish the cause, whether it is sorcery or otherwise...

And clearly she was in demand. Christians of many different persuasions, as well as other sufferers, consulted her, with or without the blessing of their churches. A Congolese poem admits the truth that adherents to the Christian faith are not necessarily any different from their compatriots:

> O unhappy Christian,
> Mass in the morning,
> Witchdoctor in the evening,
> Amulet in the pocket,
> Scapular round the neck.

There are many others, particularly from the newer independent churches, who offer a 'deliverance' ministry. Poverty, HIV/AIDS, and environmental degradation have all led to growing demand, and the rapid expansion of the so-called African Initiated Churches owes a great deal to their healing practices. They don't use medicines but sacred objects like holy water, candles, incense, consecrated oil, prayer bands and beads, together with psalms and bible verses to recite. Their diagnosis of illness comes from the Bible itself. The 'prophets', as they are known, open it at random, read out loud the passage that falls (by God's own choice) before their eyes, and discern from it both the nature of the patient's disease and the type of treatment required. So their followers sing of *Yesu sing'anga* – Jesus, the medicine man above all others who can truly cure disease and drive out evil spirits.

What higher authority could you want than that? Yet if Jesus himself doesn't seem to come up with an answer, there are many alternatives to try, including the occult. What rules the day is pragmatism: it's about what's available, what's affordable and what works (or *might* work). A client will visit a number of doctors or healers until he or she finds one who can bring some relief. As a Tanzanian proverb expresses it, 'Round the sick person's neck are many charms'.

I have only limited personal experience of health care in Africa; but in both the countries where we've lived, medically qualified personnel and the resources available to them were in short supply. The Catholic mission hospital in Lesotho relied on Swiss doctors serving there for a few years each, and the situation was very similar in Malawi with British, American, German, South African and Venezuelan doctors springing to mind. Some Malawians had trained abroad, but usually stayed abroad afterwards. It was commonly said that there were more Malawian doctors in Manchester than in the whole of their homeland. There were no dentists at all in Lesotho, so the best you could hope for there was a straight extraction. We had an excellent Indian dentist in Blantyre, having first experienced a less reliable South Korean in the Adventist Hospital. A friend of ours had a tooth taken out by him, but afterwards found jagged fragments left behind; these were identified at another dental practice as belonging to her jaw.

As for nursing staff, one mission hospital near Lake Malawi was able to man only a few of its wards, leaving the majority closed. Not enough nurses were being trained in the country, and the more experienced of them were being lured to places like Britain to work in the National Health Service. Even then, nursing care wasn't everything it might have been. I underwent two hernia operations in the private Mwaiwathu Hospital in Blantyre, and the surgeon was not best pleased to find blood-drenched bandages and bedclothes on his visit the following morning. I remember too having to stagger unassisted down a long corridor to the toilets. The day after my second operation a British surgeon whom I knew called in the ward to see one of his patients. I called him over, and apologised for not having greeted him previously – not recognising him without my spectacles. 'But look what I discovered when I put them on today'. Here I pointed to the floor behind my bedside table which (no thanks to the nurses) I had just managed to shift forward into a reachable position. It was covered with dirt, cobwebs, and scraps of material. 'I'm going to give you some sound medical advice', he said, 'take your spectacles off again!'

Prior to these operations I'd had an initial consultation with a German doctor in our local hospital, who was able to check my midriff with sophisticated sonic equipment. This required blobs of gel to be smeared over me first – but afterwards he said, 'I'm afraid we've no towels or wipes in the hospital today, so use the curtains to clean yourself up'. I was reminded of an American girl attached for several months to the main Queen Elizabeth Hospital to gain work experience. I asked her what main differences stood out for her, compared with the hospitals she knew in the States. The biggest shock, she said, was in having to make one pair of surgical gloves last for several days, instead of getting a fresh pair for each patient. Again, I recall meeting our local surgeon in Zomba market one morning, and saying to him, 'Peter – I thought you'd be busy operating in the hospital right now?' 'So I should be', was his reply, 'but there's no water in the taps today'.

It was also true that in many hospitals pharmaceutical supplies were in short supply. One story that circulated was of the monthly planning meeting in the Ministry of Health being interrupted by the minister, who announced unexpectedly that he was off to a conference in Washington with several top officials, all of them therefore 'requiring' first class air flights and accommodation. The effect of this was immediately to halve the budget that month for hospital deliveries within Malawi itself. However, even when supplies had been distributed as normal, they didn't always remain on the shelves. Pharmacists, like other hospital staff, weren't always paid, and compensated by selling items from their stores on the black market.

Fortunately therefore we kept fit most of the time, although an early fever was wrongly diagnosed as malaria. 'Surely', I asked, 'I'd need to have been bitten by a mosquito first?' A project we initiated with an orphan project in nearby villages employed a carpenter to train teenage boys to make mosquito-proof gauze shutters, which were then supplied to wards in the hospital. They also enabled tools and technical skills to be acquired, providing the boys with some potential income

Whereas during our time in Lesotho HIV/AIDS had not been identified – the main issue there was to keep local water supplies free of cholera – by the time we reached Malawi there were nearly a million orphaned children under the age of sixteen. Between four and five hundred of them were to be found in the villages just a few miles east of Zomba, for whom in two successive years of famine my wife raised around £6000 from family and friends for a feeding programme to cover the three 'starvation' months (January through to March) before the next harvest was due. Death at a young age was never far away and came close when it hit people and families whom we knew. A priest visited the college one day and looked at the group photograph of the thirty or so men from his own admission year. He went through the pictures one by one: 'He's dead ... he's dead ... he's dead ...' a total of around a dozen of his contemporaries, none of them much past their mid-thirties.

For four years we looked after Carolyn, a teenage orphan: hardly a month passed without yet another of her relatives dying. Only her grandmother, one aunt and a number of young cousins remained alive. Carolyn herself, who passed her secondary school certificate, was under the common impression that you could catch HIV from touching the clothing of an infected person – which meant that people were often reluctant to care for the sick, and in any case wouldn't admit the nature of their illness to others. In a largely pre-scientific culture it was especially hard to grasp two factors about the deadly virus: it appeared invisible, and its effects were seldom immediate, since it might be dormant for several years. It was far more straightforward to blame sickness on the better-known phenomenon of human vindictiveness. Unsurprisingly, even every third minister or priest was reputed to carry protective charms on his person.

Things are very different in the UK. Yet while resources are so much greater and life expectancy is probably double what it is in Africa, there are still many whose condition seems to have no remedy. Alternative therapies are not quite so much in evidence in this country, but demand for them remains high. In my Somerset parish I visited a woman who told me firmly that she was not a Christian but had Buddhist leanings. Shortly afterwards she remarked that on the coming Sunday she intended to visit a nearby church for a faith healing service. 'But you told me you weren't a Christian?' I queried. She then explained herself, outlining her health problems and the failure of her own GP to find a satisfactory treatment. Before she saw a consultant privately ('which is very expensive') she reckoned it was worth trying the church ('because after all it's free, and you never know, it might work').

I could understand her frustration, because for all the improvements in medical provision there are yet many ailments (such as my own headaches) which are poorly understood. A report from the School of Health and Related Research in Sheffield a few years ago claimed that about 20% of treatments offered throughout the Health Service didn't have a shred of evidence to support them, and that 'frequently, even when new research indicated clearly that doctors should stop using a particular treatment, nothing changed'. Dozens of examples were cited of treatments still being widely used, despite it being clear that all they gave patients were side-effects. One medication prescribed for me not long ago listed seventy-six possible side-effects – on a long sheet of paper resembling an ancient biblical scroll. Another recent report reckoned that doctors are mistaken over the cause of (about) one in four hospital deaths.

There are certainly growing pressures on most health services. Obesity and drug-addiction have mushroomed in scale; street violence is on the rise in urban areas;

environmental pollution triggers a variety of reactions, some of which have yet to impact more seriously; within a 'shrunken' globe, disease can spread more quickly than ever before. At the same time, medical research has discovered many new forms of treatment to enable people to live longer – but alas! very often they are highly expensive. The combination of these and other factors (such as the shortage of doctors and nurses) means that it is often a struggle to get treatment or even advice.

The story is told of the writer Marcel Proust, who at a young age underwent a painful operation on his nose which the physician insisted would cure him of hay fever for life. It didn't! Proust subsequently took the view that true knowledge in any walk of life depends not merely on book learning, such as doctors learn in medical school, but on sharing experiences of suffering and pain. A retired GP in Wye would, I think, concur. Indeed, reflecting on his life's work he once remarked, 'You have to learn to listen carefully to what the patient's telling you. If you let them talk for long enough, you'll find out what's wrong with them'.

We once had a forthright neighbour well in her 80s, who'd been taken to a private hospital after collapsing at home. I went to visit her a few days later, and she seemed more her usual self: 'They tell me I've got septicaemia: I don't believe a word of it, so I'm going home tomorrow'. Sheer will power was sufficient medicine!

From time to time I've received some curious diagnoses myself. In my twenties an outbreak of spots across my forehead was explained as a shaving rash, although I suppose the doctor in question (a lady) might be forgiven for not being entirely *au fait* with masculine shaving habits. Again, a recurrent ache in my right heel was once put down to poor circulation, with the recommendation that I should buy longjohns. When I eventually mentioned this at the hospital, the two physiotherapists in attendance were quite hysterical with laughter for several minutes, and remarked that not all GPs knew very much about feet. Or when, a few years ago, I suffered for a few months from bowel problems I saw a series of part-time GPs in our local surgery; prior to the eventual colonoscopy they variously informed me that I had (a) stomach cancer (b) cancer of the bowels (c) Crohn's disease. This was distinctly alarming at the time, but in the end I was relieved to discover it was a mere infection.

One heart blip way back in time took me to a hospital, where I was under observation for a week. At the end of my stay the verdict was pronounced: it was a mystery virus. Fifteen years later the blip recurred, and this time I saw a cardiologist as an out-patient. 'People who have heart problems stand a high risk of getting a stroke', he told me, 'so I'm giving you some tablets to take every day'. 'But if you don't really know what caused this blip,' I argued, 'how do you know what the risk is? After all, it's fifteen years since I had a problem'. 'Your chance of getting a stroke is at least 5% per annum', he said. 'Well, that's not really very much, is it?' 'You have to understand', he came back rather crossly, 'that 5% each year adds up to a 50% chance of a stroke sometime in the next ten years'. 'In that case', I responded carefully counting on all my fingers twice over, 'we'd really need to start the sum when the blip first happened, and that means that when another five years have passed it'll be twenty years on. So presumably there's a 100% certainty of a stroke pretty soon?' At that point I think the maths was getting a bit advanced for this particular expert, and his next patient was due. I did, however, return the tablets to the pharmacy, since the accompanying leaflet warned of possible side-effects, including 'malfunctioning of the heart' rather high up on the list. I surely now live on borrowed time?

It took very much longer to get advice regarding the more serious challenge of the headaches. As the condition worsened over the years, I managed to see an allergy consultant, in fact a parishioner in Somerset who had just retired. She told me that during most of her working life she'd been the only such consultant in the whole of the south-west. She asked me to compile a daily record of what I ate and how I felt, and after three weeks we met again for her to analyse the results. Her method was so simple that (had I known or thought about it) I could have used it myself long before we met: she expected a possible cause to trigger an effect within about three hours. Her answer was coffee, or more precisely caffeine. I changed at once to decaffeinated coffee and red bush tea. After several months I realised this wasn't the answer, and now know that her approach was methodologically defective. Some foods take very much longer – twelve or more hours – to trigger an adverse reaction.

There were then a couple of neurologists I saw in London, but they merely prescribed strong painkillers. The most helpful consultant to date was found in Somerset, who spotted that some of the pain was an allergic reaction to… yes, the strong painkillers previously prescribed by his colleagues in London. He had harsh words about them, remarking that not many GPs either knew the potentially addictive property of virtually all analgesics, with the possible exception of paracetemol. Ten years later the NHS finally bit the bullet, with a report in 2012:

> It has been estimated that up to 1 in 50 people experience headaches caused by medication overuse.

They still, however, didn't seem to be too interested in the root causes of pain:

> Concerns from patients about possible underlying causes can lead to unnecessary hospital investigations. These can mean people experience delays in receiving adequate pain relief from what can be an extremely disabling condition.

Surely a concern about causes doesn't necessarily lead to a *hospital* investigation? And if it can be deemed 'unnecessary', doesn't this reflect rather badly on the doctor making the referral? Why should patients who wish not merely to gain relief from pain but to eliminate it altogether be regarded as such a threat?

Several well-intentioned GPs meanwhile suggested prophylactic measures – but on a pragmatic basis: 'Try these, and if they don't seem to help, come and see me again'. None of them did work, which didn't surprise me when I read the patient information in the packets, which seemed invariably to list headaches as a possible side effect. Back in 1771, Tobias Smollett began his comic masterpiece *The Expedition of Humphrey Clinker* with the line 'Doctor, the pills are good for nothing', which no doubt resonated with his readership then, just as it still does often enough today.

In addition to these GPs, there was also one zealous dentist who'd been on a recent course to treat night-time teeth grinding. I'm not sure whether she really thought that might be my problem, or whether I was the first patient she could use as a guinea pig for her newly acquired technique. It was certainly expensive, and so uncomfortable that getting to sleep with a bulging mouth was problematic. I gave it up after a month, fighting off her proposal to refer me to her professor in Bristol at a cost of several more hundred pounds.

A sympathetic colleague then stepped in to arrange a free appointment with an elderly friend of his who practised in Harley Street. This was an awesome opportunity, as I'd always thought Harley Street consultations were reserved for celebrities and merchant bankers. It was certainly a very thorough examination, lasting ninety minutes. His conclusion was that I needed to be on what he termed a cave-man diet. His thesis was that, whereas most human beings had adjusted to modern diets, a few of us (such as myself) were still *neanderthal*, and therefore needed to think back a few thousand years to what our ancestors might have been eating long ago. We ought to avoid dairy produce and be careful about grains and cultivated crops. The principal advantage of this restriction was that one could tick the appropriate boxes on any aircraft flight, and gain priority during the serving of meals. There weren't really any other advantages, as the treatment was once again ineffective. I suspected too that even if my complaint had been the growth of horns and a tail, the prescription might well have been the same.

Of course, other (alternative medicine) practitioners have done their best, with acupuncture and homeopathy, but to no avail. Old ladies have suggested remedies such as drinking coconut water and using herbal mixtures, while a Polish waitress recommended eating lots of apples. I gave most of these a try, being desperate to find an answer however unlikely.

Indeed, as a teenager I had once been cured miraculously (or at least inexplicably). For a year or more I had suffered from terrible catarrh, and the statutory health services, including the local hospital, had failed to stem the flow. In desperation my parents arranged an appointment with a naturopath. They left me with him, and after I had described my case history I was made to lie face down on a couch while he probed my spine from the base upwards. As I didn't see any logical connection between that and my sinuses, I began to suspect his sanity — even more so when he started to manipulate my neck with his thumbs, pressing my head deeply into the pillow where I gasped for breath. The phrase 'homicidal maniac' flashed through my mind. He then announced that he had corrected the position of one or two small bones, and all that remained was for him to take a blood sample. The session concluded with his instructions on how to take a few drops each day of the two colourless liquids he was providing. He added that he would know how I was progressing by observing my blood sample in his black box. I carried out his instructions 'faithfully', but in the absence of any faith whatsoever. I thanked God that I had escaped the clutches of a madman. *Yet within a fortnight I was better.*

Since then, still searching for a headache remedy, I've not been prepared to write off the unconventional — including resort to any saints reputed to be patrons of medicine. If they too have seemed unable to help, perhaps it has been because — as St Paul expressed it — this 'thorn in the flesh' was given 'to keep me from being too elated'. Even so, the principal drawback of pain is its invisibility to others (including bishops), who may not always appreciate the exhaustion that accompanies it.

I still believe in the possibility of miracles, even if they are a rare phenomenon (or perhaps are rarely appreciated, effecting predominantly spiritual, rather than physical, transformation). In Lesotho our African helper told me one day of her sister, whose newborn baby was rapidly wasting away in the mission hospital. It was now nearly two weeks old, but taking no sustenance at all, and the doctors had advised there was no more they could do: death was imminent. I hurried over to anoint the child and to offer prayers, hoping that this would at least bring some consolation to his mother. The following day there was an early knock on the door. It was the sister, complete with a bouncing baby who had started to recover and to feed within an hour of my visit. The hospital had discharged them on seeing the dramatic improvement continue overnight. While nothing quite as remarkable has been reported to me after any subsequent ministrations, it is clear that in many instances the reception of the holy oils has brought peace of mind and resolved much anxiety.

Moving latterly to live in Kent has providentially also led to some personal relief. One of the doctors here, so I discovered on visits to housebound parishioners, was often praised not only for his exceptional kindness but also for his diagnostic skill. I resolved to get an appointment with him myself. When I entered his consulting room, he was already studying my medical notes and said, 'I see you avoid eating cheese. I suggest you look up on the internet other food products which contain tyramine. It could be this that lies behind many of your headaches. Unlike many other doctors, I did a pharmacology course as part of my training (and was top in that subject!), and it's the sort of allergic reaction I look out for'.

Immediately I reached home I googled the magic word and found that most of the resultant websites were American. One of them, based on research in Chicago, was headed The National Headache Foundation. It offered expert advice for cranial oddities like myself, with a risk assessment of most types of commonly available food. Tyramine (a form of amino acid) develops, so I learnt, particularly in aged, processed or smoked products. So after making that rebuffed suggestion forty or more years ago, now thanks to American science and to an astute British doctor, an allergy had at last emerged as one of the factors alongside several others. On a subsequent visit to my adviser, he fine-tuned his diagnosis and even apologised for the fact that 'the medical profession has failed to help you for so long'.

By chance, I happened to be reading Longfellow at the time: I reflected on the youth he describes struggling upwards 'mid snow and ice', bearing 'a banner with the strange device, Excelsior', yet who never made it more than halfway. This prompted a certain fellow feeling; I wondered in fact whether 'Excelsior', which sounds suspiciously like a wonder drug, might not have been the wrong medication for him? Or was he just heading in the wrong direction altogether? Perhaps in my case Pseudo-Pliny's advice, offered in the 9th century, might be the answer after all:

> Headaches you will enchant: take some earth, touch your breast three times and say, 'My head hurts, why does it hurt? It does not hurt'.

This was precisely the basic tenet of V.S. Pritchett's 'Church of the Last Purification', a (fictitious) sect in his short story *The Saint:*

> The success of our prayers had a simple foundation. We regarded it as Error – our name for Evil – to believe the evidence of our senses … we knew that deafness and blindness, cancer and insanity, the great scourges, were constantly vanishing before [our] prayers.

So maybe that's the church for me?

CRUCIAL CHALLENGES

In the early 1970s, when I first served in ordained ministry, there was disaffection among some clergy about pay and conditions. I've no recollection of details, beyond the suggestion that industrial action might be necessary, in the form of a go slow. This was never implemented because it was soon realised that it would have zero impact: as one priest put it, 'No one would notice any difference'. Clergy are of course associated in the public mind with church services, particularly on Sundays – so it's plain that being a priest is a one-day-a-week job anyway, and you can hardly complain of overwork or underpay. While this popular association with worship isn't misplaced and has plenty of official backing (although the hierarchy's expectations may be a shade higher), in reality it's not the only thing a priest has to do.

I sometimes think that in the Catholic Church the impression is given that if a priest says a daily mass, hears a few confessions, and stays celibate for the rest of the week, he's done his job. Back in 2009 we had a Year of the Priest to refocus on what it was all about, and I'd rather hoped that there'd be some fresh insights. The only thinking that inspired me was by the Australian Jesuit Fr Gerry O'Collins, well-known as a theologian who taught for many years in Rome. He produced a book called *Jesus our Priest*, and in it points out the following:

> His priesthood began with the incarnation. He didn't become a priest at some later stage, but from the start he already was and acted as a priest. In particular ... proclaiming the kingdom, healing the sick, forgiving sinners, feeding the hungry and the other activities that filled the years of Jesus' public life belonged to his priestly ministry as much as his institution of the Eucharist.

That's a holistic view that seminaries don't necessarily always bring out. The training is geared to doctrine, scripture, liturgy, and how the sacraments are to be offered. There's canon law, and spirituality, and something on preaching and pastoralia. But beyond the seminary, life can be rather different, often with unforeseen challenges and the opportunity to exercise unanticipated priestly roles, even if playing the piano for the annual village pantomime (as I did for several consecutive years) might be considered beyond the call of duty.

Looking back at my own training, I can pinpoint one or two inadequacies. I was never warned not to accept any invitation to a Women's Institute Summer Party. This was the nadir of my entire ministry: just imagine being the only male present at an orgy of home-made wine – I fled, mentally comparing myself to the Holy Family escaping the awful fate that surely awaited them at the hands of Herod. Nor was I ever properly prepared for Christmas party games in the church hall. A few months after my ordination, I found myself in the church hall in a team of parishioners competing against other teams. The MC would call out an object, such as a clean white handkerchief, or a spectacle case, or a five pound note, and the first person to rush forward with one and present it to him won a point for their team. He called out 'an endorsed driving licence'. It rapidly became apparent that no one in the room had such a blot on their escutcheon. Except that I did, on my own person and in my own trouser pocket. This was a moral dilemma I had never faced at college: should I now produce it for the MC to inspect, and gain a point for my team? Or should I let it burn a hole in my pocket and conceal the appalling truth about the unworthiness, indeed the reckless depravity, of the new curate? The lure of a point was too great, and the same rush of adrenalin that had led me to speed at 37 mph in a 30 mph zone driving out of Oxford took me racing into the centre of the hall, shamelessly to reveal that I was a greater sinner than them all. How was this a priestly act? Perhaps it was the refusal to set myself up as one 'holier than thou' – although admittedly I thought of that afterwards.

A few years later I was in a parish of my own. Only a week or two after the institution came the annual church fete, which included a children's fancy dress competition. As the vicar I was asked to be the sole judge, a weight of responsibility I'd never borne before. The children were herded into a small paddock, and we were surrounded by a sea of faces – the mums, obviously ready to tear me from limb to limb if I didn't get it right. There were several prizes to be awarded: girls aged 5 and under, boys aged 5 and under, girls up to 8, over 8, boys up to 8, over 8 – something like that. I thought it was pc to start with the smallest girls, so I surveyed the candidates and selected my winner. 'I'm going to award the prize for the smallest girls to this little girl on my right. So what's your name?' – I turned smilingly to her. 'I'm not a girl, I'm a boy', said this little horror, in one sentence annihilating any credibility I might have had. I still lie awake picturing the scene. Fortunately the mums exercised considerable self-control, and the village proved to be forgiving.

The following year I was invited to judge the carnival floats before they processed to the recreation ground. There were a dozen or so of these, including a few entries from other villages. I'm afraid I took a prior policy decision, which was effectively to rig the result. I decided that, in the event of a close call, first prize would have to go to a home entry, and not to any outside visitors. My only defence is that without any guidance from the years of formation I had to fall back once again on my own resources, apprehensive of the possible damage to my standing in the village. 'Peace at any price' was, I suppose, my unwritten motto.

It begins to sound as if by now I was in a moral quagmire, but these initial skirmishes were really the testing ground for weightier business that came later. In Africa there were serious issues where one had to align oneself firmly on the side of justice. At the seminary in Roma we employed a few local women, among them Justina who helped in the house. Justina was a widow with three children; her husband had, like many Basotho men, worked in the South African mines and not untypically had died of lung poisoning. Justina was therefore back in her home village in Lesotho, where according to local custom she was entitled to a piece of ground on which to build her own rondavel. She told us that she'd approached the headman, who'd been fairly obliging – on condition that she slept with him, which she refused to do. I asked if it was possible for me to get something sorted out with the chief, assuring Justina that we'd pay for the basic building materials. She came the next day and told me that he could see me in a couple of days' time, at ten to two in the afternoon. That struck me as distinctly odd, as it would to anyone who's lived in Africa where time is generally less precise. 'Later on in the day' would have been a more normal appointment. So I queried it with Justina. 'Well, Ntate', she said, 'ten to two is one fifty pm. What he's saying is that, if you give him a hundred and fifty rand, he'll provide me with a plot of land'. I wasn't going to start bribing anybody, so instead I called on the chief's superior further down the valley, only to find that he was scarcely sober and plainly wouldn't remember anything he'd said.

The final move was to head for the Lands Department in the capital Maseru – not to see the government minister but the civil servant in charge. There were a couple of young women working in his office who asked me to wait until he was free. The wait was very instructive. There were a couple of filing cabinets in their room, one of which turned out to contain tea, coffee and biscuits, the other to have nothing in it but fashion magazines. There was a radiator turned fully on, although it was summer: I deduced that this was a departmental status symbol, which needed to be on proper display. The building, by the way, had been paid for by the British taxpayer, and had recently been opened by Malcolm Rifkind. One other visitor arrived during my wait – a local Mosotho, poorly dressed, whom the ladies vilified and rapidly evicted. I was treated rather better and as a result of the visit Justina got her land, and before we left Lesotho she was living in her own house.

Sadly, another – and certainly unsought – challenge was to be involved in student expulsions. I inherited responsibility for a seminary which had been neglected for some time; and, not only was it necessary to overhaul its teaching programme and its provision of worship (which led in a year or two to the construction of a new chapel), but the bishop specifically asked for unsuitable candidates for the priesthood to be weeded out. His actual words were 'I've enough problems already with the existing clergy: one third of them have drink problems, one third have money problems, and one third have problems with women. Don't let me in for any more of those'. There was one student in particular who seemed less than fully committed to his vocation. He was frequently absent, and at weekends he had various lady visitors, all of whom he introduced as his 'sister'. At first I took this in a literal sense, then allowed that he might be using the word idiomatically as meaning someone from his village, but finally was driven to the conclusion that they were in reality just girlfriends from anywhere. Certainly they were a distraction to him as well as to other students. I asked him what had led him to join the seminary. His reply? 'My father pointed out that teachers in Lesotho receive no pension when they retire, whereas clergy do. So he told me to get myself ordained'. Of course, this didn't preclude the possibility that he might grow into a vocation. All of us, including priests, may initially have mixed motives in what we do, but that's the way God often works. Musa, however, showed no sign of changing his casual attitude, hence I had reluctantly to recommend to the bishop that he be asked to leave. This was certainly not popular with some of the local girls, who hung around the seminary entrance for a while, and told me I was a white racist.

A typical Lesotho woven scene with the logo *Khotso* ('peace')
Designed by Peter Hancock (our architect) for St Andrew's Chapel, Roma
The South African government sent a spy over to check out what we were building!

Lesotho was not a country where seminarians could afford a laid-back, casual approach. The government sat lightly to the constitution, and no free elections had taken place for years: a state of emergency had been declared when the ruling party was defeated in the elections of 1971. During our time a law was passed restricting political gatherings to no more than three people. Intimidation was so rife that even within the seminary open discussion about the problems facing the country met with guarded response. Almost every week our students – and those who attended Sunday mass – reported incidents occurring in their home villages. Usually these followed a familiar pattern: a night-time raid by government supporters against those suspected of being in opposition, with people disappearing for questioning, sometimes never to re-appear. Our bishop Philip received threatening anonymous letters, and found his van tailed more than once by the paramilitary. If my own sermons ventured from time to time into political territory, there were usually friendly warnings from the congregation reminding me to go carefully.

The most startling event that happened to us was one evening in our house, which was adjacent to a student hostel on the university campus. The back door suddenly opened, and a student covered in blood burst in and hid under the kitchen table. Fortunately he was not pursued. He explained that the government youth wing was attacking students suspected of dissident activities. They had seized him in his room and beaten him up, and he'd only escaped by jumping from a first floor balcony and running from the building. We offered to clean him up, but he insisted as a law student that before doing so we should first take photographs of him and send copies to the embassies in Maseru.

The government of course strenuously denied that such intimidation ever took place, and the local police station played their part by eventually 'losing' the student's file. Although I made the contacts that he had requested, my faith in the diplomatic service was not as great as his. I had already met the over-cautious and exceedingly discreet British High Commissioner at a lunch ('Lovely day, isn't it?' I said – to which he replied, 'It would appear to be so for the time being'), together with his flamboyant American counterpart who poked me in the ribs and congratulated me giving voice to his tunnel vision of missionary work: 'You boys are doing a great job keeping the commies out'. These encounters must be coupled with another occasion when I'd visited the High Commission, after our son had been stoned just outside the campus by local village boys. The underling I spoke to then suggested such things were bound to happen if the boys' mothers let them play outside after tea, whereupon I tried to conjure up an image of cucumber sandwiches on a manicured lawn. Hence my reservations!

I wouldn't necessarily describe Lesotho's police force as corrupt, but in Roma it was certainly 'relaxed'. One day our horse Ivan, who occasionally broke loose from his tethers, seemed to have vanished altogether from the university campus where we were based. I reported this loss to the local police station, who instructed me to let them know when I'd found out who'd stolen him; then they'd go and arrest that person. There was actually no need to lay any accusations in the end, as Ivan turned up at his stable the next day. We discovered a similar relaxed approach in other dealings with officialdom: our telephone, for example, was frequently out of action for a couple of weeks at a time. Once, when a much longer interval had passed with a faulty line, I made a personal visit to the exchange in Maseru. 'How long's it been like that?' they asked. 'Well, almost a month now,' I replied. 'That's over four weeks, isn't it? – OK, we'll look into it', they promised. The implication was that any shorter breakdown in their system was normal and not worth investigating at all.

In case the above accounts sound unduly critical of African attitudes, perhaps an anecdote from our Irchester days offers a useful comparison. A surprise visitor to the Vicarage one day was a policeman who came with an unusual request. Our house looked across to the village police house, where the resident officer had just received a threatening letter, thought to have been written by a gypsy who'd recently faced justice over his dodgy horse trading. We were asked if a police car could be kept for the day in our garage, while a rota of officers would keep watch on the police house from our sitting room window. The man on duty first fulfilled every expectation, never once taking his eyes off the threatened building. The one who followed in the afternoon was pretty good, but took time out to sit down and have a cup of tea. In the evening, the officer sat in an armchair writing up his notes, without apparently glancing even once through the window. So if 'relaxed' attitudes may be judged appropriate in the UK, who would deny them to others?

When we reached Malawi fifteen years later, political tensions were very much in the air. For nearly 30 years after independence Malawi was ruled by 'life-president' Kamuzu Banda, and it took considerable effort to introduce a more democratic arrangement. In fact, one unsung hero of the struggle in the 1980s was a Kiltegan missionary priest called Patrick O'Malley, who – along with being the Catholic chaplain – taught literature in the university. He sent me a copy of his memoir *Living Dangerously*; and I realised on reading it how quite unexpectedly it was his engagement with other writers, as well as with his own students, that proved to be God's way of moving mysteriously at that crucial time 'his wonders to perform'. Banda had become a ruthless dictator who brooked no criticism and suppressed all opposition. The churches remained silent, but it was O'Malley and his colleagues who rekindled hopes of justice and freedom, and gave courage even to the bishops. It was poetry in particular that became a vehicle of coded communication, its language and imagery potentially conveying subversive meanings to those capable of appreciating them. 'Suffer us not to mock ourselves with falsehoods', wrote T. S. Eliot – words which O'Malley was able to convince his students were of contemporary relevance. While Banda was ever ready to ban modern dramatic writings, he was unaware that certain classic plays, such as Julius Caesar, involved the assassination of dictators no worse than himself. In the end, the Catholic bishops realised there was a huge groundswell of support behind them, and it was their pastoral letter read throughout the country that led to Banda's resignation. In my view Patrick O'Malley played an exemplary priestly role.

It was under Banda's elected successor Bakili Muluzi that we found ourselves at the start of the 21st century, well into his second term of office. The new constitution specifically limited the president to a maximum of two consecutive terms – precisely to prevent another life president taking over. In Africa, as no doubt elsewhere, many politicians start with high ideals but rapidly succumb to the temptations of high office. Muluzi was no exception, and he saw that he could legally hold on to power if the constitution were to be amended. To this end he illegally banned public discussion of the issue and ordered the police to suppress any dissent. There were of course strong protests from church leaders and from civil society who cherished their hard-won rights. (Ironically, the traditional form of democracy in Southern Africa was the *pitso*, in which village men would sit down and thrash out the pros and cons of any proposals until – hopefully – they reached *consensus*. Much better, surely, than Western ideas of majority voting, which chiefly endorses tribalism? When our friend Bishop Patrick Kalilombe, however, introduced 'small parish groups' into his Lilongwe diocese he was deported by Dr Banda.)

My own involvement in Muluzi's constitutional crisis came unexpectedly through my un-anticipated appointment as parish priest of Zomba (together with its two dozen out-stations!) – in addition to continuing full-time duties as a lecturer. One morning the verger reported to me that armed police were now on church premises. Immediately I set off to see the divisional police chief to request their removal, pointing out that Christians were agents of peace and non-violence, and that it was quite unacceptable to bring weapons of any sort on to church property. His first line of defence was that they were there to protect our building from angry students – for example, to prevent the breakage of our windows. I observed that we had never had any quarrel with students, and that in any case we had no glass in our windows, which were actually cement blocks with slits for light and ventilation. He then said that it was his job to prevent public meetings taking place, which in Zomba meant gatherings of university students. This was the real target of my visit – to remind him that the police's prime duty was to uphold the constitution, under which there was a fundamental right of peaceful assembly, and indeed a freedom of speech which included the right of peaceful dissent and protest. I added that it was in any case highly unlikely that if students exercised any such rights they would so at St George's, since it was on the opposite side of the town to the university Were students at all likely to walk two miles to a meeting when there were plenty of alternative venues closer at hand?

At last the truth emerged: his officers had been instructed to patrol the approach roads to State House, which was one of the presidential residences not far from St George's, in case anyone chose to attack it. It was now clear to him that they were taking advantage of the warm sunny morning to rest on the grass and the benches outside our church. An officer was dispatched to get them moving again. It may seem to have been a storm in a teacup, but it did provide an opportunity to reflect on the presidential powers and the constitutional rights of the people – hence to challenge the police about their own role. The importance of priestly vigilance is borne out in a later incident, when students protested about some other issue, and Zomba police dispersed them with live bullets. One student died, and the official line was that the police had reacted in self-defence. The post-mortem examination by an expatriate doctor revealed that he was shot in the back, obviously running away. But that version never got out to the public – a story again endlessly familiar across the world.

There was a rather less dramatic occasion when I encountered the CID in Zomba. To my surprise they were housed in a modest outhouse at the rear of the police station, more like a white-washed cowshed than an office. It was a Wednesday morning, because on the Sunday I'd been there earlier to report a break-in and theft while we were down at church. I had mentioned that the only person aware of our unprotected property was the watchman, who was absent at a family funeral. The police had not merely questioned him but had already put him in prison – and now his wife was with us, pleading for his release. The officer in charge explained that he'd been arrested as one under suspicion, although the stolen goods (a radio and several CDs) had not been found. 'So you have no firm evidence?' I suggested. 'No, but he's the obvious culprit,' came the answer. 'What are you going to do?' was my next question, 'The law says he can't be held for more than 48 hours without being charged'. 'What would you like us to do?' 'Surely it's not a matter of what I like, it's a matter of complying with the law'. 'All right then, we'll let him out tomorrow. It'll teach him a lesson. But can you have a look at the prison book and find his name: I'm not sure exactly where he is right now'. Once that task was accomplished, he decided it was lunchtime, so saw us out of the office, locked the door and (for extra high security) placed the key under a stone just outside.

As a matter of fact, the watchman was treated leniently by local standards. A month previously we'd been woken in the middle of the night by the blowing of whistles, and men racing round the house shouting. In the morning, we asked what the fuss had been. The watchman said that he'd heard a sound in the outside toilet, so had sounded the alarm for the squad to come up with truncheons and helmets from the centre of town. On arrival they'd swarmed out of their truck and burst into the said toilet where they'd found the watchman from next door, overcome with paroxysms of diarrhoea. Having beaten him with their truncheons, they'd sent him back to use his own toilet. Surely a lesson he was unlikely ever to forget?

As you can see, life in Malawi had its lighter moments. It certainly wasn't all gloom and doom in the Malawian church either, where, despite the ongoing disputes between different factions, there were some delightfully unanticipated moments. After preaching at the opening of a new church in a neighbouring parish, I was sat down in front of the altar and showered with gifts. Everyone in the congregation danced forward with something from their gardens, and I went home laden with at least two dozen cabbages, quantities of other vegetables, four dozen eggs, a couple of live hens and a live cock. The only problem was then to find homes for all these goodies. Nothing had prepared me for such generosity, which is actually so typical of African hospitality. What is freely shared with visitors and travelers is seen as 'a loan to be repaid' - not necessarily to those who provided it, but to others who may be helped likewise.

I recalled the kind reception of a colleague visiting a remote area of Zambia linked with his English parish: after a long and hot dusty drive, he finally reached this outpost. Modern facilities were not to be seen, with water available only in a bore-hole half a mile away. But in the centre of the village, just outside the church, parishioners had rigged up a screen, concealing a plastic bath and hosepipe. They invited him to go behind the screen to wash and change, explaining that it was a homemade shower room. When he gave the signal, a relay of ladies poured into the bath the water they'd fetched from the bore-hole, enabling him to refresh himself as effectively as if he'd checked in at a five star Hilton Hotel.

Although Africa may not run to parish fetes or Christmas party games, it has an astonishing vibrancy of its own. There is a liveliness and spontaneity not always evident in the sober routines of English church life. Singing, for example, will erupt naturally out of the joy of being together in the Lord's presence – such a contrast to an organist I once inherited in England whose response to any breath of novelty was threefold: 'They won't like it; no one will sing it; I can't play it'. Even a parish music group who contributed monthly to the service seemed unduly regimented. The lead guitarist insisted on counting the beat very audibly to start them off, and even did this before each psalm response. The result was that we never simply acclaimed 'I will walk in the presence of the Lord', but invariably 'one, two, three, four, I will walk in the presence of the Lord', thus turning it into a route march.

The contrast between Africa and the West is best illustrated in the response from the Vatican some years ago to a request from the Congolese church to allow dancing in the liturgy. The ruling came back, that dancing was out, but 'a rhythmic ordered procession' might be permitted. What may have eluded the authorities' consideration in Rome is, of course, that in Africa a rhythmic procession is a dance.

After returning to England, I discovered that in our Catholic parish of Sherborne there were existing African connections. The Malawian president Muluzi had sent his daughters to school there, and the king of Swaziland himself had spent two years (as Crown Prince) learning English at the International College. Indeed, one of his first teachers was a member of our congregation, who explained that his presence in the town was meant to be a closely guarded secret, hedged by strict security. He lodged therefore, not on college premises, but in a rented house whose name was promptly and prominently re-labelled, with bold lettering for all to read: it said 'Swaziland House'. Mswati was enthroned soon after his return home, and to the horror and shame of everyone who'd known him in Sherborne turned rapidly into a ruthless and extravagant dictator with a growing number of wives, for each of whom a palace, expensive cars and staff were provided out of the public purse. The least we could do was to lend support to his critics and indeed his victims, and over several years funds were sent to the Catholic diocese of Manzini.

I paid a short visit there in 2008, staying initially with bishop Louis. He proved to be well acquainted with one of our ex-Roma students, now a senior Anglican priest. So early the next morning the bishop called him on his mobile phone. In less than two hours Mandla joined us for breakfast. He was a Dlamini, and therefore a cousin of Mswati. Was he not concerned about the polarisation between the king and the majority of his people? 'Yes, of course', he said, 'but it's very difficult to make Mswati listen. I used to get regular invitations to royal events, and two years ago I had the opportunity for a brief conversation with him. "Your majesty may have noticed some public unease about the very high cost of your new motor cars. Would it not be possible to travel rather less luxuriously?"' 'And his reply?' I asked. 'The king just looked at me, and walked away, since when invitations to the palace have ceased'.

While we were having this conversation, and catching up on family news, bishop Louis had gone out to the main police station. He'd been summoned there to explain his actions on the previous day. A prominent Christian of a different church had been thrown in prison without charge, and church leaders across the board had gone to the prison to visit him, but without success. A photograph of them grouped outside the prison gate was taken at the time on the bishop's mobile phone and had appeared in a newspaper along with an accompanying report. The bishop said as he left us to talk: 'I may be back in an hour – or they may detain me'. We were relieved when he rejoined us. We knew the outcome had been very much in the balance.

My visit concluded with two nights spent in Fr Moses' parish. Moses met me in Manzini and stopped off on our way back at a supermarket to stock up on food. He needed enough, not just for the two of us, but for the three ravenous orphan lads who lived with him. His one concern was that I should find the menu to my liking. When I explained that I'd enjoy whatever they were eating themselves, he still insisted on buying something that would make me feel at home. He settled on a huge tin of strawberry jam. 'I know you'll like this', he said, 'because all English people like jam'. As it happens, I do. But it tasted of so much else – the kindness and thoughtfulness that is the real Africa.

SABBATICAL SURPRISES

When I was growing up, our family never took holidays abroad. We had no car, so we travelled by train to some coastal resort in Britain and then either walked out from our guest house onto the cliffs and downs or took the occasional excursion on a bus or a steamer. I remember a little of North Wales, and then much of Dorset, later on enjoying the Pembrokeshire coast, and eventually the West of Scotland.

The first time I ever travelled out of the country was with a university folk dancing team that took part in an international festival in West Germany. We were the only group from England, but most other European countries were represented. As this was the mid-1960s, the then communist authorities in the Eastern bloc made sure that their teams were well up to standard: hence, the Czechs and the East Germans were all professional ballet dancers, in an entirely different league from ourselves. Where we hopped around more or less on the beat, they performed amazing feats of perfectly timed athleticism. Nevertheless, the locals who were watching indicated that they felt more at ease with our performance and applauded us far more generously than we deserved. They said, 'We could see you were all really enjoying yourselves'. We didn't, however, bother to explain that we'd steadied our nerves beforehand with ample draughts of lager, which may have contributed to the general merriment. Our speciality was the Morpeth rant, which I can still just about manage; we added a particularly British touch, carrying furled umbrellas as we danced – we couldn't think of any other 'national costume'.

A year or so later, now employed as a teacher, I ventured with colleagues on an expedition to Ireland. First we hired a boat on the river Shannon. It was meant to have six berths, one for each of us, but when we arrived to collect it the boatman explained that during the previous week its propeller shaft had been damaged. 'So I thought I'd get a new one. I reckoned it up, and – would you believe it? – when it came, it was just two inches too short'. If only we'd known in time, we could have sent him a tape measure! He promised to get the old prop shaft repaired, and to have our boat ready in a couple of days' time. Meanwhile he offered us a four berth boat with a two man tent to pitch on the towpath.

Two of our party weren't due until the next day, when we'd arranged to meet them by a particular bridge upstream. So those of us already there slept on board while the latecomers had the tent just for one night. They arose much earlier than they had intended, however, because, just as dawn was breaking the sound of a motorbike was heard. As the noise increased it became obvious that it was travelling along the towpath at considerable speed directly towards the pitched tent. It was indeed fortunate that our friends were not heavy sleepers... We returned somewhat apprehensively to the boathouse, but all was in order with the prop shaft and we were able to navigate the river from Lough Ree in the north to Lough Derg in the south. We performed our good deed for the day after reaching the former, where we discovered a film crew at work taking shots of a Viking longboat. This was manned by actors who seemed to lack any natural sense of rhythm or timing in their attempts to row across the water. One of our group, James, who had rowed for London University and coached the school first eight, took them in hand. His instructions, along the lines of 'in – out, two – out, three – out', seemed to have a magical effect.

Related boating skills had also come into play the previous year when we had less ambitiously taken a narrow boat on the Shropshire Union canal. Here there were a number of locks to navigate, and one Sunday afternoon a fibre glass cruiser stayed too far back in one of them as the level dropped, caught its prop shaft on the lock gate, and gashed itself below the water line. It struggled forwards out of the lock, and promptly sank at the entrance to the pound, effectively blocking all the traffic. We found two long ropes, and between us organised the bystanders into tugging them. One rope went under the cruiser and lifted it off the bottom, while the other was for towing it out of harm's way towards the bank. Whereas on the canal, we passed about two boats each hour, the Shannon was so deserted that it amounted to as little as two per day. Nor were there many locks, which was lucky, as in Ireland the lock keeper has to be summoned from his work in the fields, which might be up to half a mile away.

After this adventure a taxi took us to a farm outside Galway town, where we had booked a horse-drawn caravan to take us around Connemara. We were not surprised to find some running repairs were needed here too; this time we had to take the horse to the smithy to be re-shod. The delay meant that by the time we reached the town it was the peak rush hour. There were many cars, some of them parked, not to mention several traffic lights. None of us had any previous experience in steering such a vehicle, so we were highly nervous of causing serious damage. But providentially the horse had been this way before and knew what to do.

On the other hand, we soon discovered he was not partial to uphill climbs and would often stop sulkily in his tracks until he thought we'd all dismounted (which we only pretended to do). On one particularly steep climb we were overtaken by a cyclist; but on reaching the summit and starting the descent, we soon found ourselves rattling along at an uncomfortably fast pace. It wasn't quite a gallop, but it was a good imitation of a western movie. Our brake had little effect, perhaps because the sink overflow pipe dripped directly onto it. If we were terrified, how much more the cyclist with whom we rapidly caught up. He simply threw himself, bike and all, into the ditch as we thundered past. We raised the issue of the brake's ineffectiveness on our return, but the farmer explained: 'Well now, you wouldn't be wanting it any tighter, or you'd stop him altogether and then he'd never be starting again'.

There was invariably hospitality and kindness as we travelled around, and wherever we needed a field for the night it was provided. On one particular farm we were puzzled how to take advantage of the farmer's generous offer – there was no gate to the field he indicated, which was entirely surrounded by dry stone walls. 'It's not a problem', he said, 'I'll just knock the wall down to let you in'. 'But what happens when we leave?' we asked. 'Don't you worry – I'll build it up again'. More than once we inquired of locals who passed us on the road to find roughly how far we had yet to travel before reaching such-and-such a village. We rapidly learnt that the answers corresponded to what they thought we'd like to hear. Indeed, regardless of the actual distance, it was invariably much the same reply, 'You'll find it over the hill there, just half a mile away'. Sometimes it was nearer five or ten.

The following year I was in Ireland again, this time further south in the hills south of Killarney. This was a project with teenage boys under the umbrella of the Brathay Exploration Group. I'd been recommended as a leader as a result of an *apparently* successful scout camp I'd supervised in Snowdonia. This had been my last outing with the school scout group, and we'd pitched our tents in a field shared with a town troop from Macclesfield. They were proper scouts who knew the drill and did everything by the book. We, by contrast, were pretty casual; for example, I recall several lads eating their entire food ration for the week in a single day and having to beg from the others for the remainder of our stay. I also had a shrewd suspicion that much smoking was taking place, with cigarette ends concealed afterwards under the ground sheets. Towards the end of the week, the local district commissioner carried out his inspection. Afterwards I received a glowing report, which I can only suppose was intended for the town troop, who must by mistake have received ours and been thoroughly embarrassed by its contents.

At any rate, Brathay took me on, and our group met in Fishguard to catch the ferry to Cork. On arrival we piled into a local minibus, which was once again a truly Irish experience. Our driver stopped at every single filling station, not to add more petrol but to top up with oil, which was constantly leaking out of his engine. I estimated he must have lost at least a gallon of it on the journey. But we made it – to a remote farm about four miles from Killarney itself, where we set up camp. This was to be our base for daily expeditions up to a mountain tarn, which it was our task to survey, previous mappings having somehow failed to do so. A rowing boat was available, but otherwise we had to provide our own kit. As well as marking out weighted twine for accurate depth sounding, it was also necessary to post observers on the shoreline to record the exact position of the boat. The oarsmen for their part attempted, not always successfully on the windier days, to stay on a steady course. On the whole, we welcomed the wind, as otherwise there were clouds of midges.

There were two days of intense rain which prevented any sightings on the tarn, so we crowded into the farmhouse kitchen where simple fare was provided at midday. Throughout the year the menu was always the same: jacket potatoes, cooked by the fire all morning, with vegetables in season (this meant either cabbage or turnips), plus a wedge of home-killed pork (much fat, a fragment of meat, and bristles for flavouring). Later in the day we might be offered a mug of tea and a slice of home-baked soda bread. The couple had just one son to help them on the farm. He told us proudly that he'd once visited Cork, but otherwise Killarney marked the limits of his social life (we walked there ourselves one evening, and found men in the bars singing Danny Boy, with tears rolling down their cheeks). His ambition one day was to travel to Dublin. Of course, this long preceded the heady years of Euro money and the radical changes to the Irish economy.

Despite our unsophisticated equipment, we achieved our mapping goals, with the maximum depth of the tarn registering around 100 feet. On our return journey to Cork the minibus seemed in better health, and we caught up there with a massive funeral procession through the streets, complete with black-plumed horses drawing the hearse. These may now be something of a rarity, as the pace of life quickens.

Apart from Ireland, another early overseas destination was the Pyrenees, using Cedric's 'chateau' in the foothills as a base. Cedric, who was uncle to a university friend, had left England in the 1930s, finding it 'too crowded'. His working life was in Paris, but his bolt-hole was half a mile outside Rébenacq, on a road that ran south to Laruns not far from the Spanish border. One Thursday we proposed venturing into the village, but he discouraged it: 'It's market day, it'll be too crowded'. On our return, he asked how things were there. 'We saw a few people, but less than double figures'. 'Well, I did warn you about the crowds', he said in all seriousness.

Life here was as unsophisticated as it was in Ireland. One year we arrived during the grape harvest and were invited to tread the grapes in Cedric's stone winepress. This required us to put on wellington boots and to walk backwards in circles, stamping down with our heels as we went. Everything was thrown in, including any grapes that were unripe (for their juice) and those that were shrivelled and over-ripe (for their colour), plus a few bags of sugar to sweeten the final mix. His wine, not surprisingly, had a distinctive earthy taste, but one could get used to it. It was also the season for shooting migratory birds, which held great appeal for Cedric's gardener, although we thought it very unsporting for him to fix clay decoy models of birds in the woods above. Further up the valley we met flocks of sheep coming down from the high pastures for the winter, and one memorable meal was shared with the shepherds in the local inn where they left their cheeses to be turned and salted regularly.

The real appeal of *Le Balagué* lay in being able to hike in the mountains. Sometimes this required a hair-raising drive up steep roads to find a parking place. My worst experience was in ascending a 1 in 3 gravel track in bottom gear, knowing that if I stalled, I might skid or slip backwards in the attempted re-start. That wouldn't normally matter, but here the track, narrow enough already, was on the edge of a ravine that lay hundreds of feet below – and no crash barrier. However, the agony invariably preceded the ecstasy. Walking on the border here with Spain was always breath-taking.

He who treads on the heights of the earth, the Lord is his name

One year I climbed the highest peak Vignemale with James. Having borrowed ropes and an ice-axe from Cedric, we set off one afternoon, aiming to reach the refuge before nightfall. We were delayed by the one way road system above Lourdes, however, which – at least in those days – allowed traffic to flow in each direction in alternate hours. So as night fell we were well short of our intended shelter. Yet fortune smiled, in the shape of a shepherd's hut which, with a fire blazing all night, kept us warm until sunrise the next day. From here it was a steady six hour walk to the summit, our ascent being slowed over the glacier where we had to cut steps in the ice. (I didn't want to repeat an earlier incident, where in crossing a col my foot had slipped on the snow causing me to descend about half a mile in a very short time down the valley until I was able to brace myself against some rocks. Even so, the chamois we saw invariably travelled faster still on these slopes.) We had but a short time to linger on the summit before the afternoon mists and clouds gathered, as they usually did in the Pyrenees, but the views from it were magnificent in every direction.

> You mention some Ben (in Gaelic a hill), but from the entangled appearance of the Letters I cannot discover the name, and shall therefore call it Ben Blot; we did not see it. To mount a very high hill, is an adventure of dubious success; you are very often repaid with fog and vapour for your trouble [wrote Sydney Smith].

There were no such expeditions in the immediate aftermath of ordination: holidays took us to the West Country, into Norfolk and to the North Yorkshire moors. But then Lesotho, 'Kingdom of the Sky', beckoned. Here even the lowlands are essentially high veldt, at an altitude of 6000 feet, with the remaining two-thirds of the country rising several thousand feet more. There were many Saturdays when we set out by ourselves or with friends to walk in the mountains. Once or twice we were caught in terrifying thunderstorms, with lightning bouncing off the rocks around us, necessitating temporary shelter in a nearby cave.

Once we came across a man lying dead, who'd fallen (or been pushed?) over a cliff. We also encountered a wedding party, where we were offered raw strips of beef to eat, and a village feast, where the chief handed me a pinch of some strange grey powder. I gave it a tentative lick, whereupon he roared with laughter and told me to sniff it. It was snuff! One day in the south of the country we found women singing as they threshed their corn, who gave us *joala* to drink. This is beer brewed from maize. It looks like cold milky coffee and tastes unpleasantly bitter – but it kept them going all day.

Another time, above the notorious *Modimo N'Thuse* ('God help me') pass, where thieves sometimes pounced on slow uphill traffic as it negotiated the endless hairpin bends, we hired ponies and rode to the Quilane Falls. In the pool below there was a gathering of the Zionist Church, decked out in their white and coloured robes. We studied the ritual of immersions for some time, and concluded that it seemed to be a penitential, rather than an initiation, ceremony.

Often we parked vehicles at opposite ends of a route, and exchanged keys when we met halfway. But once, after a long riverside walk, we found our friends' car had been damaged. There had been a failed attempt to steal two of the wheels, which wobbled frantically as I started to drive. Without a jack or indeed tools of any description, we had no option but to continue walking many more miles until we reached the road from Ramabanta, where eventually we hitched a ride home on the back of a lorry. Our daughter Patricia aged 5 was disappointed in not being able to extend her hike beyond the 22 miles already covered. We came to appreciate her point of view on the steep hill down into Roma valley, where our driver probably broke all records for the speed of his descent in the pitch dark.

While occasionally there was wildlife to be seen in these Maluti mountains – such as lammergeier circling overhead, or baboons in the undergrowth – potential habitats were in increasingly limited supply. By contrast, Malawi much further north boasted tropical forest, savannah, riverine marshes and (its jewel) Lake Malawi itself. We managed to explore several parts of the country during the more recent years we spent there. Only one hour's drive away from our house was Liwonde National Park, bordering the Shire river. Our visitors could rely upon seeing bird life in abundance here, and always antelopes, kudu, warthogs, hippos, crocodiles and elephants.

In the southern end of the park I was once on my own with an unarmed guide walking through the bush. The previous week there had been lions around, but he 'believed' they'd moved east into the hills. After a couple of hours, after emerging from the woods we approached a shrub-covered mound. 'Now that', he explained, 'is exactly the sort of place where young lions like to keep a look-out and lie in wait for their prey'. As it happened, none was on duty at the time. One week later, this over-confident guide met with disaster. He was tracking elephants with a small English party when a bull elephant turned and attacked them, killing one of the women. This being Malawi, however, his licence to operate was not revoked.

At other times, the authorities did display a concern for public safety. We took a couple of trips on the old (1950s) passenger tub MV Ilala, which each week sails northwards from Monkey Bay taking essential supplies (sacks of maize and live chickens among them) to the lakeshore villages. Our departures were delayed by several hours until the government inspector was satisfied adequate repairs had been carried out – for example, to the deck rails. At Nkhata Bay on our first trip we loaded up with sacks of sugar for delivery across the lake in Tanzania, but the chief engineer considered the ship was overloaded and refused to sail with it. As the weather was calm, we took a chance and made the crossing safely there and back.

Not many days after we had disembarked, a terrible accident occurred in the night. The two so-called lifeboats were ferrying people ashore when a violent storm blew up and capsized one of them. Only the men aboard were able to swim, so a score or more of women and children drowned. Our feeling was that, as these boats were invariably overladen, there may have been even thirty or forty who died; but at the inquiry the captain insisted that precisely twenty-two had been on board. Was it a sheer coincidence that this was the very number each of the ship's boats was licensed to carry?

Three years on, we sailed with the Ilala to Mozambique, to a remote corner that still bore the devastating marks of the civil war. We saw one of the most astonishing sights of the lake – cylindrical columns of mating flies rising up to a hundred feet or more above the water. The centre of each column, so we were told, was where the males clustered together, viewed by females on the periphery who were talent spotting, their ideal partner apparently needing to be as symmetrically-shaped as possible. The first night ashore was also rather fly-ridden, but the next day the air cleared and we walked on the clean white *nkwichi* ('squeaky') sands. Little did we know then, as we saw for ourselves shortly afterwards, that crocodiles flourished in the water only half a mile along the shore. Crocodiles, though, are essentially lazy, and prefer to keep an eye on places that are more regularly frequented by human beings. Hippos, we'd already learnt, can be less predictable. Over on the opposite side of the lake we'd seen half of a dugout canoe abandoned on the beach. A local boy told us then: 'My father was out fishing in his dugout, when hippos swam past, and one of them attacked, biting the boat in half and killing my father at the same time'.

The only dangers encountered on the Malawi mainland were manmade. As we travelled towards the western escarpment at Dzalanyama we found the tracks increasingly waterlogged, and finally ground to a halt in the mud. Inevitably we were soon surrounded by a crowd of children who enjoyed pushing us out and were duly rewarded. The very opposite happened on Nyika Plateau, where we were heading for one of best viewpoints when we found the grasslands around us rapidly catching fire with us trapped in the middle. It happened to be the time of year when this was deliberately induced, but without any immediately visible warning to visitors. The only way to escape was to drive straight forwards down the track, which had a thinner covering of grass and fewer flames than elsewhere. I trusted to luck that our fuel tank would be spared, and we made it to safety.

It was also a truck ride that was to give us a few unplanned thrills down south. Our house, on the slopes of Zomba mountain, faced south [NB not in that hemisphere the direction of the midday sun] and presented us with a lovely vista of the Mulanje range in the distance. Here were the highest mountains between Kilimanjaro and the Drakensburgs, stretching a good thirty miles across. We made three trips into them, each time staying in the mountain huts provided. A climb of three thousand feet up to the plateau was necessary from any of the valleys below but, with the local economy relying on visitors to hire porters, the burden of carrying one's kit was shared. Our first porter was named Hanky (confusing when one addressed him by name). His ambition was to read computer studies at college. He was tall and fast, and quite unconcerned when the straps of our Chinese-made rucksack, newly bought in Zomba market, collapsed. He simply balanced the weight on his head instead as he skipped along. It was the fastest hike we'd ever experienced. When on our descent I inquired how long it might take to reach a stream flowing down below, he said: 'It'd take me twenty minutes, but we're going so slowly it may well be more like forty'. There was actually an annual porters' race, which took them up the steep mountain path, before contouring around and down again to cover in a few hours a route that took us three days. One year the winner went on, with no training other than his experience as a porter, to compete in his first-ever marathon in Lilongwe. He won, in a time of two hours fifteen minutes.

For our longest trip in Mulanje, which was a traverse of the whole range, we took two porters, as of course there had to be sufficient food for several days. The weather was perfect, and we successfully made it, descending to the small town well east of our starting point. It was then about the middle of the day, and with no organised public transport we needed to find a truck heading back west. I inquired in a shop, where they pointed out a driver waiting to load up passengers. He needed, he said, a dozen to make his trip worthwhile, so thought he might be setting off in an hour or two. I offered him extra for our fares if he went slightly sooner, and a deal was struck. I was perched in the open back, which proved to be a better place than in the one passenger seat (where Sarah sat, unfortunately far more conscious of the vehicle's deficiencies, starting with an entire absence of springs in her seat and a crazed windscreen). Our nerves were tested most of all as we approached the narrow plank bridges over the various streams. The driver invariably halted first, because his radiator leaked (shades of Cork!) and he needed to top up with water. But we had become aware that his steering was also defective, and we seldom advanced consistently in a straight line. On a section of ordinary track, with hardly any other traffic around, that was not a problem; but crossing an unprotected narrow bridge did raise doubts in one's mind. Nevertheless, I argued statistically that he'd crossed these bridges a number of times before in the same vehicle – indeed, once already earlier that same day – and so the chances immediately looked rosier. I am glad to report that my calculations were justified.

Thus, we survived the hazards of the African continent. We kept free of malaria, bilharzia, and cholera. As others did too, I always carried a stick when we were out walking to ward off any potentially rabid dogs. In the house there was a small risk of rabies carried by bats that occasionally came down the chimney, so that gloves were worn in handling them should that be necessary. Towards the end of our time, we stopped over in Ethiopia to explore the so-called 'historic route' and here our unfamiliarity with local conditions induced a serious mistake. We chose to ride mules up to a mountain pass in search of an ancient hermitage. The mules saved our legs, but gave us scabies – unpleasant and itchy, but treatable.

The seven years spent on the continent came therefore with challenges not previously encountered. But our blessings undoubtedly far outweighed any setbacks, and gave us so much more: not least, a resourcefulness to cope with the unexpected, and deeper friendships than any previously experienced.

COUNTING THE COST

Africa was my safe haven, a place of refuge away from the stormy seas of English church life. It was where I went primarily to teach, yet in the event it provided the setting where I learnt far more than I ever taught. It was a liberating experience of a culture with often different values and expectations, although these were evidently beginning to succumb rapidly to Western influences. It was certainly a less stressful way of life, even if there were many material limitations – frequent power cuts, water shortages, much more basic shopping, pot-holed roads and dirt tracks, a virtual absence of books and bookshops (to name but a few).

When returning to the UK, the major readjustment was always on the flight back. There by one's seat was the duty-free catalogue, with a plethora of perfumes, electronic gadgets, and jewellery, all of which begged the question Why? Why, for example, would anyone want a pearl-encrusted biro? Would it improve the legibility of their hand-writing or inspire their literary efforts, or for that matter encourage them to deal with their correspondence more promptly? The duty-free trolley symbolised the cultural divide between a world that valued possessions and a world that valued people. (Nevertheless, on arrival in Malawi in the year 2000, I visited the Blantyre office of the internet provider SDNP, and after paying their fee was connected to the internet by the time I reached home an hour later. Over ten years later, when we moved house in England but remained on the same phone package with TalkTalk, it took them an unbelievable six weeks to connect us to the internet even after the landline went live. On the other hand, phones hardly ever worked in Lesotho, while the inefficiency of banks, government offices and the postal service was legendary.)

It is of course facile to exaggerate any differences, but I certainly owe a personal debt to Africa, even while admitting to having been a privileged outsider. Without pretending that the Garden of Eden was ever located there, one sometimes caught glimpses of how human affairs might be more felicitously ordered. Once, after being generously accommodated in the Catholic seminary in Namibia to continue studying inculturation in the African church, we visited a game park further north in the country near Etosha. We were fortunate to be allocated a room overlooking a water-hole, which provided an entrancing spectacle for the whole of one morning. Emerging at separate intervals from the bush, groups of different birds and animals came unhurriedly to refresh themselves at the pool; among them were baboons, and zebras, various antelopes, giraffes – and much later in the day, several lions. What struck me was the absence of conflict over this precious resource. All the creatures that relied upon it took their turn, and – so it seemed – waited considerately until others had moved away. Perhaps it was this invisible queuing system that appealed to my British instincts. Even so there was the sense of a world at peace with itself, ready to share and share alike.

Such an ideal is elusive; in Lesotho one soon encountered the reality of African life. For example, vegetation there is now sparse. Much of the country lies above 6000 feet, giving rise to its popular description as 'kingdom of the sky'. Yet with overgrazing in the mountains, and few tree plantations in the valleys, the lowlands have become eroded by dongas – deep gulleys where flood water has washed the soil away. Bird life is noticeably absent too, partly because there are relatively few nesting places but also because herdboys, who are still sent up into the mountains during the summer months, depend upon birds and mice to supplement their otherwise basic diet of maize meal.

A similar situation occurred in Malawi, with deforestation largely the result of clearing land for crops to feed a growing population but also through the demand for fuel (often as charcoal, which was more compact). Village boys also deployed different methods to catch their birds. Rather than relying upon the deadly catapults of the Basotho, they took sticky sap from the *kachere* (wild fig) tree, smearing it on twigs placed near ponds and streams. In the course of a morning dozens of small birds might be caught in this simple trap as they perched ready for a drink. We were fortunate to live on the lower slopes of Zomba mountain, and to have a greater abundance of birds in our own garden, including several different owls at night. There was also the occasional monkey, and a nest of so-called 'house snakes' which indeed appeared inside my study through a subsidence crack in the floor. We had to guard these against them being killed, as this was too often the likeliest reaction to be pursued locally. Malawians have a regard for all forms of wildlife except for snakes, all of which they unhesitatingly describe as dangerous black mambas. In fact, house snakes are a good insurance against rodents.

One day I noticed a long procession of army ants passing our back door, with a small snake close by. It seemed to me there was quite a feast awaiting him, but ten minutes later the reverse had happened – he'd been completely eaten by the ants. To deflect them from passing through our house, which had occurred once before, I followed the local practice of sprinkling barriers of wood ash near the doors and windows. It was generally reckoned that a single line of these ants, which often stretched for tens of yards, might contain several million individuals. Once we were walking on the plateau above Zomba and needed to cross a footbridge over the Mulunguzi stream. The problem we faced was a line of army ants doing the same thing, so we simply ran as fast as possible to minimise any contact with them. When well clear, all of our party had to strip off, as the ants by then were well up our legs and crawling even higher.

Other ants, along with termites, are less threatening. Indeed, the season is eagerly awaited when flying ants emerge from their nests, as they provide a tasty source of protein. At other times too – particularly if harvested crops have failed or been exhausted – recourse is made to less likely food supplies such as roots and uncultivated leaves, and rodents of any kind. In Lesotho a stray cat once made her home with us, giving birth to a litter of kittens. One or two of these disappeared without trace, possibly eaten by a nearby villager.

Apart from game parks, where larger animals gain some protection, there are few sightings of wild mammals; yet Africa still teems with insect life, and an entomologist in Malawi once estimated that up to 30,000 different species of insects might be found there – the current known count being a little more than 12,000. I asked him how many of these were likely to bite human beings: 'About fifty', he thought, 'including perhaps twenty different types of mosquito – although only anopheles females transmit malaria'. So day-to-day existence is probably less challenging than a midge-plagued summer in Scotland!

Although Malawi is in the tropics, it is not as universally hot and humid as might be imagined. On leaving our Somerset parish, one ex-naval officer suggested otherwise, but at 3500 feet above sea-level the winter months were cold enough to warrant log fires (as also in Lesotho, where snow often falls during the same season). Traditionally, village houses were well insulated against both excessive heat and cold, with thick mud or stone walls surmounted by thatch. Growing scarcity of thatching material, along with a slowly developing cash economy, meant that corrugated sheets were becoming more and more common. It also meant that interiors were exceedingly hot at the height of summer and freezing in the winter.

In Lesotho, therefore, I tried my hand as a small-time builder. The first construction was a small thatched rondavel in which the children could play. Unfortunately, it soon needed a roofing repair, as the lively little boys next door to us enjoying playing with matches and managed to scorch half the grass roof before we could extinguish the blaze. Two other projects soon followed at the seminary, now expanding with students from Soweto (courtesy of their bishop, at this time Desmond Tutu, who as a former lecturer in Roma was always supportive of our work). The college truck was housed in a garage built by the students, and then our horse likewise gained the benefit of a stable. Both these edifices had tin roofs and secure wooden doors.

In a continuing flush of building fever, the next project was an extra bedroom for use on hot summer nights and for guests. This was a rather larger rondavel with a roof made of reeds bought in bundles from a waterside village quite a few miles away in a different valley. Once the walls were up, the roofing supports had to be fitted – and here the project nearly ended when my rickety ladder collapsed and I landed on a jagged spike that gashed me a fraction of an inch above the heart. After that, I engaged a local thatcher to finish the job, with our seminary ladies adding the final wet mixture of mud and cow dung to the walls and to the floor inside. This layer of 'paint' was applied with actual sheep skin, then decorated with patterns using a kitchen fork before it dried. It was customary to renew this protective coating prior to Christmas each year.

One final construction was the building of a small coracle for our children to use on the nearby dams. I copied the design from a book about St Patrick, using local willow which, although not native to Lesotho, is abundant in the valleys after being introduced from Cape Province. Waterproofing was effected by an outer cladding of tar-covered hessian. To my surprise it floated and could easily be steered with a paddle.

The real challenge remained: to construct a proper seminary chapel that would also serve as the Anglican church for university students and parishioners in Roma valley. The existing arrangement was the sharing of a small hall within our grounds, once kindly donated by the neighbouring Catholic convent. The other main users were a play-school on weekday mornings, a Seventh Day Adventist group on Saturdays, an occasional book fair and a ladies' craft cooperative. This meant tidying the premises and reordering the furniture in advance of every single service – which included each day of the week of course. Expatriates were keen to see a large thatched rondavel erected on our small campus, but the bishop was clear that it must be a 'proper' Western architect-designed building. Such different perceptions about African life and culture were not uncommon. It was heartening to discover that in matters of music and pastoral outreach, if not architecture, there was a lively, innovative Lumko Institute in the Transkei which was helping churches to engage much more with local traditions.

We were fortunate to find a Catholic (actually ex-Anglican) architect in the capital Maseru whose real love was to design places of worship. He had several such constructions already completed elsewhere, one being the imposing Catholic chapel nearby on the university campus. This was octagonal in shape, and therefore offered an approximation to worship in the round. Peter's idea for our own chapel was a simpler diamond, rising to a lofty height, whose essential structure would be four laminated half portals joined at the centre. The walls would thus not be load-bearing, and could be moved outwards to provide future extensions. This indeed happened two decades later, by which time the parish congregation had doubled in size.

It was clear from the outset that the project would be too ambitious for any local firms. Reliable electricians and plumbers were hard to come by in our domestic experience, both in Lesotho and in Malawi. If, in *The No.1 Ladies' Detective Agency*, Mma Makutsi is highly regarded for her 97% secretarial achievement, that figure also seemed to be the ceiling for any tradesman we ever engaged. In Zomba, for example, when new staff houses were constructed, it was no surprise to find hot water emerging from the cold tap, and vice versa, but it was slightly unusual for the toilet to be perpetually flushed with heated water. Again, a Malawian colleague there occupied the house once intended for ourselves, but we were relieved not to have faced the series of bangs and flashes that accompanied his first depression of the main light switch. In Roma our water might have been heated by a simple solar panel on the roof, but it had been fixed at an angle that defied the laws of gravity and thus inhibited any flow of water. And whenever any drains were blocked in our compound, I found my own efforts at clearing them were usually more effective than those of the local ground-staff.

This was somewhat dispiriting, because there was an abundance of potential labour in the university works department – indeed, a work force of nearly 150 men. This figure was subject to a steady increase, for the simple reason that, whereas our friend Patrick tried to run the university refectory efficiently and sacked drunken or absentee staff on a regular basis, the local chief refused to accept the dismissal of any of his villagers. They were therefore redeployed as ground-staff elsewhere on the campus. This enabled them to spend many happy hours drinking and playing cards behind the works shed, occasionally invited by their quietly charming and highly qualified boss (with a master's degree in civil engineering from Edinburgh University) to do some work. I once overheard his less-than-forceful approach to his otherwise unoccupied team of workers: 'I gather there's been some leakage of sewage onto the main track through the campus: I wonder if any of you could spare a moment to have a look and see what needs to be done? So sorry to disturb you all…' It was sad to regard the fruits of such lethargy. Many of the buildings had been donated by overseas agencies or governments, but since their construction negligible maintenance had allowed many of them to lapse into a sorry state of repair. The underlying attitude, one began to suspect, was 'You built it in the first place, you should look after it' – arguably making a preference for indigenous architecture using traditional skills a more realistic and sustainable approach.

For our new chapel, Peter had to look to his proven Maseru contacts, and obtained several quotations from building firms run by expatriates or South Africans.

The tenders were all suspiciously close to each other, varying only by a few hundred rand. It was obvious that our project had been discussed in the bar at the Maseru club, so Peter put in a word to his Portuguese Catholic ally: didn't he appreciate that this was a chapel, not a nightclub or a bank? 'In that case', came the airy reply, 'we can cut the figure by half – but we won't make much profit, you understand?' The agreed sum was then forty thousand rand, which in those days was the equivalent of ten thousand pounds. Our appeal for funds met with a surprisingly ready response from around the world. The whole cost was met in roughly equal parts by our own missionary society USPG, by the Anglican Church of the province, by the United Church of Canada, and by the Lutheran Church in Germany. In addition, my parents generously paid for seating which was made in Lesotho, as was the *Khotso* tapestry designed by our architect to hang behind the altar. At one point, work had to be halted for a few weeks until the final donation was secured, but soon afterwards we were ready for the dedication to proceed. Fr Eugene Lapointe, one of our Catholic colleagues at St Augustine's Seminary, was the preacher.

Away from our compound within the university we were also responsible for a small congregation at the mission hospital further up the valley, while an hour's rough riding over rocky ground in the truck took us to a couple of out-stations in the mountains. At Popa there was a simple rectangular church constructed by the congregation themselves, and at Ngope Tsoeu we gathered in one of the huts belonging to a elderly villager called Alice. The latter was a simple arrangement, but less satisfactory than having a dedicated chapel in that one came to discover that not all the villagers got on well with Alice and so absented themselves from her house. We usually picked up others on our way, giving us a very full truck. On our arrival the catechist would strike the 'bell' – a large metal sheet hanging from a post – to summon the body of the congregation. About half an hour later a stream of people might be seen crossing one of the high ridges bordering the valley, with another twenty minutes' walk to reach Mè Alice' rondavel. On their descent we could hear them talking and singing, since sound travelled so clearly in the unpolluted mountain air. (I recall once talking in normal conversational tones to a man on the opposite hillside, at least half a mile away.) More unexpected though at Ngope Tsoeu was the provision of a donkey one Palm Sunday, on which I had to ride in our outdoor procession. I stayed on, much to the amazement of the villagers, who said afterwards: 'He's a real brute – we thought he'd throw you off'.

Whereas in Lesotho we served a scattered rural population, in Malawi our base in Zomba was much more urban. In colonial days it had been the capital, and now numbered at least 50,000 people. After Kamuzu Banda moved his headquarters to the newly constructed city of Lilongwe (thus plunging the country into debt from which it has never since fully recovered), many of the old colonial buildings were taken over for research purposes or for educational use. The parish of St George's, Zomba, however, stretched much further afield, with a steadily growing number of village out-stations, some of which had their own simple chapels for worship. On the outskirts of Zomba too, the population was increasing, so that at least two new churches were built in our time. The only assistance the congregations there received was in the occasional transport of materials (so I might arrive for Sunday mass with a few sacks of cement) and money to pay for roofing timbers and sheets. Otherwise bricks were molded and burnt by the people themselves, and the construction work was undertaken by voluntary local labour. Remarkably little bureaucracy seemed to hinder the process. Very soon it became possible for these new buildings to become the centre of new parishes, separate from St George's.

My main responsibility, however, lay with the theological college, which – although an ecumenical venture – was in fact dominated by the Presbyterian majority, who weren't always sympathetic to Anglican concerns, such as a need for pastoral and liturgical training. Out of a full-time staff of nine or ten I was the only Anglican lecturer, and whereas our Anglican numbers were limited to about two dozen, the student body usually totalled nearly a hundred. Malawi is exceptional in its Presbyterian strength, which derives from its Scottish ancestry. David Livingstone, on discovering that the Zambezi gorges and cataracts impeded his progress westwards, turned northwards into the Shire, its tributary river which flows out of Lake Malawi through the continuing rift valley. 'What's that?' he is said to have asked, pointing at the lake. 'Stupid question', thought his African guide, who politely replied, '*Nyasa*' – meaning lake. 'I shall call it Lake Nyasa!' declared Livingstone (perhaps a trifle patronisingly?). On his return to England, Livingstone stirred up missionary (and commercial) enthusiasm, as a result of which both UMCA (the Anglican Universities' Mission to Central Africa) and the Church of Scotland's mission were both launched. Theological collaboration in Zomba began in the late 1970s, and indeed came to include other seminaries in diploma and degree programmes validated by the university.

Although some of the teaching was excellent, and usually non-partisan, there was a Calvinist ethos which expressed itself strongly in doctrine classes and in college worship. There was an exaggerated academic emphasis which insisted on students learning both Greek and Hebrew, beyond any elementary acquaintance that might assist in the use of biblical commentaries. Chapel services reflected very little that resonated with Anglican practice, and since pleas for a more varied approach fell on increasingly deaf ears it fell to me to begin the process of setting up an independent Anglican establishment.

I was at first reluctant to do this, recognising the difficulties that lay in store – to find adequate buildings, staffing, finance, library facilities and so on. We did at least have a superb site with panoramic views available further down the same road, and indeed closer to the university, whose library resources, so I negotiated, could be made available to us. This conveniently flat tract of land was about to be vacated by the Zomba Dam Project, nearing completion on the high plateau above the town. (Strictly speaking, it wasn't at all necessary. A French team had surveyed the water requirements of the municipality, and had concluded that, if everyone at the army camp turned off taps when they'd finished using them, there'd be plenty of water for the rest of the population. The government had considered this an unlikely scenario. So the World Bank had then provided a generous loan, or – putting it another way – had facilitated a new debt.)

The diocese had stipulated in its lease of the land that any buildings erected should be dual-purpose, in other words, could be easily converted to academic or residential use afterwards. This clause had not been observed, but I was fortunate in attracting funding from my alma mater in Cambridge, viz. St John's College, where the students agreed on a donation of £12,500 from their Southern Africa Education Fund. This was matched by the same amount from the college council, which encouraged an English missionary charity to allocate a grant as well. The funding enabled the existing buildings to be turned into accommodation for several staff and a number of students, together with office space, two classrooms, a chapel, and a library. Sarah meanwhile took hundreds of cuttings from our garden, and spent hours planting them out with our gardener to create an attractive natural environment replacing the dusty lorry park. Leonard Kamungu Theological College (named after the first Malawian priest who became an active missionary in neighbouring Zambia) opened a year or two after we returned to England, and ten years later is still a going concern, albeit facing recurrent financial difficulties. At the same time, one of our own former students is the local bishop.

My own calculation was that, even if the injection of overseas money was necessary to launch the college, it was quite feasible for the four Anglican dioceses of Malawi to meet its ongoing expenses. Church membership was steadily increasing, and if each member contributed an average of one kwacha per week – more or less equivalent to one English penny – then the budget would be fully funded. Allowing for those who could afford nothing, there were those well able to contribute such an amount on behalf of twenty, fifty or even a hundred others. The problem, though, was the lack of cooperation between the dioceses: the Lake diocese soon ceased sending any ordinands at all to Zomba, because it had acquired American money to build a small college of its own in Lilongwe. It was set up apparently with the intention of providing lay training (teachers, catechists, evangelists) and occasional pastoral enrichment, but when I met the founding committee early on it was obvious that the real aim was to work as separately as possible from the other dioceses.

Leonard Kamungu Theological College, Zomba, Malawi

The new Anglican college was therefore likely to need continuing outside support and could not be launched with 'desirable but unnecessary' features. This message was hard to convey to the rest of the committee. In my absence one day they spent their time sketching plans for its infrastructure; their entire focus was upon staff accommodation, which resembled nothing so much as a five star hotel – carpets, armchairs, fridges and computers, every luxury that money could buy! One of our Anglican seminarians in Zomba had in like manner insisted quite aggressively that, once ordained, he had a right to be provided with his own car as well. This was rather too reminiscent of Lesotho, where our young men told me plainly that, as ordinands in the Anglican church, they now belonged to the Western world and had a right to a Western lifestyle. In particular, they expected two *meat* meals a day at the seminary – one alone was regarded as an affront to their newly acquired status. Even though I explained that much of the funding came from congregations within their own country – in other words, from people who were grateful to eat meat possibly just once or twice a month – they were hardly persuaded to see things differently.

Too often, alas, the church was seen by Africans as a wealthy Western organisation able to provide a never-failing cruse of financial oil. Indeed, some years after returning to England, our Catholic parish in Sherborne was keen to forge a link with a parish in Swaziland, and their bishop clearly had high hopes that we would soon raise £100,000 or more for the construction of a new church, for which the design had already been drawn up. It was evident that most of his other churches had been built along Western lines and with Western money (mainly from Ireland and from Italy). In days that are long past, religious congregations such as the Salesians had flourished within his diocese and readily drummed up funds from their home parishes, not only for churches, but for schools, training centres, clinics and residential homes. Bishop Louis explained that it was now a considerable struggle to maintain them in the absence of all but a few expatriate clergy – and yet he still wanted a new building to match these others, despite the depletion of local finances beset by a serious HIV/AIDS crisis. Unlike Malawi, or even Lesotho, the days of self-help had scarcely begun to dawn. Yet even here I was confident that an adequate edifice could be erected far more economically. I consulted Peter (our architect friend), who offered sketches of a simplified and less costly building (leaving out extras such as a baby-changing room), but even this had no appeal. Sherborne parishioners did their best but could not meet the bishop's exaggerated expectations.

Money aside, Anglican links with the mother church in England were nonetheless much appreciated in Malawi. From time to time English bishops would pay visits, including Robert Runcie as archbishop. He was remembered especially for the hilarity he aroused on Likoma Island, where the first cathedral had been built. They gave him lunch, which included the favourite national dish caught in the surrounding waters, for which he gave profuse thanks in his speech afterwards: 'I have so enjoyed eating your delicious *chamba*,' he said. Collapse of all stout parties – in fact, everyone present. Someone then kindly explained to the archbishop that the word for the fish was *chambo*, whereas *chamba*, to which he'd referred, was the illicit substance otherwise known as marijuana.

In Runcie's day, Malawi was well established as an independent country, and the vast majority of African dioceses (whether Anglican or Catholic) were served by indigenous bishops. But as local finances came under increasing strain, there was increasing pressure – certainly in Malawi – for an expatriate to be sought when a retiring bishop needed to be replaced. It almost seemed that old colonial times would have been welcomed back. Yet it was simply giving expression to the perception that an African bishop would surely lack the financial contacts available to an outsider. To some it was irrelevant that their preferred candidate knew little of African culture, spoke hardly a word of their language, and had possibly paid only one or two short visits to their country.

The tensions were greatest in the diocese of Lake Malawi, where some years earlier a maverick American 'priest' (Eugene Horn) had taken up residence. It appears that Mr Horn, who began life as a Baptist, had been ordained into the Episcopal Church, but had renounced it in 1993 just after initial visit to Malawi. The following year he became pastor of a Christian Renewal Church in South Carolina, and soon afterwards founded his own Church of the Living Word. Yet somehow he duped bishop Peter Nyanja that he was still an Anglican, who allowed him to minister as such in Malawi. His charismatic style was quite different from the inherited UMCA tradition, which emphasised liturgical order, sound teaching and diligent pastoral care. Initially he found little interest in his born again message, but when one or two priests who responded found their monthly pay augmented by him, the take-up began to swell, implanting the unintended message that foreigners are good news for clergy finances. (It was through him that funds were initially made available for the new training college in Lilongwe.)

This was the beginning of a sad, and increasingly bitter, division (both in the Lake diocese and beyond) that came to a head when the see fell vacant. A London priest whose parish had sent funds out more than once became the candidate of choice for a significant number. Others pointed out that he stood in quite a different tradition from their own and knew little of the country. The quarrel raged on, with the election suspended for a time, until finally an African was appointed. Before then, however, a missionary priest – Rodney Hunter, a friend of ours who had served the people of Central Africa devotedly for many years – was murdered. While insufficient evidence was presented in court to convict his killer, he was undoubtedly martyred for his opposition to the unhealthy lure of imported money. The verdict, declared some four years after the tragic event of November 2006, stated:

> There is no dispute that he died of a violent death [a fact previously denied by his opponents, including liberal Anglicans in other parts of the world]. It was a result of poisoning and physical manhandling – suffocation ... What is in dispute is the identity of the culprit.

The situation remained volatile long after Rodney's death. A visiting bishop wrote:

> I went to Nkhotakota to do ordinations last year (2010) and was horrified that Andrew [a young man, formerly a Muslim, who had received much help from Rodney] and another Christian were chased from the service and had they not escaped would probably have been beaten. I preached a blistering attack against the chasers and deplored the fact that the clergy only looked on and made no effort to stop it.

Andrew next to Rodney Hunter's grave in Nkhotakota
Initially a potter in Nkhotakota, Andrew was helped through his school certificate, then gained a degree at Mzuzu University, and after overcoming many difficulties was ordained priest in 2016 for the Anglican diocese of Northern Malawi.

The wrangle about who should succeed as bishop was only incidentally a clash between liberals and conservatives. At heart it was about money, and was fuelled by a sense of injustice, along with a fistful of misconceptions. When Sarah was teaching English to her class of ladies in Zomba, she invited them to sketch the relative sizes of different countries. England occupied a huge area on their map, whereas the whole continent of Africa was confined to a tiny corner of it! So the battle over a bishop was for some clergy a fight to secure their proper entitlement, wages which an *azungu* would have no difficulty in supplying. Sadly, Rodney's ascetic lifestyle was not considered suitably rewarding by everyone.

The culture was changing. In the past, wealth acquired by any individual was for the good of the community – his family, his village, his tribe. Those with a selfish streak were regarded with suspicion: perhaps their fortune had come by evil means, such as recourse to witchcraft or sorcery? Yet as vistas opened on a wider world, it became evident that there was wealth beyond imagining being enjoyed elsewhere, some of it plundered from African resources. It was therefore fitting that those who engaged with that world should have a share of the wealth. So when presidential palaces multiplied in Malawi, and ministers each gained a fleet of Mercedes or top-of-the range 4x4s, ordinary people tended to see this as a matter of national pride, rather than as a reversal of African community values.

When district councils were set up throughout the country, presumably to improve local facilities, the mayor's main preoccupation in Zomba seemed to be with own perks. He managed to claim a free car, free water, free electricity, free phone calls, plus a generous per diem allowance for every day spent out of the country on council business. Why he needed to go abroad was never clear, but one imagined that if he had a relative in South Africa his holiday could be arranged at a considerable profit to himself. Of course, he would no doubt make a careful study of traffic lights while he was there, regardless of whether the low volumes of traffic in his home town might benefit in any way from their future installation.

One should not forget the triumphant announcement of his fellow mayor in Blantyre, responding to complaints about increasing traffic congestion there. 'It shows that at last we're a real city'. Of course, if the traffic was flowing well, the local police were quite capable of creating chaos themselves, as happened one time when Colonel Gaddafi was in the country. They made vehicles queue on one of the carriageways approaching a roundabout for ten minutes before his expected arrival, only to turn white with panic on hearing his cavalcade coming unexpectedly from that very direction and thus about to run into the rear of the patiently waiting queue. The roundabout then hit a record peak of activity! At other times traffic police were busy on the main roads collecting fines for non-existent offences, invented imaginatively on the spot. Cracked wing mirrors and dirt on the rear windscreen were among their favourites – but where else would their salaries be funded?

In South Africa the police once relieved me of £25 – the entire contents of my purse – for not stopping 'long enough' at a T junction on a remote highway near Swaziland. I was outnumbered three to one (as they kindly pointed out), with no other cars passing in any direction for at least ten minutes. Fortunately I had heeded the warning of a South African colleague about the high risk of being car-jacked, and kept most of my cash in my shoes. So my fine was a mere fraction of the initial demand. Later, back home, my colleague apologised for failing to point out that the police in his homeland were regular collaborators with the criminal fraternity.

My wife also achieved a remarkable first in her response to a Malawian policeman who delayed her on the way to collecting me from hospital. He claimed that our vehicle licence was not in order and demanded that she should take him to the police station in Blantyre where she would be questioned further. He was angry when she ignored the turn to his headquarters, and presumably dumbfounded on arrival at the nearby hospital where she went in to find me, as he was left imprisoned in the truck, consistent with her usual practice of locking it when unattended.

The question remains: has the formation of nation states in Africa simply created an elite tribe of politicians and civil servants (and perhaps some clergy) whose goal is self-enrichment? And if so, is this goal in fact the legacy of colonial ambitions to enrich our own country at the expense of others?

CATHOLIC CONNECTIONS

Anyone growing up in a village tucked away in the deep English countryside might not find evidences of the past so easily or in such abundance as in St Albans, the town where I was born and went to school. There, in particular, are the Roman remains of Verulamium; and there is the vast abbey church with its medieval wall paintings. Whereas one might be forgiven in a rural setting for supposing that Christianity had always taken the form of Anglicanism, no such assumptions were plausible in my own home town. From an early age I knew of Alban, first British martyr, whose death dated back possibly as far as the early 3rd century. In his day Christianity was certainly not the state religion and was only beginning to take root within these shores. We learnt of his loyalty to fellow-believers despite the blandishments of fortune that might have attended his apostasy, and of their courage in guarding his earthly relics. When monastic life began to flourish, we heard too of Nicholas Breakspear, a monk born in St Albans, the only Englishman ever to have become Pope, as Adrian IV from 1154-9. There were also immensely powerful frescoes of the crucifixion added shortly after his time on the Norman nave pillars, upon which I gazed every Monday and Thursday morning for six years during school prayers in the abbey. Nothing else of those simplified Anglican devotions remains in my memory, except the frequent outbursts of the headmaster complaining about lax participation in the hymns and the attempts of fascist-minded prefects to maintain discipline en route.

There were other ways, though, in which the school stretched my mind and imagination. There was a year when the abbey organist (Peter Burton) taught us divinity, which for him meant the wonder of biblical poetry. I still recall his favourite verse, Amos 4.13:

> For lo, he who forms the mountains, and creates the wind, and declares to man what is his thought; who makes the morning darkness, and treads on the heights of the earth – the Lord, the God of hosts, is his name.

Tragically, Peter died trying to rescue one of his choirboys in difficulty in a swimming pool.

His successor as divinity teacher, a one-time top sprinter turned chain-smoker, was one who encouraged us to think for ourselves. His most renowned local exploit was as a lay reader in one of the ancient parish churches of St Albans, where, to demonstrate his disagreement with the vicar's views, he set fire to the parish magazine while occupying the pulpit and let it burn to ashes. The congregation was unperturbed by this gesture, but very critical of his leaving the remains on the church floor below for someone else to sweep up. Despite his heavy smoking and declining athletic prowess, boys at the school almost succeeded in getting him elected Sports Personality one year in the local paper's annual competition: he was well in the lead until a fortnight before voting came to an end, when – sadly – the headmaster discovered what was happening and withdrew his name. Subsequently, in the sixth form, I was fortunate in having the new abbey organist, Peter Hurford, for a course of musical appreciation, which expanded my horizons far beyond the limited confines of Wesley's hymns. His focus was on the rich choral tradition of the Western Church.

Of present-day Catholics I then knew little, but at least the horizons were potentially wide enough to include them. The only regular encounter was on my way home from Methodist worship, when I frequently passed the crowds emerging from one of the many Sunday masses at the Catholic church. I never ventured inside it, since it was regarded as the temple of an exotic, indeed alien, faith by Protestants in the 1950s. Nor were any of my school mates Catholics, so far as I knew, although one boy was a Jew (whom I recall was always set on becoming a dentist). It was later in my teens, when preparing to be a Methodist local preacher, that I found volumes of Ronald Knox's collected sermons in a Cambridge bookshop. These not only provided inspiring models of preaching but somehow made the Christian faith itself accessible and attractive. Here was plausible exposition of fundamental doctrine, along with lively sketches of some of the saints, plus penetrating insights into present-day Catholic life and devotion. So when I finally became accredited as a local preacher, my choice of Bible for the presentation ceremony was, somewhat to the Methodist authorities' consternation, the Knox version. It was through his eyes that I came to read the gospels from a wider perspective, and to discover a sacramental focus largely missing from my upbringing. It was not a matter of repudiating the past, but of discerning where the future now lay. In fact, as a Catholic, no longer tied to a state church of perhaps a little too much pomp and riddled with internal divisions, I rejoice once again in my nonconformist roots.

Other factors also played a part in fostering a sense of vocation. In my second year at college I shared rooms with another undergraduate (Peter) reading maths, who belonged to a Congregational student society. On Sunday evenings they organised teams to take services in village chapels around Cambridge, and it was when cycling back from one of these that Peter skidded on an icy road, and was killed instantly by a following car. I found it a devastating experience – the loss of a good friend in what was my first experience of death. The college chaplain (Keith Sutton, who in time became bishop of Lichfield) was kindness and compassion itself over the weeks that followed, and the first person I'd met who seemed to offer a possible role model for someone increasingly experiencing the study of pure mathematics as merely a challenging intellectual game, but hardly in touch with real life (which is where I wanted to be). The following example may suffice to illustrate my vocational dilemma: can you imagine an entire life pursuing nothing but algebra?

Proc. Camb. Phil. Soc. (1964), **60**, 1032

Printed in Great Britain

1032

Products of linear forms

By R. SCHOFIELD

St John's College, Cambridge

Communicated by J. A. Todd

(Received 18 March 1964)

The following result gives criteria for the factorization of polynomial forms as products of linear forms.

THEOREM. Suppose $F(x_1, ..., x_n)$ is a square-free homogeneous polynomial in the variables $x_1, ..., x_n$ over a field K. Then necessary and sufficient conditions for F to be expressible as a product of linear forms in some algebraic extension of K are that, for some i with $F_i = \partial F / \partial x_i \neq 0$ and all $j, k = 1, ..., n$,

$$[F]_{i,jk} = F_i^2 F_{jk} - F_i F_k F_{ij} - F_i F_j F_{ik} + F_j F_k F_{ii} \equiv 0 \pmod{F}. \tag{1}$$

Nonetheless, a mathematical education, and the discipline of clear logical analysis, is by no means irrelevant in many walks of life. I look back on those years of highly focused study as an important foundation for all that has followed afterwards. One personal discovery has certainly remained applicable throughout. I became very aware that the process of thought (in mathematical terminology, that of 'problem solving') is at times beyond one's own rational powers. The unconscious mind also plays an important part in suggesting new ways of looking at a situation, to the extent that my best or most imaginative ideas seem always to have been 'gifted', often when awakening from sleep, rather than 'invented'.

Perhaps I was fortunate too in studying mathematics in the immediate aftermath of a flurry of renewed interest in the logician Kurt Gödel's epoch-making paper *On Formally Undecidable Propositions of Principia Mathematica and Related Systems* (1931). It is a highly technical study, but irrefutably leads to the conclusion that 'informal' meta-mathematical reasoning is sometimes needed to overcome the inherent limitations of logical thought. Or, to put it differently, it means that the resources of the human intellect cannot be fully formalised – and hence that the God question cannot be resolved according to the canons of scientific reasoning.

There was a certain pressure to remain at college doing mathematical research, but – not being clear where I was heading – I opted for breathing space in the form of school teaching. The first job offer was from Haileybury College, but all that seemed to be highlighted at the interview was the existence of a separate bachelors' dining room. Oundle School had more respectable intellectual credentials, including ground-breaking work with computer programming and a leading role in the development of new syllabi. It was during my three years there that I took the positive step of becoming an Anglican. The ethos was familiar from school days in the Abbey and later from college chapel, and the more extreme step of becoming a Catholic wasn't yet a viable option not least because of the pain it might have caused my parents. The move was a deliberate prelude to seeking ordination, because it was the encounter with Oundle pupils that prompted me to re-assess my own Christian upbringing and to cherish it as something apparently of little concern to the majority of those I taught. Their main priorities, in no particular order, seemed seldom to be other than beer, girls and money (but of course 'peer pressure' may have played a greater role than I realized at the time); whereas my own background both at school and at home had stressed (for example) the importance of service to others.

Theology in Oxford in the late 1960s focused principally upon biblical studies and patristics, whereas ministerial formation had a broader scope, including an ecumenical dimension. For the first time ever I crossed the threshold of a Catholic institution (Blackfriars, home of the Dominicans), and later stayed at the Seminary of St Sulpice in Paris during one Orthodox Holy Week. This happened in the immediate aftermath of the 2nd Vatican Council when rapprochement between the churches was high on everyone's agenda, leading (among other important dialogues) to the Anglican – Roman Catholic international conversations known as ARCIC. In the 1970s these bore fruits of mutual understanding and seemed to engender a whole new atmosphere in inter-church relations. I recall being inspired by bishop Alan Clark of East Anglia – I think he was then the Catholic Co-Chairman of the talks – describing the progress being made, together with his disarming reply to a question I put afterwards: 'Is it possible for a Christian to belong to two different churches?' He simply said, 'That's the kind of question that makes me want to hide behind the dustbins'. His tacit admission that there was no clear-cut answer was in its own way reassuring: so (rightly or wrongly) I think of myself as an available Catholic priest, yet still also in a way as both a redundant Anglican priest and a vestigial Methodist. For that matter, I reject the tribalism that masquerades too frequently as 'nationalism': I am a citizen of heaven, the homeland of all Christians. Indeed, St Augustine of Hippo commented that anyone who prays the 'Our Father' is our brother or sister in Christ.

Within the Church of England the fraternal spirit was not always in evidence. For example, my initial curacy might well have been at St Mary Redcliffe in Bristol, where I accepted the invitation of the then vicar. The bombshell fell a few weeks later, when he cancelled the arrangement, saying that he'd now found a Cuddesdon man instead. Since both he and the existing curate were from Cuddesdon themselves, it would be more 'comfortable' (an intruder from St Stephen's House might be disturbing?). This was a shock, as I had not experienced such blatant Christian cronyism previously. However, I came to understood it as an act of that divine providence that takes us (as the risen Christ indicated to St Peter) to places where we may not initially 'wish to go'. Other twists and turns in my later ministry have also proved to be much more fulfilling than I might ever have anticipated.

A Moral Tale

An old (Chinese?) legend tells of a man whose horse ran away. 'What a disaster!' said his neighbours, 'What a loss – you won't be able to plough now or go to market'. 'Well', said the man more philosophically, 'Not necessarily'. A few days later his horse re-appeared, bringing with it several wild horses who had grown used to its company. 'What a find!' said his neighbours, 'You'll be rich now, you can sell some of these and make your fortune'. 'Not necessarily', said the man. A little later, his son was trying to break in one of the new horses, when he was thrown and fractured his leg. 'What a disaster!' said the neighbours, 'Now you've got no one to help you on the farm'. 'Not necessarily', said the man. Shortly afterwards, the emperor's men arrived in the village looking for conscripts to the army. They took all the fit young men, but left the one with a broken leg. 'What a stroke of luck!' said the neighbours.

No prizes for guessing what the man said in reply!

It was not entirely surprising that this same vicar was eventually elevated to the episcopacy, presumably as a 'safe pair of hands'. I suppose that in his defence it could be argued that Cuddesdon and St Stephen's House (alias 'Staggers') do have quite a different ethos, although as a Director of Ordinands later myself it was then made clear to me that in recruiting curates a 'one at a time' rule should always apply rather than any 'pick of the bunch' approach. For the record: one Christmas, while Cuddesdon college was staging a sombre play on the life of Jeremiah, at Staggers we put on a pantomime. My role was to be a mini-skirted nun, whose brief outing on stage was to perform a song-and-dance routine with these well-known lyrics:

> You are my honey, honeysuckle, I am ze bee,
> I'd like to sip the honey sweet from those red lips, you see.
> I love you dearly, dearly, and I want you to love me,
> You are my honey, honeysuckle, I am ze bee.

It might also be noted that our principal, the 6 foot 8 inches tall Derek Allen (who kindly performed our own marriage ceremony) was not universally popular in the wider church. He was sometimes seen as lax on discipline, although he was deeply spiritual, highly knowledgeable – and much given to generous hospitality. This too came under criticism. There were a few students who complained that his wine orders were excessive and set a bad example, considering how much poverty existed in places like the Third World. One day, there was a new delivery of wine cases deposited in the college foyer. Derek was accosted there by the chief complainant, and gently invited him to inspect the labels. The cases were all bin ends – from Chile. 'John,' he said, 'do tell me if I'm wrong. But isn't Chile – the Third World?'

For once he was politically correct, but the same wasn't always true of his students. This was most apparent during our 'speech and elocution' classes, conducted by a prim middle-aged spinster (Miss Fison, sister of a one-time bishop of Salisbury) whom it was ever our object to 'wind up'. Christopher, for many years since a Catholic priest in East Anglia, was particularly successful in doing this. One morning we were asked to think of a topic on which we could improvise a two minute talk. 'Well, Christopher, what have you got in store for us?' 'My subject, Miss Fison, is "Why I hate black men"'. There was a stunned silence while Miss F reeled in shock, before asking in a low consoling voice, 'Was there some Unfortunate Childhood Incident, Christopher?' 'O no', he replied reassuringly, 'I've always been like that'. On another occasion Miss F was demonstrating techniques of correct breath control. She laid down flat on the floor and asked us to observe her diaphragm. Christopher happened to be nearer than anyone else, so she invited him to place his hand on her prostrated form and to tell us what he felt. We all sensed that this was somewhat unwise, especially when Christopher gave the candid reply, 'Well, I think it must be your corset, Miss Fison'.

In her enthusiasm she once pressed the principal to institute an annual 'elocution prize', for which we were all required to compete. It was rapidly agreed among ourselves that it would be kind to let a student (by the name of Robert) win; he had the misfortune always to speak through his nose. The rest of us duly fluffed our lines, dropped our voices, mispronounced words, stuttered or took breaths in mid-sentence – and Robert was the clear winner. For some reason, the competition was never repeated in subsequent years. And perhaps word travelled as far as Bristol about the risks entailed in engaging a Staggers curate?

After the failure of the Redcliffe appointment, divine providence was kind in providing me with an alternative, an enticing and congenial curacy in Northampton. Here a jovial spirit of teamwork prevailed with Mirfield colleagues and indeed with clergy and laity across the town. Thus, the Council of Churches was no mere talking shop, but had set up a hostel for the homeless and had made regular provision for drug addicts in a central church coffee bar. In our own half of the town south of the river Nene there were regular shared services, with a joint Good Neighbour Scheme functioning in every street.

Fr Dan from Northampton Cathedral was part of this enterprise. We came to know each other quite well through lunching in pubs, making him the first Catholic priest I could call a friend. I rapidly came to realise that his ministry was remarkably similar to my own. One story he told was of being despatched by his Dean to chase up the lapsed. He searched the civil electoral register for likely looking Irish names; having found a whole street of O'Malleys, O'Flanahans and O'Learys not far from the Cathedral, he set out to ring their door bells. At the first house Mr O'Malley was indeed at home but turned out to be a large West Indian without any Catholic roots. The same story was repeated at every house in the street, a West Indian enclave linked to a black Pentecostal church. So Dan's mission was a self-confessed failure. There was a little medieval chapel on the edge of our parish which had been loaned to the Catholic Church; this was his particular charge, and here he recounted another, not unfamiliar, clerical dilemma. With a congregation of around sixty, he'd one Sunday assumed there'd be ample provision in the tabernacle for their communion. His assumption was misplaced. Only two or three Hosts remained, so a latter-day feeding miracle seemed the only answer: his Irish luck held out!

From Northampton I was posted downstream the river Nene, which curiously changes its pronunciation from a short to a long 'e' somewhere towards Wellingborough. Here it was possible to establish a good rapport with the Catholic priest in Rushden, and permission was readily forthcoming for him to use our parish church for a weekly mass in Irchester. He also facilitated an interview for me with his bishop back in Northampton, my first such encounter. I was ushered into the episcopal presence by a housekeeper. It seemed a very large Victorian drawing room, where the bishop waved me into an armchair next to his. The housekeeper wheeled in a trolley bearing tea things, and my host instructed me to pour him a cup, and then to help myself. If the tea pot wasn't silver, then it ought to have been. We discussed the viability of my being received into the Catholic Church, but this was long before the papal concession which allowed married clergy of non-catholic churches to be considered for priestly ordination. He suggested instead that without too much difficulty he could arrange a teaching post for me in a Catholic secondary school (St Edmund's, Ware was mentioned). It was a kind offer, much appreciated, but not really corresponding to what I perceived as my own vocation.

After a few more years in the same parish, the opportunity arose to serve in the wider church, and with our two children we sailed from Southampton out to Cape Town, thence by a train misnamed *The Orange Express* (occasionally overtaken by cyclists and even pedestrians!). At Bloemfontein we transferred to a truck which took us across the border to our final destination Roma in Lesotho. Here I was to run the small Anglican seminary known as *Lelapa la Jesu* – 'the little household of Jesus' – built in the 1970s on land donated by the Catholic Church after the apartheid government of South Africa had expelled students from the surrounding front-line states. We were near the large Catholic major seminary of St Augustine, and once I'd realigned our programme of studies we were able to work closely with them and to share certain lectures. The whole of Roma valley was indeed quite holy ground, boasting Catholic schools and convents, together with a Catholic mission hospital where we were allowed to offer a monthly Eucharist (after screening off the existing tabernacle) and to visit the wards.

Our seminary occupied part of the university campus, which had grown out of a post-war teaching training college. Hence a few of our more able students moved into degree courses, taught predominantly by Catholic priests who were Oblates of Mary Immaculate. I joined the staff there as a lecturer in New Testament studies, and came to know several of the priests very well. One year I went with Fr Dennis Fahy to a regional conference held at the university near Manzini in Swaziland. We travelled in his car, but after an hour I took over the driving after discovering that his speed never exceeded 25 mph. During the conference we stayed at the OMI Novitiate, for which I was particularly grateful when I found how heartily the Catholic priests ate as compared with the nearby ascetic Anglican sisters, who had also offered hospitality. The sisters' idea of breakfast was a cup of coffee and a biscuit – no bacon and eggs for them. The one surprise at the flourishing Novitiate was that African seminarians there spoke English in strong Irish accents, copied from their mentors, so that anyone from Limerick would have felt very much at home.

Back in Roma I learnt much from colleagues at St Augustine's – especially the French-Canadian Eugene Lapointe and the English Dominican Edmund Hill, whose writings may not always have achieved the status of recommended reading in the other Roma. There were also exciting workshops (run by the Lumko Institute) on helping the Church to be musically inculturated and pastorally more effective through the involvement of lay people. Once again it was apparent that in practical terms the challenges facing our respective churches were very similar. A couple of examples may suffice. Talking with the rector of St Augustine's (Bernard Mohlalisi, who was later to become archbishop), I asked whether the more remote Catholic congregations relied as heavily upon the provision of holy water as did the Anglicans to see them through between one monthly mass and the next, and whether this didn't distort their sacramental expectations to some extent. 'Never mind about theology', was his reply, 'we're all up against the Zionists. If our people don't get buckets of holy water to keep them going, they'll convert to the Zionist Church overnight. They don't just drink it, they wash in it'. Again, I inquired whether there were any black sheep among his flock of seminarians, as there certainly were at *Lelapa la Jesu*. 'Yes, certainly', he said, 'and last night one more student disappeared – evidently for good, because he took the desk, the bed and the chair out of his room with him'.

The perception of local people too was that the Anglican and Catholic Churches had much in common. Once, visiting a remote trading post close to the Semonkong Falls, spectacularly high waterfalls in the centre of the country, I exchanged views with a Mosotho Catholic one evening in the bar. He first wanted me to know how well he had been schooled, and so recited all the books of the bible in order from Genesis to the Apocalypse – a feat in which I might have stumbled myself. This was followed by an alphabetical list of all the countries in the world, which was well beyond my scope. Having established his credentials he pronounced authoritatively on our respective churches: 'Our two churches are exactly the same, except that you have married priests whereas ours are celibate'. When I raised the question of St Peter and his well-known mother-in-law, he responded; 'We don't want our priests to look like Peter who was married; they should be like Jesus who was single'. This seemed to clinch the matter, except that it left Peter's own status rather up in the air. It was of course an issue I discussed with Fr Bernard. He wrote on my behalf to his superiors in Rome, who came up with detailed canonical advice but without advancing the possibilities open to a potentially converting married Anglican. There were yet a few years to go before the rules were relaxed.

Back in England I was offered and accepted a living in the diocese I had left earlier. This time I was again thwarted when the new bishop intervened and demanded that the patron appoint his own candidate to the benefice. The patron was a young man, unaccustomed to dealing with overbearing bishops, so he apologetically asked me to stand down. Touched presumably by a small twinge of conscience, bishop Bill sent me an overlarge cheque to cover travel expenses. We headed instead for Somerset, where bishop John was far more accommodating.

It was now becoming clear that the momentum for church unity was steadily weakening, with the Anglican Church introducing controversial new items to the agenda and claiming the right to judge these matters in disregard not only of other churches but even of the wider Anglican Communion. Although the Women Priests

Measure was passed subject to the qualification of 'reception', this rapidly proved to be an ambiguous term. To some it simply meant that it would obviously take a little time for people within the Church of England to adjust to change, whereas to others including myself it suggested a continuing need to seek consensus in the worldwide Christian community.

When after a few more years it became apparent that 'consensus' was no longer of interest, having apparently dropped altogether out of the Anglican dictionary, I realised my own frustration with the growing indifference to church unity, and wrote for advice to Cardinal Hume. Knowing that some bishops never answer letters at all, I was amazed to receive a handwritten reply within a few days. He apologised for his 'tardy' reply and suggested I should speak to the local Catholic bishop, Mervyn Alexander of Clifton. This was soon arranged through the kind offices of the local priest Fr Pat Lynch, who was a good friend to several of us in the Taunton area facing the same crisis and hosted regular lunch gatherings in his presbytery. Bishop Mervyn proved understanding, and helpfully outlined the steps necessary to seek ordination in the Catholic Church under the new dispensation. I duly noted the process, but postponed action until such time as our children should become more independent. His generous words of encouragement were reassuring: 'In your present ministry', he said, 'you are doing a good work for God'.

By now, there was little incentive to remain within the Church of England. My own bishop Jim was doing his best to replace me in my role of Director of Ordinands (work for which I'd been responsible for nearly ten years), not for any incompetence but because he preferred like-minded staff. He'd already asked a priest who shared his liberal views to do the job, so I was fortunate to be offered a college living in North Norfolk. The final step was to be approved by the churchwardens of the parish, but on arrival there I was surprised to find the entire church council assembled. The opening greeting, from the council's deputy chairman, was enough to demonstrate the futility of the journey. Whereas I'd anticipated she might be going to say, 'Welcome. Did you have a good journey? Would you like to use the cloakroom?' instead she whispered in my ear, 'We don't want people like you here'. Another bolt from the blue! It was apparent that the gathering was under the thumb of the suffragan bishop, also in attendance, who explained that the key issue was my membership of Forward in Faith. 'No', I said, 'I'm not a member, but I have friends who are – and indeed I've written an occasional article for their magazine'. 'That's quite enough', he retaliated. I asked if any of the present company had read anything I'd written (bearing in mind that the archbishop of Canterbury himself had contributed to the same magazine), but no one admitted to such a sin. So it was guilt by association, and not even the choice of a woman priest as one of my referees could be pleaded in mitigation. The aftermath of this encounter was a remonstration by the college, whose right of presentation had been thwarted on patently spurious grounds. The Bishop of Norwich (Peter) made the further suggestion that it was time for the college dean to retire. The dean (Andrew Mackintosh) told me later that he cherished the memory of this robust correspondence.

Once again, however, divine providence opened a far more fruitful possibility: the resumption of service overseas, this time in Malawi where we spent four very happy years. The different churches in Zomba cooperated well, especially in an impressive Good Friday procession from the main Catholic church to St George's Anglican church (or vice versa). At the ecumenical theological college we belonged to a network of seminaries who shared teaching programmes validated by the University of Malawi. Consequently there were regular meetings with their staff, especially those from St Peter's Catholic seminary on the far side of Zomba, which had once been the colonial capital.

The rector of St Peter's was a lively young Malawian priest – but he was then absent from subsequent gatherings, at which St Peter's was represented by a couple of Irish Jesuits. 'Is the rector well?' I asked them. They explained that he had been withdrawn when the local nuncio found that he had a regular lady friend and had fathered children in his home village. Notwithstanding my previous discussion with a Mosotho Catholic, celibacy isn't readily accepted within African societies (so that their bishops are wary of allowing married priests from abroad to enter their dioceses, for fear of undermining the established system). A woman even if not married who has children tends to be better regarded than one who is childless, while a man is only properly an adult when he has his own offspring. When my brother-in-law was visiting us, he was asked about his family. 'I have three children', he replied proudly. 'I'm so sorry', came the reply – three being considered a very small family indeed.

Under a new and no doubt better scrutinised rector, St Peter's recovered and its numbers grew. One consequence was an increased workload for staff elsewhere involved in marking their examination scripts. It fell to me to be the second marker for canon law papers. This was a challenge, as even the dimmest student must have known more than I did. The ploy I adopted was to assume the first marker's competence and to follow his assessment, adjusting it for clarity of presentation. A script that made sense to me was surely worth a mark or two extra.

Problems at St Peter's may have been resolved, but within the Anglican diocese the situation deteriorated. Following the decision to divide the diocese of Southern Malawi, there was a major dispute about the appointment of the new bishop responsible for Zomba. Influential university personnel who attended St George's had already made life difficult for its rector, and now, having missed the deadline for submitting the name of their preferred candidate, they objected to the appointment of Bernard Malango, a Malawian who was already archbishop of the province. After his enthronement he asked me to be priest-in-charge of the parish (the largest and wealthiest in the diocese), on top of my existing role in the college, in the belief that an expatriate must surely have some expertise in crisis management. My initial attempt to pour oil on the waters was an appeal in church to think of the damaging publicity surrounding this dispute, which was not helping the church's witness to a gospel of reconciliation. One or two of the university clique audibly hissed and booed at this point, the only such occurrence in my entire ministry. They recognized afterwards, however, that they had overstepped the mark, and apologized.

But there was more to come. At the outset of their opposition, the church treasurer had (under their instructions) frozen the bank account from which payments to the diocese were made, and unknown to me had also placed restrictions upon the verger. I discovered this one afternoon, when our college sacristan reported that the verger now insisted he could only replenish our communion wine *if requested first in writing*. With mass due in less than an hour, I had no alternative but to seek supplies elsewhere. I drove across to the Catholic cathedral, where the dean came to my rescue. He gave me what was needed, and far more, saying 'Take this with my blessing. It's as if I'm saying mass there myself'. Having left an increasingly argumentative and fractured Church of England for an unexpectedly divided Anglican Church of Malawi, his response came like manna from heaven, and was perhaps the moment when I resolved finally to seek reception into the Catholic Church.

On leave the following Christmas I travelled to Plymouth to meet the bishop. Unlike the similar meeting in Northampton some twenty years earlier, it was an informal occasion. No housekeeper, no trolley laden with china, not even a dog collar in sight: the bishop was in his shirt sleeves and said, 'What would you like – tea or coffee? I'll get you one'. Although we were committed to Zomba for a further year, he asked me to keep in touch. On finally returning to England I tested the Anglican waters for one last time and reported my availability to six Anglican bishops whom I knew. Only one replied – discouragingly, so it was clear confirmation that the steps I'd already taken towards becoming a Catholic were in the right direction.

The bishop proved to be sympathetic and agreed to take things forward. After a further meeting or two the necessary formalities were completed quickly. (I did reflect, however, as a result of the tardy or non-existent replies received to my letters addressed elsewhere that St Paul's example ought to be better known among those claiming to be his apostolic successors; and that he ought to be widely adopted as the patron saint of letter-writing, given his own ready responses to any missives he received. Southern Electric used to have a phrase for it, 'if it matters to you, it matters to us', a slogan which headed their paperwork.)

Within three months of submitting the file to Rome the dispensation signed by John Paul II was in the bishop's hands. The pope used the word 'willingly' according to the English translation, but I have never known whether that meant 'enthusiastically' or merely 'in an unconstrained manner'. Several months spent improving my knowledge of sacramental theology were followed by attendance at St John's Seminary, Wonersh where I topped up on canon law. On the Sunday evening when I first arrived a student social was being held. Entertainment (to my surprise) was provided by a young lady who sat on a bar stool and recited a poem entitled Lipstick. Her message was that different colours carry different spiritual meanings. I also learnt at Wonersh that the vital thing is to know the telephone numbers of one's diocesan chancellor and his corresponding episcopal vicar. At the end of the year, I reviewed progress with the bishop, who decided that canon law had been pursued far enough. 'Stick to scripture', he said, 'it's much better'.

I didn't appreciate then that this distinction reflected the main tension within the Catholic Church which continues between the legalistic and the scriptural mindsets despite the 2nd Vatican Council having to some extent redressed the balance. A difference persists in the preferred vocabulary: those who favour Tridentine ways wax strong on 'holiness' and 'discipline', whereas the *aggiornamento* party use words such as 'love' and 'compassion' more frequently. 'Mercy' and 'joy' are favourite words for pope Francis, although his readiness to 'accompany' people on their spiritual journeys has sadly met with fierce opposition in some quarters. One suspects that those who criticize Francis would have equally criticized our Lord, whose teachings and example they have perhaps not studied as closely as they might.

Ordination soon followed, together with considerable acceptance as a married Catholic priest. Of course, there remain those whose acquaintance with apostolic precedent is limited, and there are also a dispiriting number of bishops and others who perpetuate the idea that celibacy is not only at the heart of priesthood but essential to it. It was disconcerting to be invited, for example, to a diocesan renewal day only to find on arrival that I was scarcely regarded as eligible to participate. A few celibate priests understandably feel uncomfortable with one who is married; those of this ilk whom I've met tend, rather sadly, to be younger priests rather than those of riper years. For the record, Southwark archdiocese where I now live and minister has been very welcoming and from the outset has made me feel thoroughly at home. (The

Dean of Canterbury cathedral, whom I knew slightly from the past, also said very generously on my first visit there, 'treat this place as if it were your own'.)

The only pronounced resistance to my change of ecclesial allegiance came unsolicited from a vicar who denounced me as a traitor and treated me to an uninterrupted half hour rant against all things Catholic, including the local parish priest and diocesan bishop. It was reminiscent of a similar response from a Methodist teaching colleague many years earlier when I became an Anglican. But the strangest encounter of all happened one Monday morning in Missoula, the town in Montana where our son and family were living at the time. I called in at the Catholic church office to check mass times, and to introduce myself: 'I'm a Catholic priest visiting from the UK'. The conventional response from the parish secretary might have run along the lines of 'You're very welcome. Have a coffee. Would you like to meet the pastor?' So I was somewhat wrong-footed when she said, 'That's what they all say'. Totally mystified I inquired further: 'All who?' 'All them paedophiles out there'. The scales dropped from my eyes as I realised that Missoula, or possibly the whole of Montana, had been hit by a serious clerical crisis. My immediate response was ill-judged: 'Maybe I should explain. I'm a married priest staying for a couple of weeks with my son and his family here in Missoula'. This was like a red rag to a bull. 'A married priest!' she said. 'What kind of creature is that? Are you some kind of deacon?' Lost for words, I feebly suggested, 'Maybe we're both on a learning curve this morning'.

The following Sunday we tried the university chaplaincy instead. A Jesuit priest called Jim gave us a friendly reception and invited me to concelebrate – 'so just help yourself to an alb'. Kitted out thus far, I asked if he ran to a chasuble. 'Chasubles?' he said. 'O no, we don't do that kind of thing here'. 'And what about seating?' 'Just introduce yourself to some nice folk in the congregation and sit alongside them. When you feel like it, you can wander up into the sanctuary'. I wandered as instructed – and continue wandering, and wondering: will I ever know what kind of creature I am?

> 'Who are you, aged man?' I said,
>   'And how is it you live?'
> His answer trickled through my head,
>   Like water through a sieve.

SQUARING THE CIRCLE

A married priesthood has existed in the Catholic church since the time of St Peter. Yet 'a leading Catholic intellectual' in America (to use *The Tablet*'s description of George Weigel) seemed unaware when he wrote on the subject in 2012 that the primitive apostolic outreach was conducted by such men. Weigel dismissed all married priests as 'Catholic Lite', writing off their formation as too brief and their preaching as 'inept'. Presumably he would have sacked Simon Peter from his seminary on the grounds of fickle behaviour and wilful misunderstanding long before he was ever given the chance to preach at Pentecost with the miserable response of a mere three thousand people?

However, despite the continuing presence of married clergy within the Orthodox Church and their greater abundance within the Catholic Church than for many a long year, it still comes as a surprise to some of the faithful that I have a wife. Most parishioners readily accept this, together with other developments of recent years. It is certainly pastorally useful to be able to offer a hospitable home and to have a fifth columnist able to report on life in the back pews of church (which includes listening sympathetically to ladies in the congregation, who might be reluctant to talk so openly to a man about the problems that they face). It helps too to have experienced at first hand the ups and downs of family life, and to have reared children of one's own. Above all, in a world where barriers are constantly being erected to keep 'the other' at bay, one learns in a marriage to live with a person who remains of course different from oneself, even if much is held in common. In the priesthood there can be a dangerous drift towards 'clericalism', which has been a factor in the recent scandals of child abuse in so far as priestly lapses have too often been hushed up, supposedly to protect the cherished image of a race of holy men superior to the common herd. Such an idea was surely demolished by our Lord when he challenged the Levitical conventions that separated the supposedly clean from the unclean.[13]

---

[13] *The Tablet* published a letter from me in 2018: "In the Old Testament, repentance was often expressed by the donning of "sackcloth and ashes". Perhaps our own bishops could designate a Sunday when Catholics in this country could do something similar? Priests celebrating Mass could renounce their vestments in favour of a plain alb, and reduce the liturgy to its simplest form. At the end of Mass, the celebrant could take up a black bag, having distributed other bags to willing members of the congregation, and lead them out into the streets to collect rubbish (never difficult to find). On their return, a prayer could be offered humbly asking God to help remove the rubbish from our hearts and minds, and from the Church itself. Such a gesture would be pointless if it did not encourage both clergy and laity to follow ever more closely in the steps of our Lord who came not to be served, but to serve others."

From time to time, articles and correspondence about the role of a priest's wife appears within the pages of the Catholic press. It was in 2014 that I was able to write to Archbishop Peter of Southwark with what must be the definitive answer (although it will take a while to explain!). In November of that year our little church of St Ambrose in Wye reached its diamond jubilee. There is a complex history behind it. Wye, a royal manor in Saxon days, was renowned in the 15th century as the home of John Kempe who rose to be Chancellor of England and eventually Archbishop of Canterbury. Since much of his time was spent on the king's business – especially on the continent as an ambassador for peace (seeking to bring an end to the 100 years' war) – he was conscious of often having neglected his spiritual and pastoral duties as a bishop. His main act of contrition was to establish a college for priests in Wye, which flourished until Henry VIII had different ideas. It then served as a local grammar school before becoming an agricultural college of international renown, until its later owners, Imperial College, developed different ideas and sold up. (A tip for visitors to the village: if you wish to be treated with Wye's customary courtesy, make sure that the word I------l never escapes your lips. In some quarters they will never be forgiven.) During the 2nd World War the college was taken over by the army, who – as pioneers of equal opportunities – made sure that Catholic troops were provided with a chaplain of their persuasion. The regular masses held in the college attracted local Catholics too; hence a nucleus of the faithful was ready in 1946 to welcome an immigrant from Birmingham, Mrs Whatmore, who to their joy turned her stable into a chapel. This attracted a steadily growing number of worshippers, and within a few years it had become obvious that her paddock would make an admirable site for a new Catholic church.

The first step in this direction was St Ambrose Chapel, a simple hall intended to be supplanted (when funding was available) by a larger church which would serve the scattered villages of the North Downs. The latter never happened because (unsurprisingly?) the diocese developed different ideas. Our chapel is admirably compact, however, and is the friendliest church where I have ever served: furthermore, the congregation sing like angels, for the most part without organ accompaniment. They were joined on 14 November 2014, our anniversary date, by Mark Deller conducting local singers in works by Byrd (a contemporary of our own Catholic martyr Thomas Clifton) and by Archbishop Peter. The latter dropped in first to our house and was still drinking his coffee ten minutes before the mass was due to start. My wife, aware that it takes a few minutes to walk round the corner to the church and that +Peter had yet to robe, tactfully drew his attention to the time. I was able therefore when writing to thank him afterwards to suggest that we now had the ultimate answer to the question under discussion (here we are at last!): the role of the priest's wife is *to get the bishop to the church on time.*

There are some non-Catholics, however, whose appreciation of ecclesiastical issues is rather limited and who cannot grasp that their own church does not have a monopoly on the truth, or even on clergy wives. It was never easy to explain to them what attracted me to the Catholic church – its universality, which though imperfect still far exceeds the narrower bounds of Anglicans, Methodists and the like.

Quite a few of the latter still assume that my change of church allegiance can only be attributed to a misogynous dislike of women priests. Usually I respond by asking them if they imagine that was the root cause of John Henry Newman's conversion nearly two hundred years ago now. I was even accosted at an academic drinks party by a lady with some distinction as a medieval historian who reiterated the same over-simplistic accusation. She claimed that she'd never heard any argument against women priests from Catholics other than a prejudiced insistence upon the maintenance of apostolic tradition. Without referring to my own conviction that in such matters ecumenical consensus is desirable, I offered her a broader view, focusing on the significance of Christ's counter-cultural vulnerability on the Cross: had he been of the opposite sex, might not the potency of his self-sacrifice been significantly muted? Could a female Messiah have addressed the all too common violent tendencies of the male gender as effectively? My interrogator retorted that she'd 'never heard that one before', to which my baffled reply was, 'But isn't that what you requested – a different argument altogether?' Whether it was a good argument or not is another issue, but in a serious debate I firmly believe it's better to listen to all points of view and then to weigh them up *rather than* shutting one's ears to voices that need to be heard and so too hastily jumping to conclusions. As it happens, I believe that men and women share equally in the charismatic gifts of the Holy Spirit, and that this is well illustrated in the pages of the New Testament. The institutional forms of ordained ministry that to some extent supplanted these in the late 1st and early 2nd centuries evolved partly to avoid offending the social conventions of the time (which Jesus himself respected in his choice of twelve male disciples) and perhaps owed something to the way the threefold ordering of bishop, priest and deacon was justified by analogy with the Jewish hierarchy that preceded it.

An issue in our Anglican diocese after the 1992 synod decision to proceed with women's ordination was whether I (as one who had spoken and voted against the measure) could continue to be responsible for the selection of candidates for the priesthood. I pointed out that my role remained exactly the same, namely, to advise the bishop as to how far each candidate, whether male or female, measured up to the detailed national selection criteria. It was his responsibility, after further advice from a selection conference, to determine within the framework of diocesan policy whether any particular individual should proceed with formation and training.

When I left the diocese in 1999, I was glad that my efforts to remain impartial had been appreciated. One of the women priests spoke on behalf of the others at a farewell presentation in specific appreciation of my even-handedness. I had indeed done battle for some of the women, of whom some clergy supposedly in favour of women's ordination had disapproved on patently spurious grounds. One priest complained that a female candidate on placement in his parish was 'no good at preaching' – a charge which might possibly be levelled against some vicars already in post? The objection was answered by the observation that helping the candidate to preach more effectively was part of his remit as also of others involved in her training. Again, a sound candidate whose husband had crossed swords with the archdeacon was forced by him to withdraw from training on the discriminatory grounds that she had a mild heart condition (as many of us do, but there's room enough for the disabled and handicapped within God's church – ask Jean Vanier, founder of L'Arche). I took the matter up with the bishop, another apparently keen advocate for the women's cause, but in vain. My advice was then for her to wait just a few years until both the bishop and the archdeacon had retired, when I was confident she would be able to resume training. This indeed happened, and she has since proved her worth in parish ministry.

There were sadly other occasions during those years when decisions were made within Bath and Wells diocese, usually concerning appointments, on the basis of largely subjective opinions or (occasionally) hearsay. One man was denied a curate, for example, because a member of the bishop's staff reckoned that one of his churchwardens didn't get on too well with him. My observation that it could be the churchwarden who might be at least partially at fault was overruled, as was the suggestion that the incumbent in question should at least be allowed to offer his own comments on the situation. Later on, I discovered the bishop had been writing somewhat slanted references about myself. He suggested in one letter that I 'wasn't entirely comfortable in the presence of women'. What, I wondered, was his evidence? Had he considered my domestic life in depth? In reality, it was a variant way of pointing out that my views didn't always coincide with his (unless he was simply indicating that he reckoned me to be less of a ladies' man than himself?).

As a Catholic it remains important for me to work ecumenically wherever possible. The sense of obedience to Christ's expressed prayer for his followers 'to be one' remains fundamental. Soon after my priestly ordination in 2006 I took on the role of tutor for a group of *Anglican* ordinands preparing for ministry. One path to unity must surely be the sharing of teaching and ideas. If the Church of England has diverged on a somewhat different path from the Catholic church, some form of re-convergence will not come about without dialogue happening at many different levels. The task of guiding three non-Catholic students (one man and two women) for several years was an opportunity to discover how much we still had in common, to promote further understanding, and to face any particular challenges. It was, for example, a shock to the youngest of them to discover that she might have to lead a church service on Good Friday, given that she, like many of her contemporaries, had until then regarded that day as a special shopping opportunity.

Again, celebrating a common faith was the main focus of our Sherborne Churches Together. Despite considerable pressure from one or two Anglican clergy to abandon the whole project, Catholics and Methodists supported by the Anglican laity joined forces to maintain and build upon our links. One of the most effective ministers in this respect was a retired Methodist woman minister, who had given sterling service at national level already (as President of the Conference). At one gathering, I recall, we were trying to agree on a date and a venue for a summer-time united service to be held in an outdoor location. It was thought that the Abbey Green might be suitable on the first Sunday of July, since that coincided with an established Abbey festival day. Teas were already planned, so why not have the ecumenical service beforehand? Its precise timing was then the issue: many of the Methodists needed to travel elsewhere later for an important circuit gathering. But if the service were to be earlier, teas would not be ready; someone made the revolutionary suggestion that the teas and the Abbey's evening service could both be held half an hour earlier. The idea was at once vetoed: Sherborne's festival evensong was a major regional event, hence too many people would be confused by a change of timing (even though the discussion was being held in the middle of April). We therefore abandoned any compromise on timing and moved to consider other dates and possible venues. There was a park near the railway station – but this had no disabled toilet facilities. There was a new millennium garden further north in the town – but this was (I quote) *'rectangular'*, and for reasons I still cannot really grasp this rendered it unsuitable. There was an old ruined chapel within Sherborne Old Castle (my own proposal) – but an historical expert present declared authoritatively that this no longer existed. (In fact, Catholics rediscovered it a few weeks later and enjoyed a simple Latin service there with a picnic to follow.) The outcome will by now be obvious: as no outdoor event bringing us altogether could possibly be arranged, we moved to the next item on the agenda!

> # To a Retiring Colleague and Friend
>
> Christina's treasured card received on my resignation as parish priest
> *It brings back the times when we had to tough it out together*

The word 'friendship' is the key that unlocks many doors. Long ago it was the friendship and support of my college chaplain that led to my priestly vocation, and ever since it has been the friendship of fellow clergy and parishioners alike that has sustained it. The friendship I value most is that of my wife: without her I doubt I could have persevered as a priest for the best part of fifty years. For some the celibate path is God's calling, whether or not it accompanies any ordained role or any commitment within a religious community, but all of us need supportive relationships. This aspect of life sometimes seems to be missing in the call for more vocations, giving the impression that nothing matters apart from God's inner voice. My own experience suggests that human inspiration and encouragement have a vital part to play as well.

Relinquishing the parish of Sherborne after less than four years in charge was clearly not popular with the diocesan authorities (despite having indicated on taking up the role that my health might let me down eventually). Communication seemed to cease, so that for a good six months I had no idea as to when I might be able to hand over to a successor. Thereafter I continued as chaplain to RNAS Yeovilton, and took on extra duties as visiting chaplain to the nearby Catholic girls' school, where teamwork was certainly more in evidence. The following year we held a confirmation service in the chapel, followed by a lunch intended by the head to be something of an *agape*, shared by staff and our principal guests alike. The latter, however, decided otherwise – so we were distinctly 'sheep' and 'goats' at separate tables! I was greatly heartened, however, when the present bishop came specially over to Wye to greet Sarah and myself when he was up from the west country: it gave a little hint of what it might feel like to rise again from the dead.

Here in Kent there are regular social gatherings for our deanery clergy – and Sarah is delighted to have been invited more than once to join in. Likewise, there is a good ecumenical spirit in Wye itself: we occasionally worship together and eat together; we raise funds for the same causes, usually for charities working for the homeless, or for migrants and refugees. In fact, when the annual Week of Prayer for Christian Unity comes round, our prayers are not so much for 'unity' (since a century of such prayers has not thus far achieved much more than a thawing of relationships) but for local initiatives such as Ashford's night shelter scheme or for Canterbury's ministry to those suffering mental ill-health. Recognising the need for a little more generosity in contributing to the nation's housing stock, we have recently tried to persuade the parish council here to be less confrontational in its response to developers. We can only do this when we know and respect each other.

My own limitations have become more obvious with the passage of time. In my dotage it is good to have more time to think and to write. It was the move to Malawi that opened the window on this aspect of ministry, thanks especially to a German Baptist friend, Klaus Fiedler. His was an ecumenical and inquiring spirit, and he responded to the dire paucity of books in Africa by establishing publishing houses in each of the universities where he taught. While we were still in Africa he encouraged my research on issues that mattered much more there than in Western countries, such as debt relief and the very different (but highly topical) subject of magic and witchcraft; he supported my application to begin a doctorate, and since we came to Wye he has generously accepted other texts of contemporary concern, such as the present state of Christianity in Malawi, changing attitudes to war and peace, indeed how we understand the mission of Jesus himself. When I reflect on our Lord's ministry, it seems clear that initially he was both pastorally and didactically very active, yet it was his passivity, in which he surrendered his very life on the Cross, that was 'crucial'. Many Christians may well follow a similar pattern[14] — and maybe this should be the model for priestly ministry too. For myself, I value the present space for quiet reflection, and hope that this may bear some fruit for others.

(I can gladly report a tremendous response from parishioners in Sherborne who raised considerable funds for the library of a young seminary in Namibia where I researched for a short time; clergy in our Canterbury deanery also rallied well to provide them with a wide selection of books and a renowned magician — a Catholic — in Wye entertained a church gathering for free, enabling the proceeds to pay for the cost of their postage.)

---

[14] St Augustine commented on the final chapter of St John's Gospel:

> The Church knows two lives which have been laid down and commended to her by God. One is through faith, the other through vision; one is passed on pilgrimage in time, the other in our eternal home; one involves toil, the other rest; one is on the way, the other in our true home; one involves work, the other brings reward; one is a life of action, the other a life of contemplation.

> **St Luke shows the early Church fulfilling Christ's words and deeds**
>
> #1 Both of St Luke's volumes (his Gospel and Acts) begin in Jerusalem.
> *A fresh dispensation of the Holy Spirit is granted to those devoutly waiting upon God; but there is also a testing time of forty days, both for Jesus and for his disciples.*
> Jesus prepares for the descent of the Spirit in prayer, as do the apostles. On both occasions there are visionary happenings.
> *The apostles continue as a united body, preaching and healing as Jesus did. Their frequent presence in the temple reminds us that this is where Jesus found himself – in his Father's house [Lk 2.49]. Paul encounters him there too [Acts 22.17].*
> In obedience to Jesus' instruction to the Twelve to carry no money as they travel, Peter and John admit to having neither silver nor gold [Acts 3.6].
> *'What shall we do?' is asked, first of John the Baptist, then of Peter and the apostles.*
> Gospel imagery of the fishing net is renewed in Peter's vision of the all-inclusive sheet.
> *There is detention by the authorities. The Sadducees reject both Jesus' and Paul's belief in the resurrection. Each face the triple combination of the Sanhedrin, the Roman governor and the ruling Herod, as well as a hostile crowd – yet each is three times declared innocent.*
> When Stephen is stoned to death he echoes the dying words of Jesus about forgiveness, and likewise commends his spirit.
> *When the apostles are imprisoned, they are miraculously released at night, as is Peter on a further occasion – experiences akin to Jesus' rising from his tomb. Peter's release – like that of Christ – takes place immediately after Passover.*
> Philip's encounter with the Ethiopian resembles Jesus' walk with the two disciples to Emmaus: scriptural exegesis, the 'sacramental' climax, then a sudden 'vanishing'.
> *Jesus' urges the Twelve and then the seventy to 'shake off the dust from your feet' if their message is rejected. This is Paul and Barnabas' action on leaving Pisidian Antioch.*
>
> #2 Luke reflects in Acts too how 'the secrets of the kingdom of God' revealed in the parable of the sower have marked both the setbacks and the steady advance of the Church's mission. 'Those who <u>received</u> [Peter's] word were baptized, and there were added that day about three thousand souls.' Use of the Gospel phrase 'receiving the word' is no coincidence, given that Luke includes phrases such as 'the word of God grew' four further times in Acts [6.7; 12.24; 13.48; 19.20].

Neither a non-conformist within the Established Church nor a married priest in the eyes of the Catholic hierarchy can have been an entirely comfortable proposition. Yet people in the pews have often shown a generosity of spirit in stretching their own boundaries of tolerance. The afore-mentioned John Henry Newman, one of my esteemed mentors, was as famously tender of the popular religious sense as he was of the faltering way we move heavenwards:

We advance to the truth by experience of error; we succeed through failures. We know not how to do right except by having done wrong... Such is the process by which we succeed; we walk to heaven backward.

The common thread (apart from frequent recourse to Holy Writ – note the brief study of Luke-Acts) that links the several books published in this country (*Bordering on Faith, The Emerging Church, Learning Curves, Footprints of Faith*) is similar to the theme expressed in the above quotation from Newman. Down the centuries Christians (under the guidance of the Spirit) have searched to articulate their faith, 'inculturating' it in forms of devotion that resonate with their own experience as well in life styles that address the challenges and confusions of contemporary society. The process in ongoing, and inevitably mistakes and misunderstandings occur along the way. Yet there is forgiveness at the heart of the Gospel. And there is consolation too: if Jesus finds himself unappreciated by religious professionals, he is acclaimed by children:

They said to him, 'Do you hear what these are saying?' And Jesus said to them, 'Yes; have you never read, Out of the mouth of babes and sucklings thou has brought perfect praise?'

So, while encouragement is always welcome from whatever quarter, the tribute I foolishly cherish most came unsought from a first holy communion group at Leweston School in Dorset. When I left, the girls whom I had encouraged to take further steps forward in their Christian faith gave me a note of appreciation:

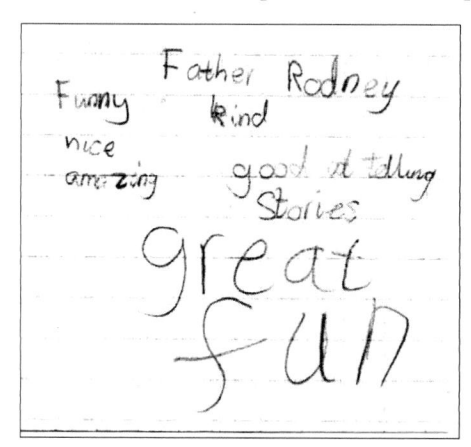

Apologies for this concluding flourish
As probably the only priest ever to have broken an ankle during a toddlers' service, I am mindful that 'pride comes before a fall'. Where St Paul could rightly claim to have 'fought the good fight', alas! I would hesitate to say the like.